ECONOMIC AND DEMOGRAPHIC RELATIONSHIPS IN DEVELOPMENT

The Johns Hopkins Studies in Development
Vernon W. Ruttan and T. Paul Schultz, Consulting Editors

Economic and Demographic Relationships in Development

Ester Boserup

Essays Selected and Introduced by
T. PAUL SCHULTZ

The Johns Hopkins University Press
Baltimore and London

The Johns Hopkins University Press,
701 West 40th Street, Baltimore, Maryland 21211
The Johns Hopkins Press Ltd., London

∞ The paper used in this book meets the minimum requirements of American
National Standard for Information Sciences—Permanence of Paper for Printed
Library Materials, ANSI Z39.48–1984.

Library of Congress Cataloging-in-Publication Data

Boserup, Ester.
    Economic and demographic relationships in development/Ester Boserup : essays
selected and introduced by T. Paul Schultz.
        p.   cm.—(Johns Hopkins studies in development)
    Includes bibliographical references.
    ISBN 0-8018-3929-7 (alk. paper).—ISBN 0-8018-3930-0 (pbk.)
    1. Developing countries—Economic conditions.   2. Developing countries—
Population.   3. Economic development.   4. Population.
I. Schultz, T. Paul.   II. Title.   III. Series.
HC59.7.B587   1990
338.9′09172′$—dc20   89-35239 CIP

Contents

ECONOMIC AND DEMOGRAPHIC RELATIONSHIPS IN DEVELOPMENT

Introduction

T. PAUL SCHULTZ

Our view of economic development and demographic change has evolved markedly in the last quarter century, in large part because of the writing of Ester Boserup. Many of her ideas are presented in her three books: *The Conditions of Agricultural Growth, Woman's Role in Economic Development,* and *Population and Technological Change.* But her many articles, essays, and conference papers equally represent her wide-ranging scholarship and innovative interpretations of historical and contemporary evidence. These essays, however, are less frequently cited than her books and thus appear to be less consulted by students and scholars, perhaps because they are scattered across such a wide variety of disciplines and publications. A selection of these essays is collected in this volume in their original published form. The goal is to make them more accessible and to encourage further study of the important problems that Boserup has addressed and clarified.

Wherever one first encounters Boserup's writing, one is delighted by her cogent analysis of—and iconoclastic perspectives on—the development process, and by her original interpretations of how constraints influence human behavior and how human behavior changes the constraints on individual and social choice. Her writing pushes us to rethink established intellectual positions, reevaluate evidence, and explore alternative hypotheses. Her command of many disciplines and related literatures is certain to bring before you new bibliographical sources, consolidated here for the first time, including fascinating unpublished dissertations, fugitive literature from international conferences, and exchanges between technical advisers and policymakers, as well as articles in traditional scholarly publications. She always provides sufficient evidence to make a solid case for her explanation of events, but there is also enough leeway in interpreting the record to motivate others to assemble new evidence to test her theories, to probe her tantalizing conjectures, and to extend her many lines of reasoning in still additional directions.

Boserup's thinking involves most centrally the interrelationships among labor productivity, population pressure, and demographic and economic behavior, as constrained by nature through climate and natural resource endowments and as limited by society through malleable human institutions such as the family, through infrastructural investments such as land improvements, and through education and technical knowledge, with their implications for productive practices. It is no simple task to assess the role of one such factor as it affects another, because repercussions often occur in both directions, in varied forms, and with different time lags. Association between these interrelated factors is never conclusive evidence of causation, but it may still be a tentative basis for advancing our understanding of these fundamental questions. In sum, Boserup seeks to answer how the process of modern economic growth (Kuznets, 1966) is influenced by the demographic and technical changes that distinguish this century from others.

Before the onset of economic development, people worked predominantly in agriculture. Therefore, a key question is what brings about the initial change in agricultural practices that causes the productivity of a worker's time to increase. The first seven essays in this book (composing part 1) consider the interplay of agriculture and population, and seek to understand the seemingly homeostatic mechanisms that have often achieved a balance between the capacities of a population to produce food and the size of that population to be fed. What circumstances disrupt this long-run balance and displace the agricultural-demographic system to reach and sustain a higher level of economic productivity? Anthropologists and historians have studied these issues with care, but Boserup is exceptional in distilling many of their insights and combining them into an overarching economic framework of agricultural growth. Malthus was the last economist to put forward a general theory that sought to account for the empirical evidence on economic-demographic development in the world. But Boserup has, in one sense, turned Malthus on his head, by showing how population pressure is responsible for many cases of technological change and patterns of land use that eventually raise the economic productivity of labor while necessitating more intensified forms of cultivation and land-augmenting investment, including the drainage of swampy lands and irrigation for multiple cropping. The historical record remains sufficiently varied and uncertain, so that neither the model of Malthus nor that of Boserup explains adequately all the evidence. But the last two decades have moved the mainstream interpretation of this process in the direction proposed by Boserup in her first book (e.g., National Academy of Sciences, 1986; Evenson, 1985; Pingali and Binswanger, 1987; Kelley, 1988; T. P. Schultz, 1981) and cautiously away from that advanced by Malthus and restated by neo-Malthusian writers who shaped public thinking after the Second World War (e.g. Coale and Hoover, 1958; National Academy of Sciences, 1971).

The four essays in part 2 focus on the constraints on food supply and agricultural productivity and how and why they have varied from region to region and from period to period in history. Boserup's emphasis on agriculture as the engine of economic development was out of fashion during the 1950s and 1960s, but is enjoying renewed popularity in the 1980s. Initially, development was thought of as a dualistic process, during which resources were transferred from agriculture to industry. Thus, agriculture was assigned low priority, and economists debated how to coordinate development investments in urban areas where industrialization held out the promise of providing productive employment for the impoverished and purportedly under-employed agricultural peasants. But development problems were not easily resolved in those countries that failed to invest in modernizing their agriculture and instead instituted discriminatory tax and price policies that reduced the incentives for farmers to invest in modern inputs and capital improvements. International assistance agencies gradually came to view these policies as inefficient and counterproductive, because they distorted price structures and penalized agricultural producers while they subsidized urban consumers. Stronger governments, encouraged by international adjustment loans, began to correct these policies in the 1980s. Boserup is keenly aware of the dangers of stimulating precocious industrial development in regions that had neither the agricultural infrastructure to supply the food surplus required for urban development or the comparative advantage to exchange for food abroad the output of these state-sponsored industrial enterprises. The problems of Africa in the last decade might have been less painful if Boserup's views had been shared by more development planners in the preceding two decades.

The seven essays in part 3 consider from different vantages the economic activities of women and the environmental determinants of desired fertility in low-income countries. Again in the company of Malthus, Boserup sought to integrate our knowledge of the microdeterminants of individual demographic and economic behavior with the macroconsequences of population aggregates that impinge on factor productivity and the incentives for various forms of investment. The social and productive roles open to women in a society appear to Boserup to influence the development path followed by the society. But the paths are many, and most place women at a comparative disadvantage relative to men as modernization proceeds. The productive activities of women include their work in the home as well as in the formal labor market. Desired fertility levels in a society are interrelated with the economic roles women perform in a society. The Reverend Malthus did not fully fathom that women and men could partially regulate their fertility within marriage in response to their lifetime objectives.

Boserup is sensitive to the anthropological literature that has recognized many means by which primitive and preindustrial populations managed to control their pace of childbearing (Dumond, 1975), though she does not defer to the microeconomic demand approach to fertility determinants (Becker, 1960; T. W. Schultz, 1973, 1974). Boserup, nonetheless, comes to much the same general conclusions as the microeconomic literature, for she finds explanations for fertility differences in individual and community opportunities open to women, men, and children, as well as the constraints set by climate, technology, institutions, and child mortality. Again, Boserup distinguishes her theories from the conventional wisdom of the neo-Malthusian school; she does not attribute high levels of fertility in low-income countries primarily to the lack of modern birth control techniques. Rather than focus attention on the deficit in family planning activity, Boserup examines closely the conditions of poor people to assess why they opted for high fertility rather than other means of investment in their future.

The five essays in part 4 deal explicitly with Africa. The development literature is more sparse on Africa than on any other major region of the world. The lack of hard data on many issues in Africa may explain part of this gap. Sub-Saharan Africa has made the least economic progress in the last two decades of any region, and there are few optimists who see things improving rapidly. Sub-Saharan Africa is only starting through its demographic transition, with mortality still very high and fertility not yet declining on a national or regional basis. It is clear that the new agricultural technologies that were developed in East Asia and Mexico, built around new high-yielding plant varieties and a package of complementary inputs such as fertilizer and pesticides, did not greatly benefit Africa. Even their adaptation to the agriclimatic conditions of South Asia and the rest of Latin America has required a long period of investment in local experimentation and extension activity. Boserup appreciated early in the 1960s that there was a wide gap separating Africa from Asia in terms of agricultural infrastructure and institutions that could support the modernization of agriculture. These trenchant observations may not have lost their relevance to the problems Africa still faces today.

Ricardo and Malthus assigned importance to the diminishing returns to labor when combined with a fixed factor—land. Whether workers sought to eke out more from a given parcel of land, whether they extended cultivation to new lands of a lesser quality, or whether they migrated to new territories at a greater distance from the market, the result would presumably be the same: a diminished real product of labor. This could be temporarily reversed by the opening up of new fertile frontiers for settlement, as in the colonial United States, but in the long run the same outcome could be expected. Boserup added to these two sources of classical diminishing returns to labor a third factor: increasing the frequency of cultivation. Her distinctive perspective is of course partly a result of the time and place of her research. Ricardo and Malthus drew their insights from the agricultural conditions of England and Europe and temperate zones of European settlement before the early nineteenth century. Boserup, with access to agricultural histories of tropical regions for the last 150 years—and hence evidence of the manyfold intensification of agriculture in such countries as Indonesia—could see that the supply of cropable land is more elastic than Malthus forecast. In the long run, changes in farming practices, buttressed by associated infrastructural investments, could expand greatly the "effective" supply of arable land.

The earliest stages of agriculture often involved slash and burn practices with long periods of forest fallow for the land to regain its fertility. These techniques continue in only a few remote regions of the world, such as the Amazon, Africa, and until recently, in the highlands of Southeast Asia. But they were once widespread. From this least intensive use of the land to the double and triple cropping in a calendar year that occurs in some tropical settings, the elasticity of "effective" supply of land is substantial. Changes in rotational practices introduced in Europe after the Middle Ages had similar but far smaller effects in extending the intensity of cultivation. Moreover, the combination of modern inputs that exploit the greater potential of tropical sunlight and temperatures for photosynthesis may be able to add further to the "effective" stock of arable land in some equatorial zones. At the other extreme, some tropical soils pose complex problems of infertility and are extremely fragile. The steady increase in the agricultural labor force in Egypt, for example, would certainly have led classical economists to forecast a decline in the real wages for an Egyptian farm worker. But in reality, irrigation developments and multiple cropping and the increased use of modern agricultural inputs have effectively substituted for Egyptian land. The share of rents in Egyptian rural income has declined in the last century, and real wages have risen (Hansen, 1968; T. W. Schultz, 1964).

The final essays in this volume concentrate on policy questions. It is difficult to demonstrate the payoff to investments in public infrastructure, because the services they produce are not readily priced and evaluated in the market, as for example, with rural roads. Boserup stresses the importance of transportation, storage, and other forms of rural-agricultural infrastructure in establishing a modern agriculture. Choices of productive techniques can also magnify the employment generated by public investments in infrastructure and thereby add more to national productivity in a country with abundant and relatively low-cost labor. Agriculture ranks high in its intensive use of labor, certainly in comparison with industry.

International development assistance from high-income to low-income countries is generally beneficial but can at times be counterproductive if it is tied to trade and thereby distorts domestic relative prices in developing countries. Food aid is seen by Boserup as a political reward for farmers in high-income countries that penalizes agriculture in the receiving countries, because the food aid lowers the price of output received there by farmers. Subsidization of farmers in the industrially advanced countries leads to the dumping of their agricultural surpluses, in one way or another, at less than their true production cost. Farmers in low-income countries thus confront a depressed price for their output in world markets and do not realize their gains from trade as a low-cost producer. Western Europe, Japan, and the United States are all, in various degrees, responsible for this growing distortion in world agricultural prices, which increasingly undermines the efficient development of agriculture in the low-income world. The soaring costs of these farm support policies for developed countries precipitate a change in policy that could be as important as the scale of development assistance. As outlined in her book *Population and Technological Change* (chapter 15), when international adaptation to demographic and technical change is frustrated by public policies, the misallocation of world resources can be great, and much of the burden falls to the low-income countries.

Supplementary Suggested Readings

PART I. ECONOMIC DEVELOPMENT AND DEMOGRAPHIC TRENDS

E. Boserup. *The Conditions of Agricultural Growth: The Economics of Agrarian Change under Population Pressure.* Chicago: Aldine, 1965.

A. J. Coale. "Recent Trends in Fertility in Less Developed Countries." *Science* 221 (1983).

A. C. Kelley and J. Williamson. *What Drives Third World City Growth.* Princeton: Princeton University Press, 1984.

S. H. Preston. "Are the Economic Consequences of Population Growth a Sound Basis for Population Policy?" In *World Population and U.S. Policy,* ed. J. Menken. New York: Norton, 1986.

D. Salvatore. "Modeling Demographic and Economic Dynamics." *Journal of Policy Modeling* 10 (1988).

T. P. Schultz. "Economic Demography and Development." In *The State of Development Economics,* eds. G. Ranis and T. P. Schultz. Oxford: Blackwell, 1988.

PART II. FOOD

Y. Hayami and V. Ruttan. *Agricultural Development: An International Perspective.* Baltimore: Johns Hopkins University Press, 1971.

T. N. Srinivasan. "Population and Food." In *Population Growth and Economic Development: Issues and Evidence,* eds. D. G. Johnson and R. D. Lee. Madison: University of Wisconsin Press, 1987.

PART III. WOMEN'S EMPLOYMENT AND FERTILITY

E. Boserup. *Woman's Role in Economic Development.* New York: St. Martins, 1970.

M. Buvinic, M. A. Lycette, and W. P. McGreevey, eds. *Women and Poverty in the Third World.* Baltimore: Johns Hopkins University Press, 1983.

J. D. Durand. *The Labor Force in Economic Development.* Princeton: Princeton University Press, 1975.

C. Goldin. "The Changing Economic Role of Women." *Journal of Interdisciplinary History* 13 (1983).

B. Hansen. "Employment and Wages in Rural Egypt." *American Economic Review* 59 (1969).

S. Joekes. *Women in The World Economy.* New York Oxford University Press, 1987.

R. Layard and J. Mincer, eds. "Trends in Women's Work, Education, and Family Building." *Journal of Labor Economics* 3 (1985).

V. Levy. "Cropping Pattern, Mechanization, Child Labor and Fertility Behavior in Rural Egypt." *Economic Development and Cultural Change* 33 (1985).

R. A. Pollak. "A Transaction Cost Approach to Families and Households." *Journal of Economic Literature* 22 (1985).

T. W. Schultz. "Fertility and Economic Values." In *Economics of the Family*, ed. T. W. Schultz. Chicago: University of Chicago Press, 1974.

L. Squire. *Employment Policy in Developing Countries*. New York: Oxford University Press, 1981.

PART IV. AFRICA

U. Lele. "Women and Structural transformation." *Economic Development and Cultural Change* 34 (1986).

J. L. Moock. *Understanding Africa's Rural Households and Farming Systems*. Boulder: Westview, 1986.

P. L. Pingali and H. Binswanger. "Population Density, and Agricultural Intensification." In *Population Growth and Economic Development*, eds. D. G. Johnson and R. D. Lee. Madison: University of Wisconsin Press, 1987.

PART V. POLICY

T. W. Schultz, ed. *Distortions of Agricultural Incentives*. Bloomington: Indiana University Press, 1978.

PART I

Economic Development and Demographic Trends

[1987]

Agricultural Growth and Population Change

THE MACROECONOMIC THEORY of the relationship between demographic and agricultural change was developed by Malthus and Ricardo in the early stage of demographic transition in Europe, and interest in classical theory was revived in the middle of this century, when economists became aware of the unfolding demographic transition in other parts of the world. Ricardo (1817) distinguished between two types of agricultural expansion in response to population growth. One is the extensive margin, the expansion into new land which he supposed would yield diminishing returns to labor and capital because the new land was presumed to be more distant or of poorer quality than the land already in use. The other type, the intensive margin, is more intensive cultivation of the existing fields, raising crop yields by such means as better fertilization, weeding, draining, and other land preparation. This also was likely to yield diminishing returns to labor and capital. Therefore Ricardo assumed, with Malthus (1803), that population increase would sooner or later be arrested by a decline in real wages, increase of rents, and decline of per capita food consumption.

This theory takes no account of a third type of agricultural expansion in response to population growth: using the increasing labor force to crop the existing fields more frequently. This was in fact what was happening in England in Ricardo's time, when the European system of short fallow was being replaced by the system of annual cropping. Fallows are neither more distant nor of poorer quality than the cultivated fields, but if fallow periods are shortened or eliminated more labor and capital inputs are needed, both to prevent a decline of crop yields and to substitute for the decline in the amount of fodder for animals, which was previously obtained by the grazing of fallows. Therefore, this type of intensification is also likely to yield diminishing returns to labor and capital, but the additions to total output obtained by increasing the frequency of cropping are much larger than those obtainable by use of more labor and capital simply to raise crop yields. In fact, the Ricardian type of intensification is better viewed as a means not to raise crop yields, but more to prevent a decline of those yields as fallow is shortened or

---

"Agricultural Growth and Population Change." Reprinted with permission from *The New Palgrave: A Dictionary of Economics*, edited by John Eatwell, Murray Milgate, and Peter Newman. London: Macmillan Press, New York: Stockton Press, 1987.

eliminated. When this third type of agricultural expansion by higher frequency of cropping is taken into account, elasticities of food supply in response to population growth are different from those assumed in classical theory.

The failure to take differences in frequency of cropping into account renders the classical theory unsuitable for the analysis of agricultural changes which accompany the demographic transition in developing countries in the second half of this century. Differences in population densities between developing countries are very large, and so are the related differences in frequency of cropping. The relevant classification for analysis of agricultural growth is not between new land and land which is sown and cropped each year, but the frequency at which a given piece of land is sown and cropped. Both in the past and today, we have a continuum of agricultural systems, ranging from the extreme case of land which is never used for crops, to the other extreme of land which is sown as soon as the previous crop is harvested. Increasing populations are provided with food and employment by gradual increase of the frequency of cropping.

In large, sparsely populated areas of Africa and Latin America, the local subsistence systems are pastoralism and long-fallow systems of the same types as those used in most of Europe in the first millenium A.D. and earlier. In areas with extremely low population densities, twenty or more years of forest fallow alternate with one or two years of cropping, while four to six years of bush fallow alternate with several years of cropping in regions where population densities have become too high to permit the use of longer fallow periods. Methods of subsistence agriculture in developing countries with even higher population densities include short-fallow systems (i.e. one or two crops followed by one or two years fallowing) or systems of annual cropping. In countries with very high population densities, including many Asian countries, some of the land is sown and cropped two or three times each year without any fallow periods.

If these differences in frequency of cropping are overlooked, or assumed to be adaptations to climatic or other permanent natural differences, the prospects for agricultural expansion in response to the growth of population and labor force look either more favorable, or more unfavorable, than they really are. In sparsely populated areas with long-fallow systems, the areas which bear secondary forests or are used for grazing may be assumed incorrectly to be new land in the Ricardian sense, it being overlooked that they have the functions of recreating soil fertility or humidity, preventing erosion, or suppressing troublesome weeds before the land is again used for crops. If neither the local cultivators nor their governments are aware of the risks of shortening fallow periods, and are not taking steps to avoid them, such shortening may damage the land and erosion, infertility, or desertification may result. In such cases, the scope for accommodating increasing populations will prove to be less than expected, and later repair of the damage will become costly, if possible at all. On the other hand, if land currently used as fallow in long fallow systems is assumed to be of inferior quality, in accordance with Ricardian theory, the large possibilities for accommodation of increasing populations by shifting from long fallow to shorter or no fallow will be overlooked or underestimated.

Labor Supplies

When population growth accelerated in the developing countries in the middle of this century, economists applied Ricardo's distinction between expansion of cultivation to new land and attempts to raise crop yields by additional inputs of labor and capital. They therefore focused on the most densely populated countries in Asia, in which there was little new land. Since the possibilities for multicropping were not taken into account, it was assumed that the elasticity of food production in response to population growth would be very low in these countries, and that the acceleration of population growth would soon result in food shortages, high food prices, reduction of real wages, and steep increase of Ricardian rent.

Lewis (1954) suggested that in densely populated countries with little, if any, uncultivated land, marginal returns to labor were likely to be zero or near to zero, and that a large part of the agricultural labor force was surplus labor, which could be transferred to nonagricultural employment without any diminution of agricultural output, even if there were no change in techniques. So Lewis recommended that rural-to-urban migration should be promoted, as a means of increasing marginal and average productivity in agriculture and of raising the share of the population employed in higher productivity occupations in urban areas. He confined his recommendation to densely populated countries, but many other economists made no distinction between densely and sparsely populated countries, assuming with Ricardo that uncultivated land must be of low quality so that a labor surplus would exist in all developing countries. The labor surplus theory contributed to create the bias in favor of industrial and urban development and the neglect of agriculture, which has been a characteristic feature of government policy in many developing countries.

However, the labor surplus theory underestimates the demand for labor in agricultural systems with high frequency of cropping, based on labor intensive methods and use of primitive equipment. If population density in an area increases, fallow is eliminated, and multicropping introduced, more and more labor-intensive methods must be used to preserve soil fertility, reduce weed growth and parasites, water the plants, grow fodder crops for animals, and protect the land. Some of the additional labor inputs are current operations, but others are labor investments. Before intensive cropping systems can be used, it may be necessary to terrace or level the land, build irrigation or drainage facilities, or fence the fields in order to control domestic animals. If these investments are made with human and animal muscle power, the necessary input of human labor is large. Even animals cannot reduce the work burden much, if fallows and other grazing land have been reduced so much that the cultivator must produce their fodder.

Part of the investments which are needed in order to increase the frequency of cropping are made by the cultivator with the same tools, animals, and equipment that are used for current operations. Estimates of investments and savings in agricultural communities with increasing population are seriously low if they fail to include such labor investments. Due to the larger number of crops, the additional operations with each crop, and labor investments, the demand for labor rises steeply when intensive land use is introduced. This contrasts with the assumptions of the labor surplus theory, which expects that the effect of population growth is always to add to the labor surplus.

When the theory of low supply elasticity and labor surplus in agriculture is combined with the theory of demographic transition, the prospects for densely populated countries with the majority of the population in agriculture look frightening. With the prospect of prolonged rapid growth of population (as forecast by the demographers) and with the poor prospects for expansion of food production and agricultural employment (implied by the labor surplus theory), it seemed obvious that sufficient capital could not be forthcoming for the enormous expansion of nonagricultural employment and output that was needed. So, because the possibilities for adapting food production to population were underestimated, many economists suggested that the best, or even the only means to avoid catastrophe was the promotion of rapid fertility decline by family planning. This in turn overlooked the links between the level of economic development and the motivations for restriction of family size.

The motivation for adopting an additional work load in periods of increasing population, and the means to shoulder it, are different as between agricultural subsistence economies and communities of commercial farmers. In the former, the need to produce enough food to feed a larger family may be sufficient motivation for adopting a new agricultural system which, at least for a time, raises labor input more steeply than output. The way to shoulder a larger work load is to increase the labor input of all family members. In some regions most of the agricultural work is done by men, and in other regions, by women; but when the work load becomes heavier, women become more involved in agricultural work in the former regions, and men more involved in the latter; in both, children and old people have more work to do. For all members of agricultural families, average work days become longer and days of leisure fewer. The whole year may become one long busy season in areas with widespread multicropping, labor intensive irrigation, and transplanting from seed beds.

For commercial producers, the motivation for intensification of agriculture emerges when population growth or increasing urban incomes increase the demand for food, and push food prices up until more frequent cropping becomes profitable, in spite of increasing costs of production or need for more capital investment. By this change in sectoral terms of trade, a part of the burden of rural population increase is passed on to the urban population. The increase of agricultural prices is by no means all an increase of Ricardian rent, but is in good part a compensation for increasing costs of production. If the increase of food prices is prevented by government intervention or by imports of cheap food, the intensification will not take place.

Moreover, in regions with commercial agriculture, work seasons become longer when crop frequency increases in response to population growth. Therefore, the decline of real wages per work hour is at least partially compensated for by more employment in the off-seasons, and by more employment opportunities for women and children in the families of agricultural workers. The discussion of low or zero marginal productivity in agriculture suffers from a neglect of the seasonal differences in employment and wages. Many off-season operations are in fact required in order to obtain higher crop frequency through labor intensive methods alone, and so may well appear to be of very low productivity if viewed in isolation from their real function. Wages for these operations, or indeed off-season wages generally, may be very low, but the seasonal differences in wages are usually large. Therefore, accumulation of debt in the off seasons with repayment in the peak seasons is a frequent pattern of expenditure in laboring families.

Low off-season wages are an important incentive for intensification of the cropping pattern in commercial farms, since much of the additional labor with multicropping, irrigation, labor intensive crops, and feeding animals falls in these seasons. But when the same land is cropped more frequently in response to population growth, the demand for labor in the peak seasons also rises steeply, perhaps more than the supply of labor. In many cases, a large share of the agricultural population combines subsistence production on small plots of owned or rented land with wage labor for commercial producers in the agricultural peak seasons, and this contributes to considerable flexibility in the labor market. If real wages decline, because population increase pushes food prices up, full-time agricultural workers have no other choice than to reduce their leisure and that of their spouse and children, and offer to work for very low wages in off-season periods. But workers who have some land to cultivate may choose to limit their supply of wage labor, and instead cultivate their own land more intensively with family labor. Since they took wage labor mainly in the peak seasons, their limitation in the supply of wage labor may prevent a decline in, or cause an increase in, real wages in the peak seasons, and thus put a floor below the incomes of full-time workers.

The flexibility of the rural labor market is enhanced if not only labor but also land is hired in and out. A family that disposes of an increasing labor force may either do some work for other villagers, or rent some land from them, while a family that disposes of a reduced labor force may either hire some labor, or lease some land to others. With such a flexible system, prices for lease of land and wages will rapidly be adjusted to changes in labor supply. But the smooth adaptation of the system to population change will be hampered or prevented if, for political reasons, either hiring of labor or lease of land is made illegal, or changes in agricultural prices are prevented by government action.

Transport Cost and Urbanization

In Ricardian theory, marginal returns to labor and capital decline in response to population growth, partly because agricultural production is intensified, partly because it is expanded to inferior land, and partly because more distant land is taken into cultivation, thus increasing costs of transport. Thus, when population is increasing, producers have a choice between increasing costs of production, or increasing costs of transport between fields and consumers. However, there is a third possibility, which is to move the center of consumption closer to land which is of similar quality to that which was used before the population became larger. Communities who use long-fallow periods often move their habitations after long-term settlement in a forested area, and move to another area where the fertility of forest land has become high after a long period of nonuse. Such movement of villages is likely to become more frequent as population increases.

In other cases it is not the whole village which is moved, but an increasing number of villagers move their habitation to new lands, where they build isolated farmsteads or new hamlets. This may accommodate additional populations until all the space between the villages is filled up with habitations, and the choice in case of further population growth is between more frequent cropping or use of inferior land, or long distance migration of part of the population.

The combination of shorter fallow periods and filling up of the space between the villages helps to create the conditions for emergence of small urban centers. Costs of transport are inversely related to the volume of transport, and roads, even primitive ones, are only economical, or feasible, with a relatively high volume of traffic. If fallow periods are very long, and distances between villages are large, there will be too few people in an area to handle both the production and transport which are necessary to supply a town with agricultural products. Urbanization and commercial agricultural production are only possible when population densities are relatively high and fallow periods short. So when population in an area continues to increase, a point may be reached when small market towns emerge, served by road and water transport, as happened in large parts of Europe in the beginning of this millenium.

With further growth of population it will again be necessary to choose between further intensification of agriculture at increasing costs, or moving the additional consumers (or some of them) to another location, where they can be supplied by less intensive agriculture, and with shorter distances of transport. So at this stage of development, new small market towns may emerge in between the old towns, or in peripheral areas together with agricultural settlement. In other words, instead of agricultural products moving over longer and longer distances, thus creating Ricardian rent in the neighborhood of existing consumer centers, new centers of consumption may appear closer to the fields. In most of Europe, such a gradual spread of decentralized urbanization made it possible to delay the shift from short-fallow agriculture to annual cropping in the late eighteenth or the nineteenth century. Areas with such a network of market towns have better conditions for development of small-scale and middle-sized industrialization than sparsely populated areas with a scattered population of subsistence farmers.

The long-distance migration from Europe to North America in the nineteenth century can be viewed as a further step in this movement of European agricultural producers and consuming centers to a region with lower population density, less intensive agriculture, and much lower agricultural costs. The urban centers in America were supplied by extensive systems of short-fallow agriculture at a time when production in western Europe had shifted to much more intensive agriculture with annual cropping and fodder production.

Technology

From ancient times, growth of population and increase of urbanization have provided incentives to technological improvements in agriculture, either by transfer of technology from one region to another, or by inventions in response to urgent demand for increase of output, either of land, or labor, or both. Until the nineteenth century, technological change in agriculture was a change from primitive technology, that is, human labor with primitive tools, to intermediate technology, that is, human labor sided by better hand tools, animal-drawn equipment, and water power for flow irrigation. In the classical theory of agricultural growth, such changes are means to promote population growth and urbanization, but they are assumed to be fortuitous inventions, and are not viewed as technological changes induced by population growth and increasing urbanization.

In the course of the nineteenth century, the continuing increase in the demand for agricultural products, and the increasing competition of urban centers for agricultural labor, induced further technological change in European and North American agriculture. The technological innovations of the Industrial Revolution were used to accomplish a gradual shift from intermediate to high-level technologies, that is, human labor aided by mechanized power and other industrial inputs. The chemical and engineering industries contributed to raise productivity of both land, labor and transport of agricultural products, and scientific methods were introduced in agriculture as a means of raising yields of crops and livestock.

The existence of such high-level technologies improves the possibilities for rapid expansion of agricultural production in developing countries as well, but because in North America and Europe these technologies were used to reduce direct labor input in agriculture, those economists who believed in the labor surplus theory feared that they would further increase labor surplus. However, the idea of a general labor surplus in agriculture in developing countries had never been unanimously agreed, and under the influence of empirical studies of intensive agriculture in densely populated regions, T. W. Schultz (1964) suggested that labor was likely to be fully occupied even in very small holdings, when primitive technology was used. Therefore, output and income in such holdings could only be increased by introduction of industrial and scientific inputs and human capital investment of the types used in industrialized countries.

Although proponents and opponents of the labor surplus theory had different views concerning the relationship between the demand for and supply of labor, they agreed in suggesting a low supply elasticity of output in response to labor inputs, because they overlooked, or underestimated, the large effects on output and employment which can be obtained by using high-level technologies to increase the frequency of cropping. The availability of new varieties of quickly maturing seeds, of chemical fertilizers, and of mechanized equipment for pumping water and land improvements, permits the use of multicropping on a much larger scale and in much drier and colder climates than was possible before these new types of inputs existed. The new high-level technologies have changed the constraints on the size of the world population from the single one of land area to those of energy supply and costs, and of capital investment.

The new inputs permit a much more flexible adaptation of agriculture to changes in population and real wages. Intensive agriculture is no longer linked to low real wages, and it is possible, by changing the composition of inputs, to vary the rates of increase of employment and real wages for a given rate of increase of total output. By using a mixture of labor-intensive and high-level techniques, adapted to the man-land ratio and the level of economic development, first Japan, and later many other densely populated countries obtained rapid increases in both agricultural employment, output per worker, and total output. This Green Revolution is an example of a technological change in agriculture induced by population change. The research which resulted in the development of these methods and inputs was undertaken and financed by national governments and international donors concerned about the effects of rapid population growth on the food situation in developing countries. Therefore, it focused mainly on improvement of agriculture in densely populated countries, where both governments and donors considered the problem to be most serious.

Agricultural producers who use high-level technologies are much more dependent upon the availability of good rural infrastructure than producers who use primitive or intermediate technologies. Transport and trade facilities are needed not only for the commercial surplus but also for the industrial inputs in agriculture; repair shops, electricity supply, technical schools, research stations, veterinary and extension services are also needed. Therefore short-term supply elasticities differ between those regions which have and those which do not have the infrastructure needed for use of industrial and scientific inputs in agriculture. In the former, a rapid increase of output may be obtained by offering more attractive prices to the producers, while in the latter, increase of prices may have little effect on output, until the local infrastructure has been improved. Improvement of infrastructure may, on the other hand, be sufficient to obtain a change from subsistence production to commercial production, if it results in a major reduction in the difference between the prices paid to the local producers and those obtained in the consuming centers.

In densely populated regions with a network of small market towns, it is more feasible to introduce industrial and scientific inputs in agriculture than in regions inhabited only by a scattered population of agricultural producers. Because per capita costs of infrastructure are lower in the first-mentioned regions, they are more likely to have the necessary infrastructure, and if not, governments may be more willing to supply it. Thus sparsely populated regions are handicapped compared to densely populated ones, when high-level technologies are taken into use.

Tenure

Changes in output may also be prevented if the local tenure system is ill adapted to the new agricultural system. Land tenure is different in regions with different frequency of cropping. In regions with long-fallow agriculture, individual producers have only usufruct rights in the land they use for cultivation, and the land, the pastures, and the forested land are all tribally owned. Before a plot is cleared for cultivation it is usually assigned by the local chief, and when large investments or other large works are needed the producers are organized by the chief as mutual work parties. If population increases and with it the demands for assignment of land, a stage may be reached when either the chief or the village community will demand a payment for such assignments, thereby changing the system of land tenure. Payments to the chief for assignment of land may turn him into a large-scale landowner, and this payment may tip the balance and make more frequent cropping of land more economical than use of new plots, or settlement in new hamlets.

When frequency of cropping becomes sufficiently high that major permanent investments in land improvement are necessary, a change to private property in land may provide security of tenure to the cultivator, and make it possible for him to obtain credits. If at this stage no change of tenure is made by legal reform, a system of private property in land is likely to emerge by unlawful action and gradual change of custom; but in such cases, the occupants, who have no legal rights to the land, may hesitate (or be unable) to make investments, and the land may remain unprotected against erosion and other damage.

In more densely populated areas, with more frequent cropping and need for large-scale irrigation and other land improvement, these investments may be organized by big landlords as labor service or by local authorities as wage labor, financed by local or general taxation. In order to change from a particular fallow system to another that is more intensive, it is likely that not only the ownership system in the cultivated plots but also that for uncultivated land must be changed, as must responsibility for infrastructure investment. Because of the links between the fallow system, the tenure system, and the responsibility for infrastructure investment, attempts to intensify the agricultural system by preservation (for political reasons) of the old tenure system and rural organization are likely to be unsuccessful, as are attempts to introduce new tenure systems that are unsuitable for the existing (or the desired, future) level of intensity and technology. Therefore, government policy is an important determinant of the agricultural response to population growth.

During fallow periods, the land is used for a variety of purposes: for gathering fuel and other wood, for hunting, for gathering of fertilizer, for grazing and browsing by domestic animals. Therefore, a change of the fallow system may create unintended damage to the environment unless substitutes are introduced for these commodities, or the pattern of consumption is changed. When hunting land becomes short, the right to hunt may be appropriated by the chiefs (or others), forcing the villagers to change their diet. When grazing land becomes short, enclosures may prevent the villagers (or some of them) from using it, or the village community may ration the right to pasture animals in the common grazing land and fallows, in order to prevent overgrazing and erosion, or desertification. These measures will impose a change of diet, and perhaps a change to fodder production in the fields.

Nutrition

Both production and consumption change from land-using to less-land-using products when population increases and agriculture is intensified. There may be a shift from beef and mutton to pork and poultry, from animal to vegetable products, from cereals to root crops for human consumption, and from grazing to production of fodder for animals. Under conditions of commercial farming, the changes in consumption and production are induced by increasing differentials between the prices of land-saving and land-using products. If the process of population growth is accompanied by decline of real wages, the changes in consumption patterns for the poorest families may be large. This may result in protein deficiencies and malnutrition with spread of the disease-malnutrition syndrome; this causes high child mortality because disease prevents the child from eating and digesting food, and nutrition reduces the resistance to disease.

The classical economists had suggested that continuing population growth would result in malnutrition, famine, and disease, which would reestablish the balance between population and resources by increasing mortality. But they also envisaged the possibility of an alternative model, in which population growth was prevented by voluntary restraint on fertility. Malthus (1803) talked of moral restraint and Ricardo (1817) of the possibility that the workers would develop a taste for comforts and enjoyment, which would prevent a superabundant population. However, it was not ethical or psychological changes but the economic and social changes resulting from increasing industrialization and urbanization which induced a deceleration of rates of population growth, first in Europe and North America, and later in other parts of the world.

Government Policies

The deceleration of rates of population growth in Europe and North America coincided with a decline in the income elasticity of demand for food due to the increase in per capita incomes. As a result, the rate of increase in the demand for food slowed down, just as the rate of increase of production accelerated due to the spread of high-level technologies and scientific methods in agriculture. If it had not been for government intervention in support of agriculture, these changes would have led to abandonment of production in marginal land, and use of less industrial inputs in the land that was kept in cultivation. But this process of adjustment was prevented by attempts to preserve the existing system of family farming. Large farms could utilize high-level technologies (especially mechanized inputs) better than smaller ones, but governments wanted to prevent the replacement of small or middle-sized farms by larger capitalist farms, or company farming. Therefore, both western Europe and North America gradually developed comprehensive systems of agricultural protection and subsidization of agriculture, agricultural research, and other rural infrastructure. In spite of this support, a large proportion of the small farms disappeared and much marginal land went out of cultivation, while the support actually encouraged large farms, and farms in the most favored regions, to expand their production; they increased their use of fertilizer and other inputs, and invested in expansion of capacity for vegetable and animal production. So supply still continued to outrun demand, and protection against imports and subsidies to exports still continued to increase, while the industrialized countries turned from being net importers to net exporters of more and more agricultural products.

In the discussions about labor surplus and low elasticity of agricultural production in nonindustrialized countries, Nurkse (1953) had suggested that an increase in agricultural production could be obtained if the surplus population was employed in rural work projects. In the period until such a program, in conjunction with industrialization and a deceleration of population growth, could reestablish the balance between demand for and supply of food, he recommended that temporary food imports (preferably as food aid) should be used to prevent food shortage. Because of the increasing costs of financing and disposing of the food surplus, Nurkse's suggestion of food aid was well received by Western governments, and transfer of food, as aid or subsidized exports, reached large dimensions.

Some governments in developing countries did use food aid and commercial imports of the food surpluses of the industrialized countries as stopgap measures, until their own promotion of rural infrastructure and other support to agriculture would make it possible for production to catch up with the rapidly increasing demand for food. But for many other governments, the availability of cheap imports and gifts of food became a welcome help to avoid the use of their own resources to support agriculture and invest in rural infrastructure. Even in those developing countries with a large majority of the population occupied in agriculture, the share of government expenditure devoted to agriculture and related rural infrastructure is small, and within this small amount, priority is usually given to development of nonfood export crops, which often supply a large share of foreign exchange earnings. Exports of food crops are unattractive because of the surplus disposal of the industrialized countries, which exerts a downward pressure on world market prices. Therefore, both producers and governments in developing countries focus on the types of crops which do not compete with these subsidized exports. In regions in which the necessary infrastructure was available, employment and output of such export crops increased rapidly, not only in countries with abundant land resources but also in many densely populated countries, which shifted in part from food to nonfood crops. This general shift from food to nonfood crops contributed to a downward pressure on export prices of the latter crops in the world market.

Food imports can have important short-term advantages for the importing country. Rapidly increasing urban areas can be supplied at low prices and without the need to use government resources to obtain expansion of domestic production. Moreover, counterpart funds from food aid can be used to finance general government expenditure, and in countries with high levies on export crops, government revenue increases when production is shifted from food to export crops. However, although there might be short-term advantages in food imports and food aid, the long-term cost of neglecting agricultural and rural development can be very high. The lack of transport facilities and local stocks, and the lack of irrigation in dry and semidry areas, may transform years of drought to years of famine. When governments do not invest in rural infrastructure and fail to provide the public services which are necessary for the use of high-technology inputs, the latter can be used only by large companies (who can themselves finance the necessary infrastructure) or only in a few areas close to large cities.

Without cost reduction by improvement of the transport network and agricultural production, commercial food production may in many areas be unable to compete with imports. Commercial production will decline and subsistence producers will not become commercial producers. Instead, the most enterprising young villagers will emigrate in order to earn money incomes elsewhere. A larger and larger share of the rapidly increasing urban consumption must be imported, and food imports become a drug on which the importers become more and more dependent. The increasing dependency of many developing countries on food imports and food grants is often seen as a confirmation of the classical theory of inelastic food supply, and an argument for continuation of the policy of production subsidies and surplus disposal in America and western Europe. Food imports are seen as gap fillers, bridging over increasing differences between food consumption and national food production in developing countries; but in many cases the gap is actually created by the food imports, because of their effect on local production and rural development.

Fertility

Contrary to the expectations prevalent in the middle of this century, government policy has proved to be a more important determinant of agricultural growth than the man-resource ratio, and the response to rapid population growth has often been better in densely populated countries than in sparsely populated ones with much better natural conditions for agricultural growth. The differences in agricultural growth rates and policies have in turn contributed to create differences in demographic trends, partly by their influence on industrial and urban development and partly by the effects on rural fertility, mortality, and migration.

Because of their preoccupation with the man-land ratio, governments in densely populated countries not only devoted more attention and financial resources to agriculture than governments in sparsely populated countries, they also more often devoted attention and financial resources to policies aimed at reducing fertility. Moreover, tenure systems in densely populated countries usually provided less encouragement to large family size than tenure systems in sparsely populated countries.

In many densely populated countries with intensive agricultural systems, much of the rural population consists of small and middle-sized landowners, and such people are more likely to be motivated to a smaller family size than are landless labor and people with insecure tenure. They are less dependent upon help from adult children in emergencies and old age, because they can mortgage, lease, or sell land, or cultivate with hired labor. They may also have an interest in avoiding division of family property among too many heirs. If they live in areas where child labor is of little use in agriculture, they may have considerable economic interest in not having large families, and be responsive to advice and help from family planning services.

In sparsely populated regions with large landholdings, the rural population seldom has access to modern means of fertility control, and motivations for family restrictions are weak. A large share of the rural population tends to be landless or nearly landless workers, and if not, they may be without security in land. So they are much more dependent upon help from adult children in emergencies and old age than are landowners, or tenants with secure tenure. If, moreover, their children work for wages on ranches, farms, and plantations, the period until a child contributes more to family income than it costs is too short to provide sufficient economic motivation for family restriction.

People who use long-fallow systems in regions with tribal tenure have even more motivation for large family size than landless workers. The size of the area they can dispose of for cultivation is directly related to the size of their family, and most of the work, at least with food production, is done by women and children. So a man can become rich by having several wives and large numbers of children working for him. Moreover, unless he has acquired other property a man's security in old age depends on his adult children and younger wives, since he cannot mortgage or sell land in which he has only usufruct rights. Because of the differences in motivations for family size provided by individual and tribal tenure systems, the start of the fertility decline in regions with long-fallow systems is likely to be linked to the time when population increase induces the replacement of the tribal tenure system by another system of tenure, and a decline is then more likely if it is replaced by small-scale land ownership than if it is replaced by large-scale farming.

In addition to the tenure system, changes in technological levels in agriculture and the availability of economic and social infrastructure may influence the timing of fertility decline in rural areas. The heavy reliance upon female and child labor in those densely populated areas in which agriculture is intensified by means of labor alone may provide motivation for large families in spite of the shortage of land. Introduction of higher level technologies may then reduce a man's motivation to have a large family because it reduces the need for female and child labor. Use of intermediate and high-level technologies is nearly always reserved for adult men, while women and children do the operations for which primitive technologies are used. So when primitive technologies are replaced by higher level ones in more and more agricultural operations, men usually get more work to do and the economic contributions of their wives and children decline, thus reducing their economic interest in large family size. Moreover, in regions with little rural development, high rates of child mortality may delay fertility decline, and the large-scale migration of youth from such areas may have a similar effect if parents can count on receiving remittances from emigrant offspring.

However, the relationship between rural development and fertility is complicated. Parents may want a large family for other than economic reasons, and increases in income due to rural development or to better prices for agricultural products make it easier for them to support a large family, thus preventing or delaying fertility decline. Other things being equal, fertility is positively related to income; but in developing societies most increases in income are caused and accompanied by technological, occupational, and spatial changes that tend to encourage fertility decline, and the operation of these opposing effects may result in a relatively long time lag between rural modernization and fertility decline.

[1983]

The Impact of Scarcity and Plenty on Development

IN ALL PERIODS OF human history wide differences have existed among societies which developed rapidly, stagnant societies, and societies which reverted from more developed to more primitive levels. Even today, we see sharp contrasts between communities of hunter gatherers which have remained small in numbers, are illiterate, and apply Stone Age technologies, and societies which, as a result of a long process of interrelated demographic and technological development, have large populations and have reached high levels of development with advanced industrial technology, general literacy, and a sizable, scientifically trained elite.

Were these differences in development related to differences in accessibility of food in these societies, and if so, was scarcity or plenty of food most likely to promote development?

Two centuries ago, the French Physiocratic school suggested that the development of human societies depended upon the size of the agricultural surplus which that society could produce and, since that time, this idea has been the focus of development theory. This agricultural surplus was the total food surplus produced in a given society, and the Physiocrats saw population increase as a means to increase this surplus. However, the classical economists, by developing their theory of diminishing returns to labor use in agriculture, focused upon the agricultural surplus per head of population. Malthus suggested that population increase would gradually reduce this surplus and end by eliminating the whole surplus, thus arresting development and causing starvation (Malthus, 1803).

There was an escape from the Malthusian population trap. Technological improvement in agriculture could raise the productivity of land and labor, thus making it possible to feed a larger population. But, unless technological change in agriculture was rapid, as it is in industrialized societies, the escape was assumed to be only temporary, because the surplus created by technological progress would be "eaten up" by further population increase, due to improved nutrition.

"The Impact of Scarcity and Plenty on Development." Reprinted from *The Journal of Interdisciplinary History* 14 (1983): 383–407, with the permission of the editors of *The Journal of Interdisciplinary History* and The MIT Press, Cambridge, Massachusetts. © 1983 by The Massachusetts Institute of Technology and the editors of *The Journal of Interdisciplinary History*.

This neo-Malthusian theory is unrealistic for more than one reason. First, technological progress in agriculture would not result in further population growth in cases where factors other than insufficient food supply were the effective restraints on population. Second, the malnourished were always the poor, and they would sometimes lose more than they gained by changes in agricultural technology, at least in the short run. Thus their mortality might not decline and might even increase. Third, and even more important, the Malthusian theory overlooks the effect of population increase on technological change. We have recent examples of this effect in the Green Revolution and modern birth control techniques. Both were developed as a result of research promoted by fear of rapid population growth in unindustrialized countries. Also, in earlier periods of history, the need to feed larger populations led to technology transfers from one society to another or to the invention of new methods and tools (E. Boserup, 1981a).

Population increase has two different effects on systems of production: the one, on which the Malthusian theory focuses, is the negative effect of diminishing returns, when the existing agricultural system must feed more people. But this situation provides motivation for the introduction of more intensive systems of production and these changes may or may not raise the productivity of land and labor, depending upon local circumstances. The other effect of population increase is to make it possible to build, and finance the building of, collective investments in physical and human infrastructure of various types, especially investment in water regulation, energy supply, and transportation. Because a larger population can afford more infrastructure, it can make use of technologies which would be inapplicable or uneconomical for a smaller one. The positive effects of this will often outweigh any negative effects of a higher man-land ratio on food supply and development.

In other words, because population increase motivated and often facilitated technological change, its effects on development were often positive. We have seen many increasing populations with sufficient food supply and rapid development, and many stagnant populations with sufficient food supply and no development. But we have also seen increasing populations with insufficient food supply and no development, and increasing populations with insufficient food supply, widespread malnutrition among the poor, and rapid development. We look below at some important examples of these different patterns of demographic, technological, and nutritional conditions.

A people could adapt to increasing numbers by means other than the intensification of agriculture and the introduction of technological changes. They could increase total food supply by changing the diet from food which uses land extensively, for instance meat of large animals kept on natural pastures, to pork, poultry, and cereals. Or they could replace such land-intensive crops as cereals with tubers or roots that have higher food value yields per acre. Another possibility could be to use the increasing military strength of a growing population to conquer land from neighbors, or impose food imports from them as a tribute. Food could also be obtained in exchange for other products. Finally, growing populations could adapt population size to food supply instead of adapting food supply to population either by inducing a part of the population to emigrate to another area, or by birth prevention or infanticide. The effects on development would be very different according to which of these means of adaptation were used.

Food Supply and Development in the Ancient World

In a primitive society, food supply is plentiful when the man-land ratio is very low, but becomes scarce when the population becomes larger. Even in regions of poor soil and unfavorable climate, a very small population may be able to obtain sufficient food by applying primitive techniques. If climatic conditions preclude agriculture, a population which is sufficiently small and widely scattered can obtain enough food by hunting, pastoralism, or fishing, but in such a region food supplies will fall short as soon as the population density exceeds a very low level. In areas of better climate and soil, the limit between easy and difficult food supply will be at higher population densities, but there will be a limit where plenty gives way to scarcity, unless the methods of obtaining food are changed.

There can be little doubt that population trends in prehistory varied from one period to another, and from one people to another, as was the case in later periods for which we have better information. Some prehistoric peoples no doubt died out, either as a result of sudden catastrophes or because mortality exceeded fertility over long periods. Other peoples avoided an increase in the man-land ratio in their original habitat either by migration, by infanticide and exposure of children, or by high mortality from disease, war, or starvation. If their numbers did not increase, they were likely to continue as hunter gatherers or pastoralists, and as late as 1500 A.D., such peoples occupied most of the world except for Europe and parts of Asia. However, some peoples increased their numbers slowly and adapted to increasing man-land ratios by eating new types of foods, and later by introducing systematic food production (R. B. Lee and de Vore, 1968; M. Cohen, 1977).

Within the group of peoples who introduced food production, there were wide differences in population trends. Most of the early food-producing peoples seem to have used long-fallow systems. Such systems are still widespread in Africa, Latin America, and parts of Asia, but they cannot support high population densities. If population increases, land which has been fallowed for the usual number of years becomes scarce, so that it becomes necessary to shorten the fallow period (E. Boserup, 1965).

However, fallowing serves many purposes; it preserves the land's fertility, reduces weeds and plant disease, and protects against erosion. Before industrially made chemicals and other industrial inputs existed, the shortening of the fallow period necessitated the use of additional labor to gather and spread fertilizing matter, weed, remove diseased plants, create mounds or terraces, and perhaps water the crops or drain the land.

The need for such additional labor and capital inputs was—and still is—

a deterrent to the introduction of more intensive systems of agriculture, as long as the man-land ratio was low enough to allow the land to lie fallow for long periods. When fallow was shortened or abandoned, labor-intensive techniques had to be used. If such techniques were not known, or if they remained unused to avoid additional labor and capital inputs, crop yields declined and the land was often damaged. The result was starvation and malnutrition, unless the population was reduced by migration or infanticide, or unless food was imported or more territory could be conquered.

A number of peoples, widely scattered over the world, avoided these pitfalls when they shifted to more intensive agricultural systems. By gradually making land use more and more intensive, they supported long-term rates of population growth, which may have amounted, with some large fluctuations, to an average of 0.1 percent annually (Cowgill, 1975).

Some of these peoples, who in the millennia before our era increased from small numbers to more than a million, inhabited the Mesopotamian Plain and the surrounding mountains. A large number of excavations have shown that settlement began in the mountains with gathering and pastoralism, which were increasingly replaced by agriculture. As the population continued to grow, part of the increase was accommodated in the mountains through the intensification of agriculture and the development of small systems of flow irrigation. Another part of the population increase chose emigration to the plains, where it continued with irrigated agriculture and gradually, as the population continued to grow, built systems of flow irrigation (Smith and Young, 1972; Adams, 1965a; Adams and Nissen, 1976).

The Mesopotamians and other peoples in Asia and the Mediterranean region who had developments of this type gradually invented or imported from each other many techniques which intensified their agriculture. One of these techniques was flow irrigation, which solved both the problem of water supply and that of fertilization in regions like Mesopotamia, where the rivers carried silt, which was spread over the fields by annual overflows. Moreover, the Mesopotamians imported oxen, suitable for draft power, and iron, and they either invented or imported plowing techniques. Much later, they imported different methods to lift water, so that the irrigation networks could be further enlarged. It was long believed that these inventions enabled the Mesopotamian peasants not only to multiply many times, but also to produce food surpluses, which could feed at first a number of small towns, and later a number of large cities.

However, archaeological research in other parts of the world has revealed that large-scale urbanization occurred also among peoples who did not benefit from any of these techniques. For instance, the Mayan people in Mesoamerica built their urban centers and huge temples although they only had tools of stone and hardened clay. They had no draft animals or plows, but relied exclusively on human muscle power and Stone Age tools for all of their intensive agricultural operations and construction activities. Fertilization was not provided by the overflow of silt-laden rivers; instead, the Mayans relied on labor inputs and performed the ardous task of hand weeding. Recent research has shown that, in the period of high population density in the Mayan region, that is, in the first millennium A.D., the Mayas created walled and elevated fields and terraces, and dug canals in order to drain their fields and perhaps for transportation. In the Mayan area, transportation was effected exclusively by human muscle power, in contrast to Mesopotamia, where boats were drawn upstream by wind power and wheeled wagons were drawn by animals (Sanders, 1972; Harrison and Turner, 1978).

No doubt, life was very difficult for the Mayan peasants, and some exhumed skeletons show signs of malnutrition; but the example of the Mayas demonstrates that an urban civilization with monumental structures, a written language, and a large population could be created by peoples with very primitive tools and difficult conditions of food production and transportation (Angel, 1975).

If we compare the conditions of the Mayas in the period of urbanization with those of European peasants north of the Alps, it is clear that it was much more difficult for a Mayan peasant family to produce an agricultural surplus than it was for a European peasant family. The average population density in that part of Europe was still very low. According to the available estimates, there were only five to ten persons per square kilometer, and long-fallow and pastoralism were the predominant food supply systems. For many millennia, the Europeans had been importing food supply techniques from Asia and North Africa. They used crops of Asian origin, scratch plows operated by oxen, and iron weapons and tools. Irrigation, and the heavy work and capital investment it required, was not needed because of the humid climate, and long-fallow techniques saved them from arduous labor with fertilization and weeding. Their animals fed on natural pastures and forests. If ever we could talk of ancient agricultural peoples who had plentiful food, the inhabitants of Europe would seem to be among them. They combined a low man-land ratio with advanced technologies—according to the standards of that time—while the Mayas combined a high man-land ratio with very primitive technology.

Nevertheless, it was the Mayas, with all their handicaps in food supply, and not the Europeans, who developed an urban civilization. In Europe north of the Alps indigenous urbanization appeared only in the beginning of this millennium. In the Roman period, agricultural surpluses north of the Alps fed only some Roman settlements, and even these seem, at least partially, to have relied on supplies of cereals that came from Rome by sea and by river transportation (Finley, 1973).

The comparison between the Mayas and the inhabitants of Europe illustrates that the condition for development of an urban civilization is not the ability of a population to produce a large agricultural surplus per family. The Europeans could no doubt have done that much better than the Mayas. In fact, the tribute paid by the Mayan peasants was not at a high level per family, but the number of families who contributed to the total agricultural surplus was very large, and this is what mattered for urbanization.

If man-land ratios were low in ancient times and the population was scattered, as it had to be in order to use labor-saving long-fallow techniques, food surpluses had to be moved over long distances in order to supply a town of more than a few thousand non-food-producing persons. But in ancient societies land transportation over more than some eight to ten kilometers was unfeasible or uneconomical, and only very densely populated regions could afford to build networks of canals linking producers to urban consumers. All economic historians stress the importance of transportation facilities for urbanization, but few have noted the close correlation between population density and the feasibility of creating transportation networks (Finley, 1973).

A powerful empire could build strategic highways through sparsely populated areas, but long-distance bulk transportation of food on such highways was uneconomical with the primitive equipment of those times. Moreover, highways and other roads deteriorated quickly if the empire lacked the power or the motive to use and repair them. Thus, because of the dependence of urban centers on food transportation, a certain population density was a necessary but not sufficient condition for urbanization. To judge from the few estimates of population density that are available, it seems that small towns were established in regions with some thirty to sixty inhabitants per square kilometer. Large cities of 100,000 appeared only in regions with much higher densities, or with exceptionally good possibilities for obtaining bulk supplies of food by long-distance water transport, as was the situation with Rome and Athens (Sanders and Price, 1968).

Peasants, like the Europeans, who were using long-fallow agriculture in sparsely populated regions, could not become suppliers of basic food to urban centers. For lack of transportation facilities, they remained isolated subsistence producers. Sometimes they produced surpluses for a scattered upper class who lived in small numbers in the villages, but these people did not benefit from the cross-fertilization of ideas and the access to systematic training and education, from which elites living together in urban centers could benefit. So development occurred not where food was plentiful, but where population density was so high that many people lived together and created and maintained an infrastructure, which facilitated communication both within the centers and between different centers (Childe, 1952).

The Breakdown and Decay of Ancient Cultures

The high man-land ratio in ancient urbanized societies made obtaining food difficult, but it was a necessary condition for building the infrastructure on which these societies depended. Given the labor-intensive technologies of those times, the cities with their walls, fortifications, huge temples, and palaces could not have been built had the dense populations not provided a large labor force. Also, the necessary rural infrastructure, transportation facilities, and flow irrigation systems required a large and densely settled population to perform the manual labor.

Most ruling classes in ancient societies created infrastructures by means of obligatory labor services performed by peasants when they were not needed in the fields. Part of such labor services was directly related to food production, such as the building, cleaning, and repair of dams and irrigation canals, or work on the agricultural holdings of the upper class. But other activities performed by peasant labor were the construction of temples, palaces, castles, city walls, and transportation facilities, and military service. As the peasants used more and more intensive agricultural systems in step with the increase in the man-land ratio, the seasons without work in the fields became shorter, and a conflict arose as to whether labor should be used in the fields, for irrigation and other agriculture-related activities, or for non-agricultural purposes (Wittvogel, 1957).

The conflict became acute when flow irrigation systems became extensive. As long as only the area with natural overflow was under cultivation, good yields could be obtained with a relatively small input of labor; but when a large system had to be cleaned and repaired each year after the annual floods, the process became labor intensive for a lengthy period each year. This was true even for systems which used animal draft power. Draft animals are not an efficient source of energy, if population density becomes so high that the animals cannot be fed on natural pastures and human labor must be used to provide fodder for them. The mechanical energy supplied by animals is only a small percentage of the energy contained in the fodder they consume.

Moreover, the silt which fertilized the fields became a mixed blessing when the systems became large and the silt clogged the canals, ditches, and the river itself. Interference with the flow of the rivers meant that more and more of the silt was deposited before the rivers reached the sea, but the enormous silt deposits made cleaning the system more and more difficult (Adams, 1965a).

Comparison of an early stage of urban development in Mesopotamia with a late stage of development in China illustrates the magnitude of the labor problem. At an early stage of urbanization in Lower Mesopotamia, peasants had to perform labor services for temple building for four months each year; at that time the Mesopotamian irrigation system was not very demanding of labor. By contrast, when John Buck in the 1920s surveyed the input of labor in Chinese agriculture, he found that the months free of field labor amounted only to one and a half on average for the whole of China, and most of this period was accounted for by winter unemployment in the dry-farming areas of northern China. The irrigated southern parts of China had hardly any periods during which peasant families were not fully occupied in fields and on farms (J. Buck, 1937).

The causes of the breakdown of the Mesopotamian system in the twelfth century A.D. were war damage to the irrigation system and the silting of the rivers. When wars disturbed a flow-irrigation system, or just prevented regular cleaning and maintenance, the whole system or parts of it broke down. The population had to emigrate or starve. Sometimes malaria appeared and made the region uninhabitable, as happened in the environs of Rome when the empire broke down, and in Sri Lanka in the twelfth century A.D. after wars with India. In China, the silting up of the rivers which had been dammed with dikes resulted in huge floods in recent centuries. Damage to these dikes, due to war or poor maintenance, caused floods which killed millions by drowning or famine. In parts of India, salinization and ill-conceived British land reforms caused the decay of the flow irrigation systems, because the landlords, who had financed maintenance and repairs by means of high crop shares, lacked both the means and the motives for maintenance, when rents were fixed and gradually diminished in value (E. Jones, 1981; E. Boserup, 1965).

Although the reasons for the breakdown or decay of many of the ancient civilizations are well documented, the reasons for the abandonment of the Mayan core area more than half a millennium before the arrival of Spanish conquerors remains unexplained. The high labor demand of agricultural work with primitive equipment could explain why the Mayas had to stop building temples, and why part or all of the excess population had to emigrate; but it could not explain why the whole population deserted the area, died out, or moved to neighboring mountain areas. It has been suggested that low-lying areas had once been shallow lakes, which silted up. If so, water-borne diseases or devastating epidemics due to new contacts may have induced the population to leave the area, but there is no evidence to support these hypotheses (Harrison and Turner, 1978).

From Plenty to Scarcity in Western Europe

Heavy investments in infrastructure for agriculture made urban civilizations with flow irrigation vulnerable to demographic change. Decline in population was likely to cause a catastrophe, because the labor force became too small to maintain the network. Its humid climate saved western Europe from such catastrophes when population declined. Both in the first millennium A.D. and in most of the second, population size in western Europe fluctuated as a result of wars and epidemics, but such events caused no permanent damage to the food supply system. When population increased, fallow was shortened and pastures and forests were transformed into fields. When population declined, fallow periods again became longer, and some of the fields reverted to permanent pasture and forest, until the next period of population increase once more reversed the trend (Slicher van Bath, 1963).

The population of western Europe seems to have adapted to these changes by consuming less animal and more vegetable food per head when population increased, and the reverse when it declined. These shifts in consumption seem to have been induced by changes in the relationship between wages and prices of cereals. In times of population increase, prices of cereals increased more than wages, thus forcing wage earners to reduce their intake of animal products, whereas high wages in relation to prices of cereals, for instance in the period of low population density after the Black Death, made more money available for the purchase of animal products (Fourastie, 1969; Phelps-Brown and Hopkins, 1981).

The major shifts to more intensive food supply systems in western Europe occurred during two long periods of population growth. In the first, between the ninth and the fourteenth centuries A.D., during which population seems to have doubled twice, pastoralism and long-fallow agriculture were gradually replaced by short-fallow systems, except for the Low Countries, which had higher densities than elsewhere and introduced annual cropping. The second large wave of population increase occurred in the eighteenth and nineteenth centuries, in which numbers again doubled twice or more in most countries. This multiplication of population was accompanied by a gradual change from short-fallow systems to annual cropping with fodder production. In both periods, there was population pressure in some areas before the existing systems were replaced by more intensive ones; but, by and large, western European agriculture adapted flexibly to the demographic changes (E. Boserup, 1981a).

This adaptability of the populations to changes in density does not mean that there was neither malnutrition nor famine in Europe in the period of preindustrial urbanization. We must distinguish between long-term scarcities of food caused by increasing population pressure and short-term scarcities due to climatic fluctuations, interruptions in agricultural operations, and other disturbances in years of wars or epidemics. Such events would cause famines in regions with abundant reserves of cultivable land, and the food scarcities in western Europe in the period of preindustrial urbanization seem to have been mainly of this type.

In the last centuries before the Industrial Revolution, these short-term food scarcities were serious, but they were due not to shortages of cultivable land but to shortages of agricultural labor. Food became scarce either because the nonagricultural population grew more rapidly than the agricultural labor force, or because the agricultural labor force declined in periods when the overall population size remained constant. Urbanization had been late north of the Alps due to low population densities, but when it finally appeared in a period of increasing population density in the twelfth and thirteenth centuries A.D., there was a burst of activity during which imports of techniques and knowledge from more advanced parts of the world supplemented indigenous inventions.

The building of the towns with their cathedrals, palaces, universities, and fortifications, and the manning of arms factories, workshops, trading firms, and other urban activities were made possible by pulling labor out of agriculture. Armies also drew labor from agriculture in times of both peace and war. Although European agriculture could adapt flexibly to parallel changes in the demand for food and the supply of labor, that is, to overall population growth, it was much less flexible when it had to raise output per worker than when it had to raise total output by using additional labor.

The moldboard plow, equipped with a piece of iron which turned the soil, had been introduced, and there had been other technical improvements during the first wave of population growth. But in the centuries before the Industrial Revolution there were few, if any, agricultural changes which improved labor productivity. Therefore, the effective restraint on food production was the lack of labor to utilize the existing potential for increase in output. For lack of labor, the area sown with crops was sufficient only to feed the population in years of normal harvest, but when the harvest was small for climatic or other reasons, food became scarce, prices soared, and the poor went hungry. Also, peasants starved when they were unable to retain sufficient stocks for themselves, because these were confiscated for use by the army and the urban population, as happened in France in 1709–10 (Griegg, 1980; Tilly, 1972).

The development of London between 1500 and 1700 provides an example of the problem. Its population increased from some 50,000 to more than 500,000, and the whole urban population of England seems to have increased eightfold. But the rural population only doubled, and the agricultural labor force grew even less. Although more and more distant areas were drawn in as suppliers of London, the food situation was precarious, and in years of bad harvest the needs of London were met by reducing the food supply of the rural population (Chambers and Mingay, 1966).

It was suggested earlier that the plentiful food supply in Europe in the preurban period had not facilitated development. In the urban period, with its frequent short-term scarcities, these food scarcities did not prevent the rapid urban development that took place. Food scarcities were the result of the rapid urban development and the armaments race in western Europe, which accompanied increasing urbanization.

Food Supply and the Industrial Revolution

Much of the discussion of the impact of food scarcity or plenty on western European development is focused on the role of agriculture in the Industrial Revolution. Some historians have suggested that agriculture played a leading role. An agricultural revolution starting in the eighteenth century, or even earlier, should have stimulated the beginning of the Industrial Revolution by raising agricultural productivity, thus ending the period of Malthusian food shortages and permitting large transfers of labor from agriculture to industry (Bairoch, 1969).

To evaluate this theory, we must try to answer two questions. Did the changes which have been labeled the agricultural revolution increase productivity, not only of land, but also of labor? And did the changes which culminated in the Industrial Revolution originate in the agricultural sector? We begin with the latter question.

The Industrial Revolution was brought about by an acceleration of the rapid technological changes in western Europe in the period of preindustrial urbanization. Recurrent food shortages in this period had not prevented the growth of nonagricultural activities, but had been the result of it. That period had not, as is often believed, been one of labor surplus, but one in which urban activities and a demand for soldiers had competed with agriculture for labor. Therefore, the urban sector had not always found it easy to recruit the necessary labor, which had provided the motive for experiments with labor-saving techniques. Such techniques became more and more widespread even before the Industrial Revolution, but their use increased during the Industrial Revolution and after.

Moreover, as cultivation expanded in response to population increases, forest areas, and thus timber, fuel, and charcoal for iron production, became more and more scarce, just as the technological changes raised the demand for these products. Experiments with the use of coal for iron production had been going on over a period of 200 years, and when they finally succeeded toward the end of the eighteenth century, the shortages of energy and raw materials were overcome and the Industrial Revolution became possible. Industrial changes, therefore, had their origin in the industrial sector and not in the agricultural one, which only adapted to the industrial changes, but did not release them (Wrigley, 1962).

As to labor productivity in agriculture, it is generally agreed that the agricultural changes which had major labor-saving effects, that is, the use of nonagricultural inputs, like chemical fertilizer and oil cake, and horse-driven mechanization, only became important in the middle of the nineteenth century or later. The changes in the eighteenth century and the beginning of the nineteenth century, among which the elimination of fallow and the introduction of fodder production were the most important, were of the type which raised total output by means of additional labor inputs, so the agricultural labor force continued to increase. Because the rate of population growth accelerated, the nonagricultural population could also increase.

The change to fodder production was prompted by an increasing demand for meat and dairy products from members of the new urban middle class. This demand raised prices of animal products so much that fodder production became profitable; as a result, livestock numbers, the output of livestock products, and the availability of manure increased. But much additional labor was needed to produce grains, turnips, potatoes, and other fodder in areas which had been devoted to fallow and natural pasture. Some of this labor was supplied by population increase, and some was provided in seasons which had hitherto been idle. Women, children, and other family members who had previously done little agricultural work had more to do. Some of these family members had produced textiles and other nonagricultural products for home consumption, but when the prices of such products declined steeply, home production was replaced by the purchase of industrial products. Home workers either gave more help in agriculture, or they began to work in or for the new factories (Phelps-Brown and Hopkins, 1981; Snell, 1981; Eighth International Economic History Congress, 1982).

In this period, peasant families obtained higher real incomes mainly by working many more hours in agriculture, while real output per work hour probably declined, due to the intensification of agriculture, especially fodder production. Some figures are available for Denmark: during the period 1818 to 1836, agricultural output per male worker in Denmark declined 0.1 percent annually; during the whole period 1818 to 1876, it increased only 0.2 percent annually. If account is taken of the increase in labor input per male worker and per family due to the change in the seasonal patterns of work and the increasing use of female labor, there must have been a substantial decline of output per work hour, especially in the period first mentioned. But living standards increased for the agricultural population as a whole, due to an annual improvement of more than 1 percent in sectoral terms of trade and terms of trade with other countries. (Denmark exported agricultural products and imported industrial manufactures [S. Hansen, 1972].)

Many historians have described the agricultural changes in the eighteenth century as a revolutionary change from a Malthusian to a post-Malthusian era. This is no doubt because acute short-term food scarcities ceased, except for the Irish tragedy. Famines disappeared in western Europe, partly because the potato now provided a hunger crop for the poor and partly because the feeding of domestic animals, especially pigs and poultry, on grains provided a buffer stock in years of poor cereal harvests. Previously, soaring grain prices in years of poor harvest had forced the poor to starve. Now, fluctuations in grain prices between good and poor harvest years became smaller, because pigs, poultry, and grain-fed cattle were slaughtered in years of poor harvest, and the stock was replenished in years of good harvest. Moreover, improved transportation and increasing intra-European trade in agricultural products averted regional and national short-term scarcities (Griegg, 1980; Phelps-Brown and Hopkins, 1981).

Apart from the disappearance of the famines, it is doubtful whether the nutritional conditions of the lower classes improved. Income inequality increased during the Industrial Revolution, and the increase in production of animal food went mainly to the growing middle class.

Abundance and Development in North America

For the European settlers, North America was an area of plentiful food supply, but in contrast to ancient Europe and other sparsely populated regions, for instance Africa, the plentiful food supply did not delay, but promoted development. The difference between ancient Europe and Africa, on the one hand, and North America on the other, is explained to a large extent by the differences in the pattern of settlement. The population in ancient Europe—like most of the African population—was widely scattered, which prevented the development of transportation networks and urbanization. In North America a minority of the early immigrants scattered as hunter gatherers in the large forests, but most of the immigrants concentrated in areas close to the harbors of arrival or in places linked to these by water transportation. They were accustomed to a certain standard of infrastructure in their European villages and towns, and they made a compromise between the desire for larger landholdings than those of European peasants and a not too widely scattered settlement, which made some infrastructure investment feasible. In this way, they were able to choose the man-land ratio which was optimal for the technology at their disposal. As a result, their agricultural system was less intensive than that of Europe, their output per worker was

TABLE 1. Agricultural output in seven countries

| Country | Hectares per male worker | | Output per hectare | | Output per male worker | | Fertilizer kilos per hectare, 1970 | Workers per tractor, 1970 |
	1880	1970	1880	1970	1880	1970		
United States	25	165	0.5	1	13	157	89	1
England	17	34	1	3	16	88	258	
Denmark	9	18	1	5	11	94	223	2
France	7	16	1	4	7	60	241	3
Germany, Fed. Rep.	6	12	1	5	8	65	400	
Japan	1	2	3	10	2	16	386	45
India		2		1		2	13	2,600[a]

Sources: Binswanger and Ruttan (1978); Hayami and Ruttan (1971); UN (1976a; 1973).
Note: Hectares refer to agricultural area, i.e. to all land in farms. Agricultural output refers to output of both crops and animal products (excluding fodder consumed by farm animals). This output has been recalculated in wheat units, equivalent to one ton of wheat, by Hayami and Ruttan. Workers include adult male workers, but not women and children. The kilos of chemical fertilizer are measured in fertilizer content per hectare of arable land, i.e. agricultural area minus pasture and fallow.
[a] 1961–65 average.

higher, and the output of land was much lower—which did not matter, since land was plentiful.

I am not aware of any quantitative comparisons between American and European agriculture in the period of early settlement, but a comparison for 1880, when mass exports of cereals from America to Europe began, is reproduced in table 1.

In 1880, the agricultural area per male worker in the United States was three to four times that of continental western Europe. Output per hectare was half as large and output per male worker was larger. Land had remained plentiful in North America in spite of the extremely rapid increase of population, because gradually, as immigration continued, the settlers had moved further west in step with the creation of the necessary infrastructure. A plentiful supply of land had provided the motivation for the improvement of farm equipment, which was lacking in most of western Europe because of the small size of agricultural holdings. Mechanization of agriculture took place much earlier in America than in Europe, and the westward movement was accompanied by a gradual increase in the size of farms in the newly settled areas compared to the areas of early settlement on the East Coast. Large farms in the Midwest and on the West Coast of America had a much higher output of labor in cereal production than European farms, and when technological improvements in transportation equipment reduced the price of bulk transportation over the oceans, North America became so competitive that a serious crisis in European agriculture resulted from the mass imports of cheap American cereals. This crisis led to a further delay in the modernization of European agriculture, except in a few areas which specialized in animal production based upon American fodder grains and oil cake.

Because the immigrants concentrated in the East, before they moved further west, it did not take long for the East to reach sufficient densities for both urbanization and industrialization. Due to high rates of population growth, the development of both industrial and agricultural production was much more rapid than in Europe. The technological gap between American and European agriculture widened between 1880 and 1970, as can be seen in table 1. In 1970, the agricultural area per male worker in the United States was five to ten times larger than that in western Europe, output per hectare was one-third to one-fifth, and output per male worker two to three times larger. Much less fertilizer and more mechanized equipment were used in America. Demand for rural transportation over longer distances than in Europe and for mechanized agricultural equipment helped to develop motor vehicles, which became a leading sector in American industrialization that soon overtook that of Europe (North, 1966).

Food Imports and Development in the Third World

We have seen that the link between agricultural surplus and development is much more complicated than is usually assumed. In some cases, plenty of food has been an obstacle to development; in other cases, development has been rapid under extremely difficult conditions of food supply. We began by distinguishing between attempts to adapt food supply to increasing demand due to population growth and attempts to adjust demand to supply. The first alternative often promoted development, whereas effects on development of the second alternative, that is, emigration and birth control, were less positive and sometimes negative. But the effects of such measures vary widely according to the rate of growth of population, the technological level, and natural resources.

When we note that adaptation of food supply to demand often had positive effects on development, it should also be noted that there seems to be one important exception: in several cases, attempts to adapt food supply to increasing demand by means of large-scale food imports discouraged local food production and had negative effects on development. When Rome was supplied with food from the colonies, the Roman peasants were ruined and went to live in Rome on food aid. European food imports from America retarded the modernization of European agriculture, as mentioned above, and a similar phenomenon has occurred on a very large scale in many developing countries in recent decades when rates of population growth accelerated and increasing demand was met by large-scale imports of basic food on commercial or concessional terms.

When the demographic transition in the developing countries accelerated after World War II, it was generally believed that widespread famines would be unavoidable—some said before 1980—or that birth control was the only means to avoid them. Most economists assumed that agricultural output was unresponsive to population growth, because there was assumed to be a large labor surplus in agriculture in unindustrialized countries. Many Asian countries were densely populated, and there was little appreciation of how far agriculture could be intensified with traditional means. Many other countries were sparsely populated, but because of the general belief in the Malthusian population theory, these countries were assumed to have submarginal land which could not feed large additional populations (Dumont and Rosier, 1969; E. Boserup, 1965; E. Boserup, 1974).

These opinions had important effects upon agricultural policy. Since the scope for additional food production was grossly underestimated, little was done in most of the developing countries to promote investments in agriculture and in rural infrastructure. Government policies were aimed at encouraging urban development in order to move as much as possible of the rural surplus labor into urban employment. The resulting rapid increase in urban demand for food was filled by imports and aid. In the industrialized countries, income support to agriculture had encouraged the production of increasing surpluses. It was believed that the transfer of these surpluses by aid or trade provided the best means of preventing famines and malnutrition in the developing countries.

As a result of the urban bias in government policies in most developing countries and the increasing food imports, income differentials between urban and rural areas widened in the food importing countries. Rural-to-urban migration was large and the growth of food production sluggish and often less rapid than population growth. The gap between urban demand for food and its supply was filled by further increases in food imports. Cereal imports of developing countries increased from 40 million tons in the early 1970s to 96 million tons in 1980/81, and it has been suggested that they may increase to 333 million tons in 2030 (E. Boserup, 1975a; OECD, 1981; Islam, 1982).

The neglect by governments in developing countries of rural infrastructure had the worst effects in sparsely populated countries, in which the existing rural infrastructure was much poorer than in most of the densely populated countries. The densely populated countries have at least some regions with good transportation and other infrastructural facilities which are necessary for commercial production and even more for the modernization of agriculture. Moreover, because of the belief that land reserves were small everywhere, research in agriculture focused on raising crop yields by means of large purchased inputs, especially fertilizer. The result has been a very rapid increase in food output in some densely populated regions with a better infrastructure than is usual for rural districts in developing countries, but not in both sparsely populated areas and densely populated ones with a poor infrastructure where the new techniques have not been applicable. Therefore, densely populated regions of East Asia and some districts of India with a good infrastructure have had extremely rapid increases in food production and both rural and urban industrialization, whereas most of Africa and Latin

America, with their much larger unutilized potentials for food production, have had much less expansion, and sometimes declines of output of cereals, due to competition from imports (E. Boserup, 1981a).

It was indicated above that, in India, progress in food production varied between districts with good and poor infrastructures. Around 1970, 15 percent of the districts in India employed 80 percent of the chemical fertilizer used in the country. The level of fertilizer application per hectare in these favored districts was around one-third that of western Europe, whereas the rest of India used some three kilos per hectare, which is the same as saying that they did not use chemical fertilizers on food crops. The low level of fertilizer consumption largely explains the rural misery and malnutrition of large parts of India. The area of arable land per inhabitant in India is in the same ratio as in western Europe but, primarily because of the lack of fertilizer and high-yielding seeds, output per hectare is as low as that of western Europe in 1880, that is, before massive fertilizer inputs were applied there (see table 1). In 1970, output per hectare in western Europe was three to five times that of India, and Japanese output per hectare was ten times that of India. Because of the low per hectare output and poor equipment, production per male worker in India was one-eighth that of Japan, and only 2 to 3 percent that of parts of western Europe with similar population densities to India (E. Boserup, 1981b).

Food imports from the industrialized countries acted as a deterrent to investments in agriculture not only in the countries which received the food supplies, but also in food exporting developing countries. In nearly all the countries which today are highly industrialized, food exports have helped to finance their industrialization; but today the subsidized food exports from these industrialized countries, and their restrictive import policies for food, deter food exporters and potential food exporters in developing countries from investing in an expansion of their export production of those types of food which compete with food production in the industrialized countries. This reluctance is a serious handicap to development in countries at very low stages of development and with poor mineral resources.

The increasing dependence on imports of basic food in many developing countries does not only discourage local food production, it also enhances the risk of future food crises. On the export side, the world market in food is dependent upon a small number of exporters, who design the size and distribution of their food surpluses in response to pressure from farm interests and considerations of foreign policy. On the import side, world demand fluctuates widely from year to year, because of climatic changes and frequent crises in agriculture in communist countries. Poor developing countries with low food stocks and small foreign exchange reserves are likely to be the losers in years in which world market demand exceeds supply. Reduction of imports and soaring food prices may result in starvation among the poor. A radical change in investment policy in favor of investments in food production to replace imports seems to be the only safe means to reduce the risk of famine in these developing countries.

Conclusion

The relationship between food scarcity and development is much more complicated than is assumed by Malthusian and neo-Malthusian theories. These theories focus on the negative effects of an increasing man-land ratio on food supply, but they have overlooked or underestimated the positive effects which increasing population may have on infrastructural investment and technological levels.

We have shown, on the one hand, that human societies with easy conditions of food supply remained at primitive stages of technological and intellectual development because their populations were too small and scattered for them to create the infrastructure necessary for the application of higher levels of technology, and because their populations were small enough to be able to feed themselves with primitive systems of food supply. On the other hand, we have seen examples in early and recent history of populations which imported or invented new technologies of food supply that became applicable only when these populations became larger and the change in the man-land ratio made the use of new methods both necessary and possible. Such peoples entered a period—sometimes a very long one—in which technological improvements promoted further population growth and further population growth promoted further technological improvements in a beneficial upward spiral, instead of the vicious downward spiral on which the Malthusian school focused its attention.

Not everybody would be well supplied with food in a developing society which experienced a beneficial upward spiral in its population and income growth. Rapid urban development in Europe in the last centuries before the Industrial Revolution resulted in increasingly severe food crises in which the poor faced starvation. The advantages of technological change are never shared equally by all population groups, and both rapid urban and rapid agricultural development are likely to result in a deterioration of food supplies for some population groups. Also, in many developing countries today the rapid growth of population and the rapid growth of average per capita income go together with malnutrition and sometimes starvation among the poor. But this does not necessarily arrest development, as long as the decision makers and the population groups which employ the new technologies benefit from the technological changes.

[1987]

Agricultural Development and Demographic Growth

In the centuries preceding the Industrial Revolution, there were large differences in demographic trends, both between areas and in different periods within the same area. Some of the villages and larger regions had continuing population growth, and population multiplied several times. In others, periods of rapid population growth were interrupted by a period in which the rate of growth slowed down or population stagnated or declined. Some studies of villages or regions of the second type suggest that the change in demographic trends occurred because the area under study was approaching a ceiling for labor absorption and output set by climate, soil conditions, and profile of the land, thus promoting emigration or arresting immigration, if large-scale immigration had been the major cause of the population growth.

However, in the centuries and areas under study, the limit for labor absorption by settlement or by intensification of land use in existing villages was not set by natural conditions alone, but was dependent upon the macroeconomic setting. Therefore, it cannot be assumed that outmigration from a village or a region was push migration, unless possible changes in the macroeconomic setting are studied and found to be insignificant. The observed emigration may have been promoted, not by declining local income-earning opportunities or deterioration of subsistence production due to increasing population pressure on natural resources; it could as well have been promoted by increasing income-earning opportunities in other areas, rural or urban. Also immigration to sparsely populated areas may have slowed down, not because the land available for settlement had become less attractive, but because opportunities for labor absorption and incomes had become more attractive elsewhere. So immigration might stop, although there continued to be abundant unutilized resources of fertile land.

While migration is often thought to be the result of the demographic changes in the regions and villages under study, rather than macroeconomic influences, the latter is most often assumed to be responsible for whatever agricultural changes occurred. Many interpret the observed changes in both agriculture and population as a result of market forces, which either im-

---

"Agricultural Development and Demographic Growth." Reprinted from *Evolution agraire et croissance demographique*, edited by Antoinette Fauve-Chamoux. Ordina Editions, 1987.

proved or caused deterioration in the possibilities for sale of agricultural products. Some conclude that improvement in market conditions was the predominant cause of agricultural development in the period and region considered, while the effect of demographic change on agriculture was of little, if any, importance.

However, these are not alternative explanations, because the observed changes in market conditions might be—and to a large extent were—a result of the demographic changes. The areas with large increases of population in the period considered had population increase in both rural and urban areas of the countries to which the villages belonged. The increase in urban demand for food and other agricultural products, resulting from the urban population increase, provided incentive for expansion of agricultural production by intensification of land use in existing villages or by new settlements. Part of the increasing village population became employed in this expansion of production for sale in urban markets, while another part became employed in producing the additional agricultural output needed by the increasing village population. In this process, the cause of the changes in the agricultural system is the population increase, and the change in the market conditions is the means by which the agricultural output is adapted to the demographic change.

In the centuries preceding the Industrial Revolution, there was considerable intra-European trade and some overseas trade in agricultural products. Both the importing and the exporting countries had periods of increasing population, and in the period as a whole the combined population growth was very large. By a process of adaptation, similar to the one mentioned above, some of the urban areas with increasing population covered part of their growing demand for agricultural products by imports from other countries, and by means of agricultural development, increasing agricultural populations in the exporting countries covered the growing demand for agricultural products both at home and abroad. Also in such cases, what in studies of villages or rural areas might appear as a response to market conditions for exports was, when seen in a larger perspective, agricultural development in response to population growth.

The agricultural changes, which resulted from and sustained the multiplication of population in countries without free land for settlement, were mainly intensification of fallow systems and gradual transformation of natural pastures and forests into fields. In some regions with low population densities, incipient agriculture with long-fallow methods was replaced by cultivation of permanent fields in short-fallow systems. In other regions with relatively low population densities, short-fallow systems were used throughout the period in spite of large population increase. This was accommodated by using a larger share of the village land for fields, while reducing the part used for permanent pastures. In more densely populated regions, the increase of population induced elimination of the fallows and introduction of annual cropping, and the increasing shortage of natural pasture induced introduction of fodder crops in the fields.

In some cases, new high-yielding crops were introduced and contributed to increase of output, but it seems that, with few exceptions, increase of yields of the basic cereal crops played little, if any, role in the increase of output. Crop yields are often used as indicators of agricultural progress, and their apparent stagnation over centuries has sometimes been interpreted as agricultural stagnation. But crop yields are misleading indicators in periods with continuing expansion of the cultivated area and shortening and elimination of fallow. In such periods, it is necessary to make important land improvements and changes in agricultural methods in order to prevent a *decline* of crop yields. High yields can be obtained with primitive methods when population is so small that incipient cultivation of the best land is sufficient, but when a dense population must use most or all of the land for annual cropping, refined methods of fertilization, weed eradication, and other land improvement are necessary to obtain similar—or lower—crop yields. Therefore, agricultural stagnation or progress cannot be measured by crop yields alone, but only by an analysis which takes account of all changes in the agricultural system.

Because there were few changes in crop yields and also few changes in the quality of agricultural tools in the period considered, it may seem a paradox that many regions had increasing urbanization even in periods where population stagnated, and that urban rates of population growth were higher than rural rates in many regions. Because of poor sanitary and health conditions, natural rates of urban population growth were usually lower than rural ones, and a large share of the urban growth was obtained by rural-to-urban migration. So, except for countries with substantial increase of agricultural imports, the declining share of total population who remained in agriculture managed to produce food and other agricultural products for the whole population.

A major explanation of this apparent paradox is provided by the gradual transformation of agricultural subsistence producers to producers supplying a surplus for sale in urban markets. Costs of land transport were very high, and in earlier centuries only producers living in the immediate surroundings of a town or an export harbor had produced surpluses for sale. This gave strong incentive to intensification of land use in the neighborhood of existing towns when their populations were growing. Therefore, differences in intensity of agriculture in densely populated areas around existing towns and in peripheral sparsely populated areas were large, and the population in the latter regions remained subsistence producers a long time after producers in the former had become commercial producers.

When towns continued to grow, they were forced to pay the higher prices which were needed to obtain supplies from more distant producers either in the same or in another country, unless this cost could be reduced by public and private measures to reduce transport costs. Investments in the transport network became more feasible when population continued to increase, because transport costs are inversely related to the volume of transport, and the multiplication of both rural and urban populations in the period considered induced improvement of transport and reduced transport costs. This induced the obtaining of supplies for the towns from areas which had hitherto been producing only for subsistence. As a result, the percentage of total population which produced an agricultural surplus for sale in urban markets declined less than the percentage occupied in agriculture, or it increased. As a result, some villages were gradually or suddenly drawn into the market economy, either because transport conditions were improved or because higher urban prices for agricultural products made production for the towns attractive in spite of the high transport costs. The agricultural development in such villages contrasted sharply with that in even more peripheral villages, which continued to produce only for their own consumption and surplus delivery to landlords and governments, and could only participate in the economic development by labor migration.

Both subsistence producers, who began to produce surpluses for sale to the towns, and producers who intensified their system of production had to increase their work input in agriculture, a feature which is often overlooked in historical studies, because few studies of labor input have been made. But new labor-intensive crops with other seasons for planting and harvesting, the need to produce fodder and feed for animals, and the need for land improvement, fertilization, weeding, and other labor-intensive operations provided much work in seasons in which there had hitherto been little, if any, agricultural work. Much of this additional work was done by making more extensive use of female and child labor. Therefore, labor input cannot be measured by the number of adult men occupied in agriculture. In periods of labor-intensive agricultural intensification, annual work hours per family of a given size will increase more than hours worked by male labor, and this will increase more than the number of male workers. Therefore, agricultural output per family may increase, although output per work hour is declining because the additional operations have low productivity per work hour.

Producers were induced to increase the input of wage and family labor in agriculture either by an increase in producer prices or by a decline in the prices of nonagricultural products at the village level. If this was not obtained by reduction of transport costs, the town population had to pay higher prices for agricultural products, as already mentioned. Such an improvement of agricultural prices in relation to prices of urban products would help prevent the distortion in the relation between rural and urban incomes and the over-stimulation of rural-to-urban migration which might result from the decline in agricultural output per work hour.

The Impact of Population Growth on Agricultural Output

THE EFFECTS OF THE population explosion on food supplies depend upon many factors to be discussed below. They range from the behavior of cultivators and governments in developing countries to the results of technological research, triggered by the fear of future world shortage of food. The behavior of cultivators differs according to the degree of population pressure in the area where they are living, and it is necessary to make a distinction between the effects of population growth in densely populated areas and in more sparsely populated areas. Moreover, a distinction must be made between rural areas in which governments, by promoting investment in economic infrastructure, provide the cultivators with the opportunity to modernize agriculture, and rural areas where the local population has only the choice between adaptation to population growth by labor-intensive investment in traditional agriculture or labor migration.

The Scope for Additional Use of Labor in Traditional Agriculture

Existing agricultural systems in developing countries are adaptations to historical differences in the degree of population pressure, and the ratio between men and resources differs widely between areas. In areas with a low man-land ratio, villages are surrounded by large tracts of fallow, pasture, and forest, which are used in an extensive way because the cultivators can save labor if they maintain crop yields by long periods of fallow and let domestic animals graze and browse on pastures, fallow, and forestland. But when the local population is growing, more and more of this fallow, pasture, and forestland is cleared and improved and taken into cultivation.

In areas where agriculture is still at a primitive stage, with no use of mechanized equipment (see UN, 1973, vol. 1, table 2.18), investment in land improvement consists mainly of direct investment of agricultural labor. By investing additional labor (family labor and hired labor) in the clearing of land, in the levelling and terracing of land, in supplying water to the fields, and so forth, the cultivators can expand the productive capacity of the local

---

"The Impact of Population Growth on Agricultural Output." Reprinted by permission of John Wiley & Sons, Inc., from *The Quarterly Journal of Economics* 89 (1975): 257–70.

agricultural system and produce a larger output with a larger input of labor. In sparsely populated areas, they do this mainly by adding to the area of arable land; in densely populated areas, by sowing or planting the existing arable land more frequently, and by improving crop yields.

Such labor-intensive investment in agriculture is done with the same inexpensive equipment and with the same draft animals that are used for current work in agriculture, and the investment can often be done in a season when labor, draft animals, and equipment are not needed for other work. Thus, if local population increase provides the incentive for an expansion of the productive capacity of agriculture, labor-intensive investment can remove the constraint on output provided by the limited supply of arable land and capital. Therefore, in periods of rapid population growth, investment in agriculture by direct labor input is at higher levels than in periods of low or negligible rates of growth in the local population. This is true not only of investment in traditional food production but also in the production of special export crops. Output of these has expanded considerably in many developing countries in recent years because the increasing rural population provided additional labor for the cultivation of a larger area and for close planting of such crops.

An objection may be that, if additional labor input in land improvement can remove the constraint on output set by the supply of arable land and capital, how can there be underemployment in rural areas? The answer is partly that, for several reasons, there may be insufficient incentive to undertake such investment in land improvement, and partly that most of the un- and underemployment in rural areas of developing countries is seasonal. Labor demand in agriculture usually varies widely between the peak season (or seasons) and other seasons, and in many areas the labor supply in the peak season sets the upper limit to the area that can be sown, planted, and harvested with traditional technology. It is outside this peak season that sample surveys and casual observers find the large numbers of un- and underemployed, which are often considered—mistakenly—as evidence of a general redundance of labor (see Turnham and Jaeger, 1971, tables 2.7 and 3.11; UN, 1973, vol. 1, table 2.3).

Since the supply of peak-time labor sets a narrow limit to the area that can be sown, planted, and harvested within a given year in areas of traditional agriculture there may be little incentive to invest in order to expand the area in periods of low or negligible rates of population growth, and in such periods the output of agriculture is relatively inelastic. But when high rates of population growth result in a steady increase in the supply of peak-time labor, there is incentive to expand the area under cultivation, and agricultural output becomes more elastic.

The supply of labor in the peak season sets a limit to the area that can be sown, planted, and harvested in both sparsely populated areas and densely populated areas. One of the conditions for introducing a second or a third crop per year in the same field is that peak-time operations with the main crop can be handled quickly. Therefore, even in areas with a high population pressure on land, the demand for peak-time labor may be so keen that housewives, children, and persons with nonagricultural employment are drawn into the agricultural labor force in the peak season, and that wages for adult male labor for peak operations are much higher than wages in other parts of the year. Such wage increase is needed, if small peasants, who during that season have much to do in their own holdings, are to be drawn into wage employment in larger holdings. Because of the labor shortage in the peak season, there may be no incentive to undertake the investment in land improvement that is needed for the introduction of multicropping, but when rural population increase raises the supply of peak-time labor, it becomes possible to expand year by year the area under multicropping and thus to raise total agricultural output.

When increasing population density leads to expansion of output by the planting of crops in fallow, pastures, and forestland hitherto used for grazing, browsing, and so on, a fodder shortage may emerge. This may be countered by a change in the pattern of human consumption toward more vegetable food at the expense of animal food, the relative prices of which will increase. Moreover, higher prices of animal products should lead producers to use cereals and other vegetable products as fodder for domestic animals, and to produce new types of fodder. By changing over from collected to produced fodder, the same quantity of fodder is obtained from a much smaller area, but with an additional input of labor. For the 1960s, there seems to be some evidence of such adaptation of both consumption and production to increasing population densities (FAO, 1973, tables 1, 3, A2), but in most of the developing countries the shift to produced fodder for domestic animals has hardly begun.

Infrastructure and Labor Migration

In the least developed rural areas, the lack of economic infrastructure is likely to be the effective constraint on agricultural output. Often, the population in such areas can produce the food needed for subsistence with a relatively small input of labor, but they have insufficient incentive to produce a surplus beyond subsistence needs because the lack of infrastructure results in high costs of transport and distribution both for locally produced agricultural products and for products imported into the area from outside. In other words, the ratio at the village level between prices paid to the agricultural producers for a surplus over local needs and the prices for the products they can acquire for money income obtained by sale of a surplus is so unfavorable to the agricultural producers that there is little incentive to produce a surplus. Agriculturalists will tend to keep a low work input in agriculture and have a high degree of self-sufficiency of both agricultural and nonagricultural products. Thus, both labor and land resources may be underutilized because of the lack of economic infrastructure. If the local population is growing, agricultural output is likely to increase proportionately, in step with increasing local demand.

However, areas that produce little or no agricultural surplus due to the lack of infrastructure are rarely without any economic ties with surrounding areas. Instead of exportation of surplus produce, such areas are frequently seen to use labor migration as a means of obtaining money incomes. Young family members migrate as wage labor, either for several years or in the off-season for agriculture, and they deliver part of their earnings to the family, which stays behind in the village. Thus, labor migration provides a link between the local communities and the other parts of the country or region to which they belong. If economic development in the urban sector creates employment opportunities and raises urban real wages, the rate of labor migration from the areas with poor infrastructure is likely to increase and eventually exceed the rate of population growth. Concurrently, the agricultural surplus, if there was one, may decline as a result of the acceleration of migration. By contrast, if overall development of the economy is accompanied by improvement of the rural infrastructure, and thus of improvement at the village level of the ratio between prices of agricultural and non-agricultural products, labor migration may be reduced and an increasing agricultural surplus produced and sold.

Per capita costs of economic infrastructure are highest in rural areas with a small and widely scattered population, located far from markets for agricultural products. If local population increase is sustained and rapid in such areas, it significantly reduces the per capita costs of transport facilities and other economic infrastructure. If local or central government is induced by the declining per capita cost to improve the infrastructure in the area, the result may be to make the production and sale of a surplus of agricultural products more profitable than labor migration. In that case, the effect of rapid and sustained population growth is to increase agricultural output, both total and per worker, and to reduce labor migration.

Not only in sparsely populated areas does labor migration appear as an alternative to the production and sale of an agricultural surplus; the same is true of peasant families who live in villages in densely populated areas with better infrastructure and large surplus production. Thus, in all developing countries, there are close links between the subsistence sector, the surplus-producing sector in agriculture, and the urban sector, and barring strict administrative control on rural-to-urban migration, it is unrealistic to assume that a surplus of agricultural labor can continue to accumulate in the subsistence sector in countries with economic development and rising real incomes in the urban sector.

Conditions for the Use of Industrial Inputs

In the past, the predominant type of adaptation to population growth in developing countries was to utilize the increasing labor force to intensify land use and animal husbandry, as mentioned above. But this traditional type of adaptation to population pressure is now supplemented by another type of expansion of output obtained by the use of industrial and scientific inputs in agriculture, such as chemical fertilizer, insecticides, improved seeds, tractors, modern irrigation equipment, and extension services.

The use of such inputs drastically widens the scope for expansion of total agricultural output because it makes it possible (a) to circumvent the limitation to output set by the supply of manual labor in the peak season; (b) to obtain much higher yields of crops and animals; (c) to eliminate fallow; (d) to introduce much more multicropping; and (e) to use infertile, dry, and hilly land. By contrast to the traditional type of adaptation to population growth, an expansion of output by means of modern inputs raises agricultural output at a rate that is significantly higher than the rate of increase of input of agricultural labor. Thus more rapid urbanization becomes possible without increasing food imports.

However, most modern inputs in agriculture can be used only in rural areas that are better supplied with infrastructure than are most of the areas that supply towns and export markets with agricultural products produced with traditional techniques. Good roads to the villages are necessary, and so are local warehouses, repair shops, an extension network, and sometimes large-scale irrigation facilities.

Moreover, the price ratio at the village level between modern inputs and marketable agricultural products must be low enough for the use of modern inputs to be profitable. This second condition for the use of modern inputs is of course related to the first, since a poor economic infrastructure in rural areas makes for high prices of inputs and low prices of agricultural products, as already mentioned.

It follows from what is said above that, in a period of rapidly increasing population, there are two ways to step up the use of modern inputs in agriculture: (a) an active government policy designed to improve the ratio of prices *at the village level* of inputs and outputs by supplying better local infrastructure (including extension services at no cost to the farmer); (b) a passive government policy which allows the prices of agricultural products *in the towns* to increase significantly in terms of the prices in the towns of urban-produced and imported goods, including modern inputs to agriculture.

The first method avoids an increase of food prices in the towns, but it presupposes that governments see fit to devote a larger share of public revenue and public investment to rural areas. Economic infrastructure in developing countries tends to be heavily concentrated in a few major towns and in a few rural areas with particularly favorable locations. These may be areas in the immediate surroundings of major towns or mining districts, or in some agricultural development districts for specialized export crops. Apart from such favored locations, both rural areas and small and medium towns have insufficient infrastructure and, therefore, are unattractive locations not only for modern nonagricultural activities but also for the development of modernized agriculture based on the use of industrial inputs.

However, if economic infrastructure is thus concentrated in a few locations within a country, these become powerful poles of attraction for nonagricultural activities and for migrants looking for nonagricultural employment. As a result, pressure arises for even further expansion and improvement of infrastructure in these places, and governments are led to give high priority to infrastructure investments precisely in those areas which are already relatively well equipped. Meanwhile, most rural areas and smaller towns are likely to be starved of infrastructure investments and government services. Thus, only in a few favored areas will rapid population growth be accompanied by rapid modernization of agriculture and rapid expansion of output. In most of the country, agriculture will continue to use traditional methods, and a considerable share of the youth will migrate to the towns.

The other way to step up the use of modern methods in agriculture, that of increasing food prices in the towns, was not acceptable to governments. In the 1960s, governments in developing countries usually tried to prevent a shift of sectoral terms of trade in favor of agriculture, because it would have strengthened the upward pressure on urban money wages. Many governments avoided this pressure by allowing increasing imports of food as foreign aid, and the policy was facilitated by the existence of large surplus stocks that could be acquired on favorable terms, or even as grants. Other governments preferred instead to make a rigorous effort for increased agricultural output in the areas already favored by sufficient infrastructure. Subsidies to fertilizer and other modern inputs and the implantation of extension services and credit facilities were the main components of this policy. The result was to create a rapidly increasing gap in incomes between cultivators who could and those who could not seize the opportunity for use of modern inputs.

In the 1960s, the average annual rate of growth of agricultural output in developing countries as a group was 2.8 percent (FAO, 1973, table 1). This may be compared with an average annual rate of population growth of 2.6 percent. Thus agricultural output not only rose in step with the rapid rate of population growth, but even surpassed it a little. This result, a slight increase in the volume of output per capita, should, perhaps, not be considered a bad performance in view of the fact that most governments did little, if anything, to assist the expansion of agricultural output by broadly based improvement of rural infrastructure or by other means, and that many governments were more eager to prevent an increase of food prices than to provide the producers with incentives to expand output. During that period, the agricultural labor force increased by about 1 percent annually, so that there was an annual increase in output per worker in agriculture (gross of purchased inputs) of 1.5–2 percent (FAO, 1973, table 1; UN, 1973, tables 2.1, 2.11). But the increase in gross national product per worker was nearly 3 percent, so that a gap developed in output per worker between the agricultural and the non-agricultural sectors. There was probably little, if any, improvement in sectoral terms of trade for agriculture in most developing countries. This helps to explain the large flow of rural-to-urban migration.

Prospects for the Future

There are several reasons to warn against the use of the observed trends in agricultural development and rural-to-urban migrations in the 1960s as a basis for projections into the future. The population explosion in developing countries was still at its beginning, and many of its likely long-term effects, both in the field of government policies and in the field of technological and social changes, are yet to come. In the following pages, attention is drawn to some of the most important factors that are likely to influence future trends and, in some cases, reverse the trends observed in the sixties.

THE UNCERTAINTY OF FOOD IMPORTS

It was mentioned above that in the 1960s the existence of large surplus stocks and of easy access to food aid tempted many governments to use food imports as a means of preventing an increase in food prices in the towns and nevertheless secure the necessary food supplies for the rising urban populations. But with the gradual exhaustion of the surplus stocks and with soaring prices of many foodstuffs in recent years, the situation has changed. It is becoming less easy to acquire food imports on concessionary terms, and this means that it has become more risky to be dependent on food imports, either permanently or in years of bad harvest. As long as surplus stocks were large, they served as international emergency stocks, and governments could with some assurance rely on being able to draw on them in case of sudden shortages for climatic and other reasons. Thus, governments could avoid financing emergency stocks of their own, and they could without risk of future famine allow themselves to be less than self-sufficient in basic food. There seemed to be no urgent need to devote public money to agricultural development and to the improvement of rural infrastructure. Instead, the resources of the government could be concentrated on the promotion of industrialization and urban development.

This has now changed. In future years with no certainty of large surplus stocks, many governments can be expected to seek security in a more active policy in favor of national agricultural development. Therefore, governments will probably be more prepared than hitherto to improve rural infrastructure and to devote other government resources to agricultural development.

THE NEED FOR RURAL EMPLOYMENT

Internal factors also will induce governments to take a more positive and active attitude toward agriculture and rural development in the future than in the past. First, governments in developing countries are more and more concerned with the tension that is created by the rapid migration to the major urban centers and the rising unemployment in many of these centers. There is near consensus that agricultural and other rural development is the best way to alleviate this situation. Second, many governments are aware that concentration of both urban and agricultural development in a few favored regions, although it may have been necessary in an initial period of development effort, is not a long-term solution in the present situation when almost a doubling of the adult population is expected within the remaining years of this century. Therefore, many governments are likely to engage in a geographically more broadly based development effort with more resources devoted to rural infrastructure. This will create additional employment in rural areas and make both expansion and modernization of agriculture possible in many more areas. Thus, there is some reason to expect a more rapid rate of growth of agricultural output in the next few decades than in the 1960s.

LAND REDISTRIBUTION

However, there are not only positive factors. It must also be taken into account that continued rapid population growth is likely to create increasing social tension in many countries.

It was mentioned above, that agricultural systems are adapted to the degree of population pressure, that is, to the man-land ratio. This means not only that fallow is shorter, multicropping more frequent, and animal husbandry more labor intensive in a densely populated area than in a more sparsely populated one. It also means that within a given area peasants who own or rent small pieces of land use shorter fallow, more multicropping, and more labor-intensive animal husbandry than cultivators who own or rent larger pieces of land. Thus, when higher rates of population increase begin to raise the numbers in the rural labor force, the large agricultural units offer more scope for adding to employment and output by more intensive land utilization than do the smaller units. Consequently, some of the sons of the small peasants must lose status by becoming hired workers on larger holdings, which intensify their system of land use, or else there must be redistribution of land from the large to the small holdings, either by lease of fallow and other uncultivated land for cultivation by small tenants or by expropriation through land reform. Thus, it is no wonder that the quest for a radical redistributive policy usually gains strength in periods of population growth.

For a number of reasons, the claim for redistribution of land is bound to become more vocal in the next few decades. (a) The pressure is becoming more urgent because the high rate of population growth must continue for several decades. (b) More and more sons of small peasants will attend village schools, and this will make them all the more resentful of the loss of status suffered when they become sharecroppers or hired workers. (c) When the infrastructure is improved, more and more cultivators of large holdings can use modern inputs to intensify land use and animal husbandry as a substitute for the employment of increasing numbers of rural youth. Sometimes, the fear of labor unrest and land reform induce them to do so. (d) There are more economies of scale in agriculture with industrial inputs than in agriculture based on manual labor alone. This induces some cultivators to take over for their own cultivation land hitherto cultivated by tenants, or to acquire the land of neighbors. This inevitably leads to economic and social polarization, and to mounting demand for redistribution of land.

It is not possible within the framework of this article to draw any general conclusions about the long-term effects of redistribution of land on agricultural output, because the conditions both for successful redistribution and for increase of output without redistribution vary widely between areas.

However, it is widely agreed that the short-term effects on output of increasing pressure for redistribution are most likely to be negative. Thus, it must be assumed that in many countries increasing labor unrest and demand for redistribution will cause temporary setbacks to the growth of output in the coming decades, partly as a direct result of civil strife, partly because owners of larger holdings may avoid long-term investment in their land for fear of expected expropriation, and partly because output is likely to increase less rapidly or to even decline during the period when redistribution is carried out.

AGRICULTURAL AND FOOD RESEARCH

The long-term prospects for agricultural output are crucially dependent, of course, on prospective technological developments. The population explosion in developing countries has given rise to intensified research efforts with a view to secure the necessary expansion of output of food. But research and development takes a long time, and until now only the development of high-yielding varieties of some cereals has reached the stage when it substantially influences the rate of growth of agricultural output. Much more research and development concerning food supplies is under way, partly in agricultural research stations and partly in supplying industries, including some of the large multinational companies.

Agricultural research is centered on further improvements in crops and animals and in methods of fertilization. Research on crops aims not only at development of food and fodder plants which give high yields under favorable conditions but also on developing plants which give satisfactory, although lower, yields under unfavorable conditions, and plants with a high protein content. Most specialists within these fields take an optimistic view of the results that can be expected, and it seems likely that the rapid rate of scientific progress in the recent past will further accelerate in the next decades.

Research that may lead to an improvement of the supply of vegetable protein for human consumption is particularly important in periods of rapid population growth. As mentioned above, animal products are likely to become scarce and more expensive in periods of population growth, but the nutritional disadvantages of the shift of consumption from animal to vegetable food can be avoided by improvement in the supply of vegetable proteins. There is a 70–80 percent loss of calories when proteins suitable for human consumption are transformed by animals to animal proteins. Therefore, the increase in per capita demand for food, which accompanies increases in income, can be covered with the use of fewer agricultural resources, if the shift from vegetable to animal products is counteracted by gradual improvement of the supply of vegetable proteins either with traditional or with new types of protein-rich food.

Agricultural research stations and some large international companies are also engaged in research and development of new types of food. International research is particularly keen with regard to two kinds of progress. One is to develop substitutes for animal products from vegetable products, such as milk and meat out of soybeans. Development of such products may sharply reduce the rate of increase in per capita demand for agricultural products (in terms of produced calories) because of the elimination of the transformation loss mentioned above. The other type of industrially produced substitutes uses no agricultural raw materials. These new types of food and fodder are produced from nonagricultural raw materials such as fish, marine algae, cellulose, and yeast growing on derivatives of mineral oil. It seems likely that industrially produced substitutes for fodder may become accepted more rapidly than products for direct human consumption, for which differences of taste are more of a handicap than for fodder.

EXPANDING LOCAL OUTPUT

It is difficult to foresee how quickly substitute food and fodder will come into commercial production on such a large scale that it significantly influences food demand and supply in the world market. On the other hand, the scope for using more traditional means to cover the prospective rise in demand for food is very far from having been exhausted. (a) Although fertilizer consumption in developing countries has been increasing in recent years by 10–15 percent annually, by 1970 it was still less than 15 kilos per hectare sown in developing countries taken as a group, as against 80 kilos in the United States and 200 kilos in France (UN, 1973, table 2.14; FAO, 1971a). (b) As yet, high-yielding seeds are used in only a few areas. (c) Areas under fallow continue to be larger than areas under actual cultivation in a given year. (d) In most countries, multicropping is practiced in only a small fraction of the area that, with the use of modern inputs and methods, would be amenable to such intensive utilization. (e) The area that could be arable with existing modern technology is assumed to be at least twice the present area of arable land (FAO, 1969), and with improved technology, such as desalinization of seawater and better use of tropical land, the long-term prospect is for much larger expansion (Pawley, 1971). According to a recent estimate of the earth's land and water resources, agricultural capacity could be expanded to feed fifteen times the present world population an adequate diet (Revelle, 1973).

However, there are wide geographical variations in the costs of expanding agricultural output and the means to be used. In some countries with large reserves of land, the investment required for a large expansion of agricultural output consists mainly in the construction of transport facilities and in land clearing and other labor-intensive investment in agriculture. In densely populated countries like China and India, on the other hand, heavy investment in water control and fertilizer factories will predominate. Both in China and India, this high cost will probably be acceptable, for they fear becoming dependent on the world market for supplies of basic food. If this attitude is shared by other large developing countries, and if such policies of self-sufficiency of food succeed, the world market may well continue to be a buyer's market, except for years of exceptionally poor harvest or other major catastrophes, including those of political origin.

It is not very attractive to be an exporter of food if world market prices are low in most years and high only in years of unusually poor harvests. Therefore, if most importing countries endeavor to be self-sufficient in food in normal years, and to use food imports only in emergency, many governments in countries with good possibilities for developing export surpluses of food may avoid giving so much encouragement to agriculture that it expands beyond the needs of the home market. Thus, with the steady growth of world population and world consumption, world trade in food may come to account for a smaller and smaller share of world consumption of food.

There is a potential danger in a situation in which international trade in vitally important products with inelastic demand is a small share of total output. If world trade is a large share of consumption, exporters carry large stocks and many importing countries share the burden of high prices and reduction of purchases in years of unusually heavy demand for imports. But if world trade is small, a major economic or political catastrophe in a densely populated area may raise the demand for imported food more than can be covered from export stocks, and the result may be famine, since it takes time to expand output, even in food-exporting countries with a spare capacity of cultivable land.

Population and Technology in Preindustrial Europe

IN PREINDUSTRIAL EUROPE, periods of modest positive rates of population growth were interrupted by violent setbacks to population. It is generally assumed that these setbacks were caused by the population increase in the preceding period, because such growth implied a deterioration of the man-resource ratio, and production expanded more slowly than population. As a result, periods of population growth ended in subsistence crises, but when these reduced the population, the man-resource ratio improved and this induced a new increase in population and new subsistence crises. Technological change was assumed to have been random and too rare to have had much importance for population trends, until the great breakthrough of modern technology at the end of the eighteenth century rendered the classical model inapplicable.

There are several reasons for abandoning this model in the interpretation of European history, not only for the industrial period, but also for earlier periods. There was in fact much technological change in the long period from the fall of the Roman Empire to the end of the eighteenth century, and most technological changes were not random but rather were adaptations to the change in factor proportions resulting from population change. Population growth induced technological change either by substitution of labor and capital for land, or by enabling the use of substitutes for scarce materials. Population growth also induced technological change by permitting specialization of labor and economies of scale. Most of the large setbacks to population were in fact not the result of population growth in the preceding period, and they were more likely to reduce than to increase average incomes.

In the following two sections, I shall deal first with the ways in which population change could promote technological change in food supply, and second with the ways in which it could promote technological change in nonagricultural production of goods and services. The third section addresses the relationship between urbanization and technological change, and the fourth discusses causes and effects of large fluctuations in population size.

"Population and Technology in Preindustrial Europe." Reprinted with the permission of the Population Council from Ester Boserup, "Population and technology in preindustrial Europe," *Population and Development Review* 13, no. 4 (December 1987): 691–701.

Links between Population Change and Food Supply

The widespread belief that there was little change in the technology of food production in preindustrial Europe is explained by a tendency to identify technological change with a change in tools and other equipment. If technological change is defined as one involving both methods and equipment, there were vast changes in the technology of food production, and these were closely linked to changes in population.

When population density increased, the growing scarcity of natural resources forced the population to change its methods of food supply. In the first millennium A.D. most of the small population in Europe north of the Alps used highly extensive food supply systems. They combined crop production using long-fallow methods with gathering and hunting in the large forests that surrounded their habitats. Or they obtained a large share of their food by herding animals in extensive natural pastures. But a gradually increasing population density forced changes in the technology of food supply several times, in three major ways: (a) the use of more of the forested area for crop production and reduced consumption of gathered products and of meat from hunted animals; (b) the use of more of the natural pastures for crop production and a shift from the system of herding to that of feeding domestic animals in fallowed land; (c) reduced fallow periods and a shift first from forest-fallow and bush-fallow systems to short-fallow systems, and later from short-fallow systems to annual cropping, with a simultaneous change from grazing of fallow to production of animal fodder in the crop rotations (Fauve-Chamoux, 1987).

The demand for labor per unit of output was larger the more intensive the system of food supply. A new system would be introduced when the old had become inapplicable. Therefore, the timing of the change in system differed widely depending on population densities. Because rates of population growth were low, a system could be used for a long time before a new one needed to be introduced. In cases of major population decline, there was often a regression in technology, with partial reintroduction of earlier systems.

The more intensive systems were not only more labor intensive; they also required more capital investment, partly in land improvements and partly in new tools and equipment. During most of the preindustrial period, the land improvements were labor investments made by the producers in the off seasons with the tools and animals that they used for current operations in the peak season. Or they were labor investments imposed on the peasants by the nobility. Because work seasons became longer, the decline in output per labor hour did not necessarily entail a decline in agricultural income per year or a shortfall in the food supply. But the change in systems imposed a change in the composition of food. The poorest part of the population was forced increasingly to live on vegetable food, while the more wealthy consumed most of the scarce and expensive products of the hunt and of animal husbandry.

When the change in food production method required new equipment, such equipment was introduced by technology transfer from Asia or from more densely populated regions in Europe. Moldboard plows and harnesses for horses were introduced when increasing population density in some parts of Europe made it necessary to take the heavy soils in valley bottoms into cultivation instead of using only light soils that were easy to cultivate with scratch plows and oxen. Also, new methods of fertilization and labor-intensive, high-yielding crops were introduced by technology transfer when an increase of population density made this necessary and profitable. In all these ways, the change in factor proportions resulting from population growth promoted technological advancement.

Links between Population Change and Nonagricultural Technology

In the last centuries before industrialization, the reduction in the forested areas of Europe had gone so far that the result was an acute shortage of wood, both for construction and for energy production. In this period, the efforts to create substitutes for wood led to some of the most important inventions in industrial technology, especially coal-iron technology and the steam engine (Wrigley, 1962; E. Boserup, 1981a). At earlier stages of European history, however, the innovations in nonagricultural technology were mainly of the labor-saving type. They consisted in improvement of products and reduction of unit costs through specialization of labor. This allowed the use of specialized equipment and the creation of infrastructure, which benefited from economies of scale. These technological changes also were linked to population change, since a minimum size and density of population is a precondition for a higher level of specialization than that obtained by age and sex specialization within the family.

In the first centuries after the fall of the Roman Empire, the small and widely scattered habitations were visited only by a few itinerant craftsmen. Goods and services were typically produced by the families who consumed them. But with increasing population, villages became larger and closer to each other, as new hamlets and villages were created in the uncultivated areas between the old villages. In this way, the local market became large enough to provide a living for a settled population of specialized craftsmen. Through learning by doing and investment in specialized equipment, these craftsmen produced better quality products at lower unit cost. The agricultural producers, or some of them, could with advantage exchange food for the products of the craftsmen. When the local market became large enough to make the investments profitable, some of these specialized producers were able to reduce costs by making use of nonhuman power, such as animal power, water-power, and wind power for milling and other heavy work. These technological changes were also introduced by technology transfer from more advanced regions.

By giving up some of their nonagricultural activities, agricultural families gained more time for improvements of the land and other labor-intensive activities needed for more intensive land use. And, by more intensive land use, they could produce a food surplus for consumption by the families of nonagricultural producers. Further specialization and increases in productivity became possible when the population in a region became so large that some centrally placed villages became small towns, inhabited by traders and craftsmen.

In the first centuries of this millennium, populations in major parts of central and northern Europe began to exceed the minimum density for urbanization under preindustrial transport technology. Towns grew up in many areas, spontaneously or by design. Traders and artisans settled in these towns instead of living scattered in villages or being attached to a manor. This type of decentralized urbanization appears in densely populated regions when transport technology is too primitive to permit concentration in large centers. Some of the new towns became populated by many types of artisans, while others were dominated by the members of a particular craft. The latter towns benefited from professional contacts and specialized infrastructure, and some of them became spearheads of technological change within their particular field.

The social system was hierarchic, with large income differentials. The secular and ecclesiastical nobility obtained large incomes in the form of labor services and other dues from the peasants. They sold the food delivered by the peasants to the towns, for which the nobility provided a large share of the market in the early period of urbanization. There were also large income differentials between members of the lower classes. Some peasants, craftsmen, and traders were wealthy, while others were poor, and below these groups were the landless and unskilled workers and servants working for the middle and upper classes. When the peasant population increased in size, the total income of the nobility increased and so did the market for urban products and the size of the middle class. With growing urban demand for food, more of the wealthy peasants began to produce food surpluses for sale to the urban population.

When the demand for urban products increased, the towns attracted labor from the countryside, since urban mortality was so high that the towns could hardly reproduce themselves without immigration. Usually the rural population responded willingly to the appeal of the towns for labor, since personal freedom was greater and incomes were higher in the towns. It may seem paradoxical that the urban population could increase by immigration from the countryside, when the technological changes in agriculture were land saving rather than labor saving. But with increasing population density, improvement of transport networks became possible, and producers living farther from the towns were motivated to change from tax-paying subsistence production to commercial production, selling food and other products to the towns. It is often overlooked that market access is a function of population density and transport technology, and that these two are positively related. Both operating costs and investment costs in transport networks are inversely related to population density.

Village studies and other local studies of European agriculture often underestimate the importance of population change for rural development. They typically conclude that rural development was caused by the opening of markets for agricultural produce. Often the improved marketing conditions are themselves a reflection of increasing population both in the food-exporting and in the food-consuming areas. The growth in the European rural and urban populations improved transport conditions and thereby market access. The result was increasing commercialization of European agriculture and specialization of agricultural production. Specialization began within the most economically advanced countries; later came specialization between these and the more sparsely populated and less advanced European countries, and much later, intercontinental specialization.

Urbanization and Technological Change

In most of the preindustrial period, Europe north of the Alps was a technologically backward area, which could import technological know-how from more advanced areas; very few original inventions were made in the region. In science, the backwardness of central and northern Europe was even more pronounced. The small literate minority, using a foreign language, Latin, lived widely scattered in monasteries devoting their time mainly to religious studies.

As had happened much earlier elsewhere, however, once the population had reached a size and density that made concentration in urban centers possible, the intellectual elite increased in numbers. Both scientific and technological invention require specialization, experiment, and cooperation with a group of people who have interest in and are knowledgeable in a particular field. These conditions are first fulfilled when elite groups come to live together in a narrow area with favorable conditions for communication. The towns became locations for Latin schools, libraries, and universities, in addition to being centers of crafts, trade, and administrative services. Or the centers of learning became located in special university towns. After a period of importation of foreign science, European universities became innovators in the natural sciences, which increasingly replaced religious studies, a change of focus that promoted technological innovation.

Concentration in towns, often specialized towns, fostered the development of crafts and trade. Members of an occupational group were usually organized into a guild or corporation. These organizations have been much maligned in retrospect for their stifling of competition. Entrance to the guild was regulated by rules of apprenticeship and passing of professional tests for proficiency before establishment as an independent producer. The guilds were more or less hereditary: the apprentices were sons of guild members, while other youth became servants or unskilled assistants. Prices of products and services were fixed by the guild, with fines for undercutting. But, of course, this system also had favorable effects. It created a professional milieu and promoted quality and learning by doing and by instruction. It promoted technology transfer, because young people had to travel extensively to work with colleagues in other places before they achieved right of establishment—a parallel to advanced-level students, who visited foreign universities as a part of their education. The fixing of prices secured an income level that made savings and investment possible.

Some of the members of guilds and corporations were wealthy and had high rates of saving. This was especially so among the great merchant houses specializing in foreign trade, a very risky but also highly profitable occupation. Wealthy urban citizens financed their own merchant fleets and the infrastructure of the towns; later they became moneylenders to national governments. Ordinary guild members also helped finance urban expansion with their savings. Parents and young adults themselves saved in order to set up viable establishments that could support a family. The young, helped by their parents, had to save enough for establishment and marriage. If they could not do so, parents, priests, employers, or even the law might refuse to allow marriage, and many had to remain celibate. Even servants saved most of their meager money wages in order to be able to marry. Marriage age and rates of celibacy were high for both men and women, and this reduced fertility.

The European marriage system did not confer high status on parents of large families, unless they were able to establish all their sons and obtain good marriages for all their daughters. Irresponsible parenthood was held in low esteem. Illegitimate offspring were likely to be got rid of; if not, they and their mothers were socially ostracized. Folk methods may also have been used to limit irresponsible parenthood within marriage, but there was probably not much fertility restriction within marriage, because the late age at marriage, the high celibacy rates, and the high levels of maternal and child mortality restricted family size.

Family organization in rural areas was similar to that in the towns. Marriage customs and rules of establishment were similar. Labor investments that were needed to accommodate population increase and intensification of agriculture were made by parents and young adults in the period in which the latter remained unmarried and worked for eventual establishment as married couples with viable holdings. Unmarried young people of both sexes also went into service on other farms to earn money for later establishment and marriage. As in urban areas, those who failed were likely to remain celibate, and rural views on irresponsible parenthood usually corresponded to those of the urban population.

Thus, in rural areas rates of population growth were so low that there was ample time to adapt agricultural production to population increase through labor investment and the slow diffusion of more intensive methods of agriculture. In exceptional regions with large farms, where production was based upon the work of landless labor families, expansion and intensification of production were financed by savings out of profit. In the regions with the highest rates of urban growth, long-distance food imports were paid for by exports of urban products, as mentioned above.

Setbacks to Population Growth

It is generally agreed that the triad of epidemics, war, and famine was responsible for the crises that interrupted periods of population growth in preindustrial Europe, but there is no agreement on the importance of each of them. The problem is complicated because they usually occurred together in the same period, either in pairs or all three at once. Economic historians often describe this triad by the term "subsistence crisis," thereby tacitly implicating nutritional deficiency in assigning responsibility for the recurrent catastrophes. The virulence of epidemics is often assumed to be due to the nutritional state of the population, and warfare and famine are both assumed to be results of increasing population pressure on land. Recovery is then assumed to have occurred when the "overpopulation" was eliminated by the decline in population density, and, as a result, per capita food supply improved.

Neither quantitative nor qualitative research relating to preindustrial Europe supports the idea that land shortage was the main factor responsible for the recurrent demographic and economic crises. Many famines were accompaniments to warfare and epidemics, which prevented work in the fields, spread contamination, destroyed crops, animals, and food stocks, and starved the population in besieged towns. Other famines followed a succession of harvest failures, which exhausted stocks held by peasants and dealers and raised food prices to levels the poor could not afford. In some periods, the towns grew so rapidly that agriculture became drained of labor. The rural labor supply could cultivate sufficient land with sufficient intensity to produce enough in normal harvest years but not to stock up for successive years of poor harvest. Of course, food shortages resulting from this occurrence cannot be taken as evidence of population pressure on scarce land resources. Labor, not land, was the bottleneck.

Malnutrition and hunger among the poor contributed to the high levels of mortality both in "normal" and "crisis" years, but there was apparently little correlation between harvest fluctuations and mortality (R. D. Lee, 1981; Rotberg and Rabb, 1983). Famine had much less influence than epidemics and wars on overall population trends in Europe. But population increase caused a gradual replacement of animal by vegetable food, as mentioned above. Diminished intake of animal protein can perhaps account for the declining physical stature in the course of the eighteenth century, which is revealed by recent studies of some European populations (Fogel 1986a, b; Komlos 1985, 1986).

Internecine warfare was endemic in preindustrial Europe. Tribal wars were succeeded over time by feuds between noble families and these by national wars. The European nobility was a warrior caste to whom the peasants owed loyalty, military and labor service, and other dues in exchange for protection against enemies, which proved to be of dubious value. Low labor productivity in agriculture set a limit to the amount of labor services and other dues that an individual peasant family could pay, but a noble family could increase its income and prestige if the number of villages and towns that owed them loyalty and dues could be augmented by transfer from another noble family. Such transfers could be obtained either by favorable marriage arrangements or by force. In similar ways, royal families as overlords could increase their income and prestige through marriage or by usurping the loyalty and dues paid by noble families to other overlords. Therefore, the main preoccupations of both noble and royal families were arranging marriages, forming alliances for military purposes, and conducting wars.

Military strategy consisted of attempts to weaken the enemy by killing not only his soldiers, but also his peasants, as well as by looting property and burning farms and crops. To prevent long sieges of castles and towns, the scorched earth strategy was applied—destruction of one's own villages and neighboring fields when the enemy was approaching. Moreover, passing armies, whether friend or foe, lived off the land and looted the territories they crossed. This type of warfare resulted in heavy losses of both human life and capital stock, and the vanquished lost much more than the victor gained.

Because of the preoccupation of the ruling classes with war, much brainpower and financial means were focused on the improvement of weaponry and other military equipment, and this promoted technological change. New technology was imported or invented for maritime and land warfare. The military sector became more capital intensive with advantages of scale. The scale of wars increased, and the royal houses gained advantage over the other noble families; wars became national rather than local (North, 1981).

During this process, peasant armies serving under their respective lords were replaced by armies of professional soldiers. Wars became even more murderous and destructive, as the weapons became more effective and the soldiers, in addition to their salary, gained the right to the spoils of war. In periods of unemployment, soldiers plundered friend and foe on their own account, and often they prolonged periods of war by changing over to the losing party, if he could afford to pay them. The king's finances became increasingly strained because of the need to recruit soldiers and to make costly investments in armaments factories, fleets, harbors, fortifications, and military roads (North, 1981).

Towns were taxed heavily as a means to finance armaments and wars. They were frequently looted or even burnt down and the inhabitants slaughtered, unless they paid ransom. When the urban sector became larger and wars more costly, rulers compelled rich merchants to lend them money to finance war and pay ransom. Often they ruined the merchants by not paying them back, or expelled foreign creditors from the country to avoid payment. A good deal of the savings and capital stock was lost due to wars between European nations. This and not population increase was the main cause of capital scarcity.

The indirect losses of human life resulting from war were often larger than the direct ones. Epidemics ravaged both the armies and the besieged towns and spread to the rest of the population. The walling of towns for defense and the resulting extreme crowding of the urban population raised mortality levels in peacetime, as poor hygiene and sanitary conditions prevailed. Famines also followed in the wake of wars, as mentioned above. Epidemics were promoted not only by war but also by migration, including rural-to-urban migration, and by trade, which brought germs in contact with people who had not developed resistance against them. The epidemics attacked and killed rich and poor, inhabitants in sparsely and densely populated regions, with little discrimination. Mortality from epidemics does not seem to have been significantly related to the nutritional state of the exposed population (Rotberg and Rabb, 1983). Toward the end of the preindustrial period, the use of quarantine reduced the frequency of epidemics.

Large epidemics destroyed not only human life, but also capital stock. Fields, vineyards, and orchards became wasteland, and buildings collapsed due to nonuse and lack of maintenance. Sometimes entire villages and small towns became deserted and disappeared. By reducing the size of the population and of the work force, a large epidemic could raise wages and increase meat consumption, but it reduced the income of the nobility and royal families, and these attempted to recover by levying new taxes and engaging in new wars. The expropriation of the savings of the peasants and the urban population by the ruling class was worse in periods of population decline, when the royal and noble families desperately tried to maintain their usual display of luxury despite the decline in ordinary incomes. After the Black Death in the fourteenth century, many ruined members of the nobility turned to brigandage. The period of lawlessness and incessant war that followed bore no resemblance to the period of bliss that, according to the classical development model, should follow a major reduction of population density (Tuchman, 1978).

Conclusion

Population growth had far more positive than negative effects in preindustrial Europe. Most production was organized in family enterprises, and the organization of production in these enterprises and the marriage system kept fertility relatively low and kept savings high enough to secure the investments that were needed to adapt production to increasing population size. In periods relatively free from wars and epidemics, population increased, and economies of scale and technological change in nonagricultural activities raised labor productivity. In agriculture, modest rates of population growth allowed producers sufficient time to adapt methods and size of production to the increased demand for food. Because technological changes in agriculture replaced land by labor and labor-intensive capital investment, labor input usually increased more rapidly than output, and work seasons became longer. However, the peasants saved time by gradual reduction of nonagricultural subsistence activities. By exchange of products, they benefited from the rising productivity of the nonagricultural sectors (de Vries, 1985; Wrigley, 1985).

The recurring crises with the accompanying decline of population, destruction of capital, and decline in average per capita income were the result of local and national wars and large epidemics. The high mortality from epidemics was not due to a high man-land ratio. Wars were fought not to conquer empty land for cultivation, but to increase the prestige and income of the victors through taxation, plunder, and ransom. In other words, the European patterns of demographic and economic change in the preindustrial period are in sharp contrast to the patterns depicted in the classical model.

Demographic Pressure, Growth, and Productivity in a Historical Perspective

The Growth of the Advanced Countries

Estimates of historical growth rates in the countries which are now industrialized have been made by Simon Kuznets. Table 1, which is a rearrangement of Kuznets's material, shows estimates for long-term growth rates for fourteen countries. Typical growth rates for total national product in this period were between 2 and 3 percent annually in Europe, but over 4 percent in North America. The higher growth rates in North America went together with much higher rates of population growth than those of Europe. In fact, rates of per capita growth seem to have been similar in the two areas, but since population growth was much more rapid in North America, total American output increased much more rapidly than that of Europe.

Usually, discussions about growth rates focus on per capita growth, but both in comparing countries and in comparing different periods in the history of a given country, it is important to take account also of total growth rates. Take for instance the case of the United States compared to France. Rates of per capita growth between 1840 and 1960 were similar, but during that period the total national product of France was growing much less rapidly than that of the United States. French total national product became eight times larger, but that of the United States became fifty times larger. Due to slow population growth in France, the need to build infrastructure and the demand for other productive investment were limited, and the country was capital exporting in most of the period. The United States, with mass immigration, rapid natural population growth, and a rapidly expanding market, invested much more in its own economy, partly financed by capital imports. Because of more rapid growth of total national product, there was more scope in the United States than in France also for those types of investment and other expenditures for which demand is not proportionate to population size, such as investment in transport and communication networks, high-level education and research, and many other types of military and civil investments and

---

"Demographic Pressure, Growth, and Productivity in a Historical Perspective." Reprinted from *Human Resources, Employment and Development*. Volume 5: *Developing Countries*. Proceedings of the Sixth World Congress of the International Economic Association. Edited by Samir Amin. St Martin's Press; Macmillan, 1984: 20–32.

TABLE 1. Increase in population and national product, mid-nineteenth to mid-twentieth centuries, fourteen countries

Country	Population	National product[a] Per capita	Total	Period
		Annual percentage increase		
France	0.3	1.8	2.1	1841/50–1960/62
England	0.6	1.4	2.1	1855/58–1957/59
Sweden	0.7	2.8	3.7	1861/65–1960/62
Italy	0.7	1.3	2.0	1861/65–1960/62
Switzerland	0.8	1.6	2.6	1890/99–1957/59
Norway	0.8	1.9	2.9	1865/74–1960/62
Denmark	1.0	1.9	3.2	1870/74–1960/62
Russia/USSR	1.0	2.0	3.3	1860–1958
Fed. Rep. Gemany	1.1	1.6	2.9	1851/55–1960/62
Netherlands	1.4	1.4	3.0	1900/04–1960/62
Japan	1.2	2.6	4.2	1879/81–1959/61
Canada	1.9	1.8	4.1	1870/74–1960/62
United States	2.2	1.7	4.3	1839–1960/62
Australia	2.4	0.8	3.4	1861/65–1959/62

Source: Kuznets (1966).
[a]In constant prices.

expenditures. The low rates of population growth in France, compared to both the United States and other European countries, were the main reason for the declining economic importance of France in the nineteenth and a large part of this century (UN, 1955).

Third World Growth Rates

The high rates of population growth in North America, which went together with high rates of total and per capita growth of national product, had occurred in an area with vast natural resources and favorable conditions for attracting both skilled labor and capital from Europe. Similar conditions were not present in the Third World when rates of population growth accelerated in recent decades to even higher rates than the historical growth rates in North America, and it was a widespread belief among demographers and economists that the result of the acceleration of population growth in the Third World would be a general decline in per capita product.

Development in the 1960s and 1970s did not fulfill these expectations. The estimates for total and per capita production, published by the World Bank, show that only a small minority of Third World countries had declining

TABLE 2. Change in per capita national product, 1960–1976, by country income group

Change in per capita national product	Number of countries, by income group[a]				
	1	2	3	4	5
Decrease	4	2	2	2	1
Increase					
0–1.9 percent	12	8	3	5	1
2–3.9 percent	5	11	13	7	17
4–5.9 percent	3	2	3	4	4
6 percent and above	0	1	3	6	1
Annual increase					
Per capita increase in national product (percent)	1.5	2.2	3.2	3.6	3.3
Increase in total output (percent)	3.8	4.8	6.3	5.5	4.6
Per capita increase in US$[b]	2	7	21	68	143

Source: E. Boserup (1981a), table 15.3.
[a]Income groups were calculated by ranging the countries according to size of per capita national product in 1960, with twenty-four countries in each group.
[b]At 1976 prices.

per capita products, as can be seen from table 2. In this table, the bank's growth rates for individual countries[1] have been ranked by the size of per capita product in 1960, and the countries have been divided into five groups of equal size.[2] It can be seen that for middle-income countries (groups 3 and 4), typical per capita growth rates in the 1960s and 1970s compared favorably with the long-term historical rates in the now industrialized countries. However, it will also be seen that typical rates were lower, the lower the per capita income in 1960. Typical per capita rates for the country group with the lowest incomes in 1960 were between zero and 2 percent, and four of the twenty-four countries belonging to this group had a declining per capita product.[3]

Growth rates of total output were extremely high in most middle-income countries, and very much higher than historical long-term rates in both America and Europe. Thus rapid expansion of infrastructure and other investment would have been possible if all or most of the capital accumulation had been invested in the Third World and not, as was sometimes the case, transferred to industrialized countries.

Although rates of growth of total product were fairly high in low-income countries, the absolute additions to per capita product were insignificant. Increases measured in percentage terms are misleading when differences in levels in the base year are very different, as is the case with the income groups in table 2. It can be seen from the last line in the table that the countries in the lowest income group added on average US$2—or next to nothing—to their annual per capita production, while middle-income countries added US$21 to US$68 annually. The insignificant increases in the low-income countries did not provide room for significant improvements of infrastructure and other productive investments and services. In many low-income countries, the picture was one of near stagnation of living standards and small investment activity, in sharp contrast to typical middle-income countries with economic expansion and increase in levels of living for large shares of the population.

The low-income countries, which are nearly all located in Africa south of the Sahara and in South Asia (UN, 1976b), did not have more rapid population growth than the middle-income countries in the period here considered— rather the opposite. And, while some of the South Asian countries were densely populated, most of the African ones had sparse population. The observation that countries with low income levels in 1960 were the ones lagging behind in the following period, even in percentage terms, points clearly to the importance of historical factors in helping to explain the diverging trends within the Third World in the period of accelerating population growth.

The Inadequacy of Third World Infrastructures

A number of factors allowed some Third World countries to reach much higher economic levels than others in 1960. Both the size and quality of their human and material infrastructure were much higher and their dependence upon agricultural production much lower than that of other Third World countries. The former could adapt much better than the latter to accelerating rates of population growth in ways which permitted them not only to expand production and exports, but also to obtain high levels of per capita growth.[4]

For one type of infrastructure, but a very important one, that of transport networks, table 3 shows the huge differences between low-income, middle-income, and industrialized countries. The densities of both rail and road networks in low-income countries are extremely low compared to those of countries at higher income levels with similar population densities, and the quality of their road networks is much poorer. When networks are inadequate, most of the territory cannot be reached by modern types of transport, and a large share of the potential agricultural and mineral resources can only be utilized after expensive and slowly maturing investments have been made in the expansion and improvement of transport facilities.

The dense railway networks in the industrialized countries had already been built in the nineteenth century, and it is important to note that only those countries which acquired a dense railway network at an early date are industrialized today. Insufficient railway construction in the past outside the European continent, North America, and Japan provides an important part of the explanation of the delay in industrialization outside these areas. Apart from these areas, no country, except for the republics of Korea and Taiwan, has a railway network as dense as those of England and Germany in the middle of the nineteenth century (Girard, 1965). Later development of motor traffic did

TABLE 3. Length and quality of transport networks, in 1970, by country income group

Population density (persons per km²)	Meters of railway per km², by income group			Meters of road per km², by income group			Percentage of roads that are hard surface, by income group		
	1	2	3	1	2	3	1	2	3
0–3	0.3		3.3	21	5[a]	103	7	70[a]	21
4–15	1.6	7.3	14.4	46	79	260	9	15	31
16–63	2.8	8.4	30.9	71	74	713	12	61	58
64–255	5.1	30.3	75.8	149	347	1,060	30	66	75
256 and above		29.7	90.0		775	2,693		65	66

Source: E. Boserup (1981a), table 11.1.
Note: Number of countries included: for railways, 71; for roads, 92. The grouping of countries by income was made by a ranking of indicators by stage of development.
[a]Refers to one country, only.

not much reduce the handicap of countries with small or no railway networks, because most roads were built as feeder roads to railways, while road construction was uneconomical in areas far from railways.

In the middle of this century, when rates of population growth accelerated in the Third World, areas which had been supplied with relatively good transport facilities and other infrastructure in the colonial period could make use of their growing labor force to increase production of tropical crops and other products, for which the industrialized countries offered expanding markets. However, low-income countries with poor infrastructure and with a small foreign trade capacity could not respond quickly to the increasing demand in foreign markets. It can be seen from table 4, which covers the same countries and income groups as table 2, that nearly all countries with less than US$10 per capita exports in 1960 were low-income countries. Most had very low growth rates in the following decades, and nearly half of the countries with decline of per capita product or with increase of less than 1 percent belonged to this category of low-income countries with low foreign trade.

Similarly, differences in regional growth rates inside the large low-income countries were related to the extent to which the region had been supplied with infrastructure in the colonial period and had developed commercial production before 1960. For instance, India had only between 1 and 1.5 percent per capita growth in the 1960s and 1970s, but the Indian state of Punjab, which had been developed as a food supplier for other parts of India in the colonial period, had extremely high growth rates, in sharp contrast to Indian regions with poor infrastructure and low growth rates (Sinha, 1975).

TABLE 4. Low-export countries, by income group, experiencing change in national product, 1960–1976

Change in per capita national product	Number of countries with less than US$10 per capita exports in 1960, by income group					Other countries
	1	2	3	4	5	
Decrease	4	1	0	0	0	6
Increase						
0–0.9 percent	5	1	0	0	0	7
1–1.9 percent	3	0	1	0	0	12
2 percent and above	4	1	0	1	0	74

Sources: World Bank (1978); UN (1976a).

Agricultural Difficulties in Low-Income Countries

It was mentioned above that not only lack of human and material infrastructure but also the larger share of agriculture in typical low-income countries help to explain their lower growth rates compared to typical middle-income countries. In the period considered here, rates of growth of the agricultural sector, in particular of food production, were lower than those of population growth in many countries. In low-income countries with a large share of the population occupied in agriculture, low rates of growth in this sector had of course considerable effect on overall growth rates.

The poor performance of agriculture in many Third World countries should be seen in a historical perspective. In earlier centuries and in early decades of this century, nearly all countries which lagged behind others in development used incomes from agricultural exports to finance industrialization. This was true of England before the Industrial Revolution, and later of Scandinavian countries, east and south Europe, North America, Japan, and Oceania.

Many of these areas, both in Europe and overseas, developed a large capacity for agricultural production in order to supply markets in the industrialized countries. Later, when both rates of population growth and income elasticity of food consumption decelerated in the industrialized countries, these became less dependent upon imports, and exporters began to look for new markets in the Third World, with its rapidly increasing populations.

Access to Third World markets was obtained by offering heavily subsidized export prices and by grants of food and other special advantages. On the other hand, aid to Third World agriculture was given only on a small scale, or was bluntly refused if it concerned development of products which would offer competition to exports from donor countries. Moreover, the industrialized countries discriminated against or prohibited agricultural imports from Third World countries which competed with their own production.

Governments in many Third World countries were tempted by the favorable conditions for agricultural imports to supply their urban populations, and sometimes also their rural populations, with imported food. By this means they could avoid the need to use scarce investment resources and other expenditure for rural infrastructure and other development of agriculture. Such a policy may increase overall growth rates in countries with good possibilities for production and exports of nonagricultural products, but it will keep growth rates low in countries with the bulk of the population in agriculture.

Moreover, the difficulties for agricultural exports resulting from agricultural, foreign trade, and aid policies in the industrialized countries, hit low-income countries more than others. For lack of markets and rural infrastructure, producers were unable to change from subsistence production, with a small surplus for local sales, to commercial production with use of industrial inputs. Modern inputs in agriculture can be used only in regions with a relatively good infrastructure. Thus, agricultural productivity remained low, and lack of progress in the large agricultural sector provided a handicap to development of the nonagricultural sectors.

As a result of the farm support policies in the industrialized countries, which promoted production and exports or surpluses, a radical restructuring of world trade in agricultural products has occurred. Except for crops which grow only in tropical climates, the net flow in agricultural trade is no longer from less developed to industrialized countries, but from industrialized to less developed countries. Usually, this change is viewed as an inability of the Third World to expand agricultural production in step with the needs of a rapidly growing population; but it should not be forgotten that the main cause of this is the discouragement of local agriculture following from the policies of the industrialized countries. These are not just filling a gap between demand and supply in the Third World: they have created this gap by their policies.

International Finance for Infrastructure Investment

Low-income countries have had slower growth than middle-income countries, even in percentage terms, and chances seem slight that this trend will be reversed in coming decades. Most of the demands in the Third World program for a new international world order will benefit middle-income countries much more than low-income countries. Better prices for commodity exports are of more benefit to middle-income countries with large exports than to low-income countries with small per capita exports. Better access to export markets for manufactures benefits mainly those countries which have reached a certain level of industrialization. The demand for debt relief is also most important for middle-income countries which have obtained high growth rates in the past by borrowing heavily. But few low-in-

TABLE 5. Low-income countries, by income group, receiving development finance, 1968–1973

Range of development finance, US$ per capita	Number of countries, by income group			
	1	2	3	4
0–9	22	10	1	2
10–29	2	10	8	2
30–59	0	0	0	0
60 and above	0	1	2	3
Annual percentage increase	3.1	12.1	14.4	26.0
Grants as percentage of finance	0.7	3.8	0.4	2.3

Source: UN (1975a).
Note: Income group 1 has less than US$200 per capita annual income; group 2, US$200–399; group 3, US$400–799; group 4, $800 and above.

come countries had the chance to borrow and thus acquire a great amount of debts.

Private capital investment has mainly gone to middle-income countries and to a few low-income countries, mainly countries in which oil resources were discovered. And low-income countries have not got large amounts of official loans or of grants either, because the distribution of foreign aid, like that of private capital, was skewed in favor of middle-income countries.

Table 5 reveals that the poorest countries obtained insignificant amounts of development finance per capita, while some middle-income countries received large amounts per capita. Both private investors and official donors preferred to lend to middle-income countries, which because of their better human and material infrastructure were more likely to use capital imports effectively, and without too long a delay. Moreover, the geographical distribution of economic aid was heavily influenced by military and political considerations.

Redistribution of aid in favor of low-income countries is a hotly debated issue, but middle-income countries are insistent that redistribution must not go very far. Nor is there much support for radical redistribution of aid in most donor countries. These consider aid as a means to help political clients and to obtain new export markets, and they want to see rapid and spectacular results of their aid, in order to convince their public opinion and pressure groups that aid is worth giving. Therefore, development finance for basic infrastructure in low-income countries is not a popular use of development finance, unless such investment happens to be in the military interest of the donor country.

The international preoccupation with development aid has been focused upon national five-year plans and international development decades. In such short spans of years, a stepping up of basic infrastructure investment will have little effect on national production in a low-income country. But unless this is done, the plight of low-income countries will be prolonged indefinitely. When the World Bank shifts the focus of its development loans from basic infrastructure to other types of loans, the futures of the poorest countries are at risk, because other lenders are unlikely to replace the bank in this field of lending.

However, if more international development finance were to be available for infrastructure investment in low-income countries with slow growth, this would be a great help at the present stage of the demographic transition in these countries, in which the number of young adults is growing rapidly. Employment could be provided for this increase in the labor force if the new investments in infrastructure were made with a mix of manual labor and modern equipment adapted to the increasing supply of local labor.

It is probably unrealistic to assume that massive grants will be offered from either rich or middle-income countries for infrastructure investment in poor countries, but it is perhaps less naive to hope for much larger official loans with very long grace periods or private loans with government guarantees. It is true that such a program would be a reversal of past trends in development aid, which have been toward softer terms and grants, especially to low-income countries. It may, however, be asked whether the successful efforts to make aid softer have not contributed to the increasing hostility of public opinion in the large countries toward foreign aid. Perhaps the way out of this impasse is to attempt other types of development aid as a supplement to the stagnating or declining traditional programs.

Politicians and voters in the rich countries who object to large free gifts to Third World countries may have less objection to long-term loans or government guarantees for private loans. Moreover, industrialists and workers who are looking for new export markets but are afraid of the effects of Third World industrialization on their home markets and export markets may perhaps see some advantage in aid to projects which may boost export sales of equipment without producing new competitors, or at least not in this century.

Notes

1. Except for communist countries, which use different systems for calculation of national product than do other countries.

2. The differences in growth rates between income groups are smaller in table 1 than those in the World Bank report, from which the growth rates for individual countries were taken. This is because the weighting in table 1 is based on 1960, while the bank uses 1976 weights. The latter method distorts the differences between the groups, because countries with high growth rates have often moved to a higher group in the period between 1960 and 1976, while some countries with low growth rates may have moved to a lower income group in 1976 than they were in in 1960.

3. All estimates of growth rates for national products have an upward bias, because commercial production of goods and services is included to a larger extent and is

likely to be more correctly evaluated than production for family use. It is uncertain whether this general upward bias in growth rates is strongest at early or at somewhat later stages of development and whether it is strongest for the historical or the more recent estimates. However, it seems unlikely that this general upward bias in growth rates could explain all or most of the differences and similarities in growth rates mentioned in the text.

4. It may be objected that, besides the more general causes of differences in growth rates discussed below, a number of countries had low growth rates either because of unsuitable government policies, national or civil wars, or environmental difficulties. However, such phenomena seem in many cases to have been not only causes of, but also effects of, the low economic levels and growth rates. For instance, severe lack of human infrastructure and, in consequence, heavy dependence upon foreign staff and advisors with little if any local experience enhance the risk of unsuitable government policies, with consequent reduction of growth rates.

[1976]

Environment, Population, and Technology in Primitive Societies

WHEN THE RATE OF increase of European populations accelerated in the second half of the eighteenth century, European economists elaborated a theory of interrelationships between environment, population, and technology, which continues to be applied by many social scientists who are dealing with problems of development of primitive societies. The basic characteristic of this theory is that it deals with demographic trends as an adaptive factor: it assumes that a given environment has a certain carrying capacity for human populations, defined as the number of persons who can be accommodated in that region under the prevailing system of subsistence. Population is kept within the limit for subsistence in a particular environment by customary restraint on the number of births or by high rates of mortality, including various forms of infanticide. According to this theory, over the long run primitive societies tend to have a rate of zero population growth. The rate rises above zero if improvements in the technology of food production increase the carrying capacity of the environment, but only until the new limit is reached, after which the rate of population growth again returns to zero.

This reasoning suffers from two main weaknesses: first, the theory focuses exclusively on the technology of food production, ignoring the effects of technological changes in other areas and the effects of the environment; secondly, the theory ignores the effects of demographic change on both environment and technology.

Effects of Technological Changes on Population

Demographic trends in primitive populations are influenced not only by food technology but also by health, transport, and war technologies, and by the system of organization, which could be called "administrative technology." Until recently, health technology was so primitive that many well-fed populations had low birth rates, owing to endemic venereal disease and

"Environment, Population, and Technology in Primitive Societies." Reprinted with the permission of the Population Council from Ester Boserup, "Environment, Population, and Technology in Primitive Societies," *Population and Development Review* 2, no. 1 (March 1976): 21–36.

malaria and high mortality rates, particularly for infants. The main technique of avoiding contamination by epidemic disease was to isolate oneself as much as possible from the source of contamination by such procedures as abandoning the old village and building a new one in another place, fleeing the town, and closing the gates of the town or the frontiers of the country. Some of these measures tended to spread the epidemics more widely rather than to contain them.

Improvements in the means of transport, which open up new regions for human contacts, are likely to raise mortality rates by giving greater sway to the spread of epidemics. It is true that improvements in transport technology might sometimes reduce mortality by facilitating the supply of food to a famine-stricken region, but since such improvements make it easier for a conqueror or an indigenous ruling class to move food away from the region where it is produced, they could also result in reduction of food available for the local population, with negative effects on demographic trends.

Improvements in military technology usually raise mortality rates, particularly when they are of a kind to benefit the aggressor more than the victim. However, the effects of a given type of technological change are often complex. For instance, building walled towns probably reduced losses in warfare but increased mortality by epidemics if sanitary and other health technology was not improved. In other words, this particular improvement in military technology caused deterioration of the (urban) environment, which might have raised mortality by more than it reduced direct war casualties.

Administrative technology is particularly important in affecting mortality rates in cases of military events and food shortages. A breakdown of the organization of society might transform a local war or harvest failure into a demographic catastrophe.

The examples above may suffice to illustrate that improvements in food technology are only one among many types of technological changes that influence demographic trends in primitive societies. Therefore, it seems unwarranted to assume that population growth was rapid in primitive societies in the past whenever the rate of growth was unhampered by an inelastic supply of food. Many primitive peoples who were not underfed and who did not fully use the subsistence capacity of their territory must have been decimated by epidemics and wars repeatedly; and I surmise that such wars were waged rarely in order to conquer empty land for a people suffering from overpopulation, but more often in order to conquer slaves or inhabited land (i.e., people who could be made to pay tribute).

Thus, the most reasonable assumption about past demographic trends seems to be that some unfortunate peoples, decimated by disease and war, had negative rates of population growth and disappeared, while other more fortunate ones had positive, but fairly low, rates of growth over long periods. There seems to be little reason to assume that zero rates of population growth occurred more frequently in past history than other rates of growth, positive or negative.

In many cases, peoples with positive rates of growth may have migrated to land that became free when the previous inhabitants were reduced in numbers. But in many other cases, the effects of different rates of population growth among neighboring peoples must have been the opposite: peoples with positive rates of population growth would use their increasing numerical advantage to force neighboring peoples with declining or less rapidly increasing numbers to become slaves or wage workers in the villages and towns of the stronger people, thus further increasing the differences in population densities within a region. I shall return to the effects of such variations in population density later.

Increase in Population and Change in Subsistence Technology in the Early Development of Europe

Until fairly recently, agricultural history dealt mainly with Europe, and European agricultural history was interpreted in the light of the classical theory mentioned above. It was assumed that the primitive nature of agricultural equipment prevented the cultivation of most of the land that is under cultivation today. It was also assumed that the European population was unable to expand, except in periods when better equipment was introduced. In such periods, rates of population growth would have been positive until the new capacity limit for food production was reached, at which time the long-run rate of population growth was assumed to have returned to zero.

This theory fails to take account of the fact that much of the land that was uncultivated in prehistoric times and later was not land that could not be used with the existing types of equipment, but rather land that was used in certain years but that in other years lay fallow under the prevailing systems of long fallow (E. Boserup, 1965). Europe's population began—like populations on other continents—as hunting-gathering communities, but as early as 4500 B.C., some populations in temperate Europe seem to have adopted a system of forest fallow similar to that still in use in some contemporary primitive communities on other continents. When this system is used, a plot cleared in the forest is cultivated for a brief period and, when weeds appear, it is left to regrow into forest. The system requires a large area of land to feed a small group of people. The next step in the development of European agriculture was a gradual shortening of the fallow periods and lengthening of the periods of cultivation for any given piece of land, in step with the gradual increase of the European population.

During many centuries, systems of shorter and shorter fallow spread gradually over Europe, until finally annual cropping became widespread in the eighteenth and nineteenth centuries. The change was slow because the increase of population was slow and intermittent, and an increasing labor force was the precondition for a type of change under which the share of land under cultivation at any given time would increase and the share under fallow correspondingly decline. In regions of Europe that remained sparsely populated the land-using systems of long fallow continued to be used for many more centuries than in those regions of Europe where population increased more rapidly, whether by natural increase or by immigration. By ignoring the process of gradual shortening of fallow, the classical economists, and the economic historians who were influenced by their reasoning, failed to notice the link between demographic trends on the one hand and environment and technology on the other.

The gradual transition to shorter fallows changed the environment. Forests were thinned out and eventually disappeared, and natural grazing pastures and man-made fields replaced them. Also, soil conditions changed as forest areas were transformed either into grassland or into drained, marled, and manured fields. In step with all these changes, the primitive digging sticks and stone axes used in the food-gathering and forest-fallow stages had to be replaced by other hand tools and later by plows.

The gradual shortening of fallow served to feed larger and larger populations in Europe, but the effects of this change on labor productivity in European farming seem not always to have been positive. When fallow was shortened, labor-intensive operations of land preparation, weeding, and fertilization became necessary in order to prevent a decline in crop yields and exhaustion of the soil. The negative effects of this on labor productivity tended to offset the positive effects of improved equipment.

Agricultural historians have described cases in which reduction of population after major epidemics or wars was accompanied by a reversion to systems of longer fallow (Bloch, 1931; Slicker van Bath, 1963). This would seem to indicate that, in these cases, the previous expansion of output by shortening of fallow had been obtained at the cost of a decline in output per unit of labor. The point is important in evaluating the effects of these technological changes on demographic trends, because these changes could be expected to accelerate population growth only if they raised output per unit of labor. If the only positive effect of these changes were to allow a larger population to raise total food production in proportion to the increase in numbers, there would seem to be little reason to expect any acceleration of the rate of population growth as a result of the changes in method.

Effects of Demographic Trends on the Environment

The recent acceleration of rates of population growth in contemporary primitive communities on continents other than Europe provides much new information about the interrelationships between demographic growth and environment and technology. Both natural and social scientists have studied the changes in environment and technology that are occurring under population pressure in contemporary primitive societies, and a number of scholars are taking this evidence as a starting point for a reinterpretation of the ancient history of primitive and other preindustrial societies.

In order to provide a framework for discussion, the main primitive subsistence systems are listed below according to the difference in periods of cultivation and fallow, beginning with the most primitive systems with the longest periods of fallow and the smallest carrying capacity in terms of human populations. This framework also illuminates the preceding discussion of early European development and underlies the examination of the impact of demographic trends on technology in the sections that follow.

1. Food gathering—no cultivation, all land fallow.
2. Forest fallow—one to two crops, followed by fifteen–twenty-five years of fallow.
3. Bush fallow—four to six crops, followed by eight–ten years of fallow.
4. Short fallow—one to two crops, followed by one year of fallow.
5. Annual cropping—one crop each year with a few months of fallow.
6. Multicropping—two to three crops each year without any fallow.

The number of persons who can live in a given area of land is, of course, higher the shorter the period of fallow. It is not possible to use all the subsistence systems in all environments, but most environments are adaptable and allow a choice between several of these systems: a semidesert can be used for herding but also for irrigated crops.

If the population using one of these subsistence systems increases (by natural growth or by immigration) to the point of exceeding the carrying capacity of the land under that system, the environment is likely to deteriorate. If the subsistence system is food gathering, edible plants and animals may gradually disappear. If the subsistence system is forest fallow, the forest may gradually disappear and become replaced by bush or grassland. In other cases, grassland may become overgrazed, and the cultivation of steep hillsides may result in erosion and barrenness. In such cases, the population may have to move to another region, leaving a useless desert behind. This seems to have happened, for instance, in some parts of Southwest Asia during ten millennia of agricultural exploitation of the environment (Hole, 1968).

But sustained demographic growth among primitive peoples does not always result in deterioration of the environment, because the possibility exists that the population, when it outgrows the carrying capacity of the land with the existing subsistence technology, may change to another subsistence system with a higher carrying capacity. Sometimes this change is even facilitated by the transformation of the environment, for instance, by the replacement of forest by bush or grassland, which forces the population to shift to bush fallow or grass fallow instead of forest fallow and to introduce tools that can cope with grassy weeds.

Changes in Subsistence Systems under Population Pressure

Studies of changes in subsistence systems in contemporary primitive societies have been undertaken by many anthropologists, geographers, and agricultural experts. These studies are usually limited to a single change within a particular community or region, for instance, from food gathering to agriculture, or from forest to bush fallow, or from short fallow to annual cropping. Likewise, economic historians and archaeologists have taken an interest in changes in primitive subsistence systems that have occurred in the history of the peoples they are studying. Most of these studies are also limited to a single change, but by linking a number of studies made by different scholars, it is sometimes possible to follow the whole process of gradual change from land-using to land-saving systems in step with demographic growth within a major region. I mentioned above the changes that have taken place in the course of European history; similar changes from land-using to land-saving systems have taken in other parts of the world. For ancient Mesopotamia, evidence from many studies has been combined to show a gradual change from the food gathering on mountain slopes before 8000 B.C. to intensive agriculture based on large-scale irrigation and plow cultivation in the southern plains 4,000–5,000 years later (see Smith and Young, 1972).

It is apparent from the few examples mentioned above that the change from the food-gathering stage to intensive preindustrial agriculture has been a very slow process. It apparently took ancient Mesopotamia over 4,000 years to pass from the beginning of food production to intensive, irrigated agriculture, and it took Europe still longer to pass from the introduction of forest fallow to the beginning of annual cropping a few hundred years ago. Moreover, the geographic diffusion of land-saving systems was also very slow and, in some cases, it failed altogether to take place. Even today, some food-gathering peoples are left, and primitive long-fallow systems continue to be the basic subsistence system in large areas of Africa and Latin America and in parts of South and Southeast Asia (see Allan, 1965; Carniero, 1956; Ekvall, 1972; Gleave and White, 1969; R. B. Lee, 1970).

The subsistence systems mentioned above are distinguished not only by differences in periods of cultivation and fallow but also by differences in types of equipment used. Food-gathering peoples use little or no equipment—they may use sticks to dig up edible roots and fire to enlarge hunting or grazing areas. Forest fallow cultivators also use digging sticks and fire, but bush fallow cultivators usually use hoes or machetes. Most short-fallow cultivators, annual croppers, and multicroppers use plows and keep draft animals, and many annual croppers and most multicroppers use various types of irrigation equipment. Thus, the equipment used for the more land-saving systems of subsistence is much more complicated than that used for the more land-using systems.

It is pertinent, therefore, to ask whether primitive peoples are likely to invent new tools and new subsistence systems when their population size comes to exceed the carrying capacity of their environment with the existing system. The answer is, of course, that it is not necessary to "invent" either a new system or the tools needed for operating it in order to change the subsistence system and to introduce new types of equipment. Both in contemporary and in past primitive communities, technological innovation was rarely the result of invention but rather the result of diffusion of technology from one community to another. A growing population that is beginning to outgrow the carrying capacity of its subsistence system is likely to be receptive to the idea of borrowing technology from other communities with higher population densities and with less land-using subsistence systems (Dumond, 1965).

When we observe that even today some peoples use primitive land-using subsistence systems and primitive transport systems that were abandoned by other peoples many millennia ago, we should not ask why these peoples never invented the plow and the wheel, but why the diffusion of these technologies seems to have happened fairly rapidly in some cases and not at all in other cases. In other words, why did small groups of people who live in regions of very low population density and use primitive land-using subsistence systems never adopt the better technologies that were used by other peoples with whom they have been in contact?

Labor Productivity of Land-Using and Land-Saving Subsistence Systems

The main answer to the question posed above seems to be that the primitive land-using subsistence systems, that is, food-gathering and long-fallow agriculture, have a higher output per unit of labor input than usually assumed and, therefore, the primitive peoples who use them have little incentive to change to more land-saving subsistence systems, as long as they are few enough to obtain the necessary food by use of the land-using systems. But the advantage of the land-using systems has been overlooked, partly because of lack of proper information about labor input and partly because many of the peasants who use land-saving systems produce large surpluses that they deliver to landlords or sell to merchants, while the primitive peoples who employ land-using systems rarely produce any surpluses beyond the immediate needs of their families. It seems, however, that the surpluses produced in preindustrial peasant communities, which have been taken as proof of the relatively high labor productivity of the land-saving agricultural systems used in such communities, are partly yields on labor investments and partly the result of a larger input of labor in the cultivation of crops than that customary in primitive communities where land-using systems are used (E. Boserup, 1965, 1970a,b). In other words, it seems that the peoples who employ land-using systems would also be able to produce surpluses if they were to make labor investments and work longer hours. We shall see below why such peoples usually fail to produce any surpluses.

A number of anthropological studies show that present-day hunting-gathering communities obtain the necessary food without working very hard, even when they live in inhospitable environments. A study by Richard Lee of the Bushmen living in the Kalahari Desert reveals that the women who do the food gathering use only two to three days a week to provide the necessary food (R. B. Lee, 1970; 1972). Lee showed the alternatives available to a food-gathering people when their group size increases and the ways in which they adapt to increasing size. He measured the distances that the women must walk in search of food and the burden they have to carry under varying assumptions about group size and the average number of young children per woman. With increasing group size, a woman must walk longer and longer distances in search of the necessary food, and the choice is between spacing the children more (children born alive and allowed to live) and splitting into separate smaller groups. The latter solution would of course be excluded if the number of Bushmen in the whole territory were to become so large that there would be no free space for new groups. In that case, women would have a strong incentive to produce some crops instead of gathering all the food. It is tempting to ask if the connection found by Lee between the need to carry children around and the increasing burden of food gathering with increasing group size can help to explain the fact that it is the women who usually cultivate crops in the most primitive systems of long-fallow agriculture that follow the stage of food gathering.

Many hunting-gathering peoples produce some crops as a supplement to their diet, and it seems that when their territory becomes more densely populated and their hunting-gathering activities therefore become less productive, they come to rely increasingly on their crops and on domestic birds and animals. In other words, as population pressure gradually makes the environment less productive, they may react by adopting an alternative technology, which was already known but had hitherto been little used. This new technology will increase the carrying capacity of the environment but will probably lower labor productivity. Therefore, the new technology is unlikely to be transferred from one people to another as long as the population size permits the continued use of the old technology (Binford, 1968). The neolithic revolution—the change from food gathering to agriculture—is not a sweeping revolutionary change but a process of gradual evolution (Galy, 1969).

Turning from anthropological to archaeological evidence, we have an example of gradual change from food gathering to food production in Kent Flannery's diggings in Mesopotamian village sites from the period 7500–5500 B.C. (Flannery, 1969). In a site that contained remnants from this very long period, he found striking changes in the composition of vegetable foods, with a gradual decline in the use of wild legumes, the major staple food at the beginning of the period, and a gradual increase in grains of cultivated cereals, weeds, and plants typical of fallowed agricultural land. Flannery rejected the idea that early agriculture caused any drastic improvement in people's diet or provided a more stable food supply. He assumed that the slow change from wild food to produced food was a means to increase the carrying capacity of the environment in response to population growth, and he pointed out that the anthropological studies by Lee and others also suggest that population pressure was the factor that made prehistoric hunting-gathering peoples turn to agriculture.

The sequence of gradual change from more land-using to increasingly land-saving types of agriculture in step with population growth in ancient Mesopotamia has been traced by Smith and Young by means of the archaeological finds of equipment (Smith and Young, 1972). The plow was in use in the southern plains from the fourth millennium B.C., but hoes for short-fallow cultivation were found in much older sites in mountain villages in the area. It is more difficult to trace digging sticks by archaeological excavation because they are made of wood, but Smith and Young have suggested that holed stones found in the oldest of the village sites may be weights for digging sticks and that the lack of hoes in other very old sites may be "evidence from silence" for the use of wooden digging stocks for long-fallow cultivation. The excavations seem also to indicate that a considerable increase in population took place during the period when primitive tools were gradually replaced by better equipment.

William Sanders has traced the development of subsistence systems in the Mesoamerican region from ancient times to the Spanish conquest and compared them to the apparent demographic trends in various parts of the region, taking account of the special environmental and other factors (Sanders, 1972). He concluded that the most productive direction for research in the evolution of civilization is to study the history of population growth and its relationship to increasingly intensive agriculture.

The low labor input needed for subsistence under long-fallow agriculture has been brought out by a large number of studies from many parts of the world. Carneiro concluded from a study in the Amazon Basin that the easiness of the long-fallow system was one of the factors that induced primitive cultivators to split up their local communities and disperse over the territory when their numbers were growing, instead of changing to more land-saving systems. He suggested that because of the centrifugal effects of land-using systems with growing populations, old civilizations based on land-saving, labor-intensive agricultural systems are found in what he calls "circum-scribed areas," that is, regions where growing populations were confined in a restricted area surrounded by inhospitable mountains, deserts, or oceans and thus had no other choice than to adopt the land-saving systems in spite of lower labor productivity (Carneiro, 1961).

In comparing the labor needed to obtain food for a family by means of either land-using or land-saving systems, it is necessary to take account not only of the labor needed for actual food gathering or crop growing but also of inputs of labor that are in the nature of investments and that are prerequisites for the use of more land-saving systems of production. While no such labor investment is needed for food gathering and very little for forest fallow if the clearing of land is done mainly by fire, the land-saving systems usually cannot be applied without some preliminary labor-intensive land improvements. These labor investments range from clearing roots and stones from land before it can be plowed for the first time to building wells, ponds, dams, terraces, bunds, and so on, for irrigation. Once such labor investments have been made, it may be possible to obtain higher output per man-hour from the cultivation of permanent fields than from long-fallow agriculture on similar land, but for a primitive population that must choose between undertaking the labor investments and starting long-fallow cultivation in a new place, it is a labor-saving operation to split up the group and continue with long-fallow agriculture in two different places. The yields of the labor investments—if properly maintained—may last forever, but the planning horizon of peoples who subsist by food gathering or long-fallow agriculture is a few years at most.

Demographic Trends and Nonagricultural Technology

For obvious reasons, the more land-using subsistence systems can be pursued only as long as the population in the region remains below a certain size. There are many other types of technology, however, that require the density of population to be above a minimum level.

It is well known, since Adam Smith's famous dictum, that the division of labor is limited by the extent of the market. This applies not only to modern industrial technology but equally to specialized products of traditional crafts and provision of services. Full-time specialized craftsmen could not possibly exist in villages of long-fallow producers in the Amazon region with populations of 50–150 persons. Craftsmen and other specialists can find enough customers for full-time specialization only in large villages or in small villages in regions that are so densely populated that the distances between villages are small enough to allow one craftsman or other specialist to serve several villages. Thus, very small, isolated groups of persons who practice the land-using primitive subsistence systems cannot afford such specialized activities. Their inhabitants must remain jacks-of-all-trades, which means that their relatively high labor productivity in the provision of food is partly offset by a low labor productivity in the provision of other necessities of life. Such communities are caught in a trap, because the maximum density consistent with their subsistence system is below the minimum density needed for development in fields other than food supply. They are not likely to escape from the trap until population density in the region becomes so high (by natural growth or by immigration) that they are forced to adopt a land-saving system of subsistence.

Also, much transport technology—modern as well as primitive—can only be applied where there is a certain minimum population. Even a footpath through tropical forest can exist only if used regularly by a certain number of people (or animals). Transport by cart or wagon can develop only where the local population is large enough to build and maintain a network of roads, and the canalization of rivers also requires a large labor force. Thus, small groups living in regions without naturally navigable waterways cannot develop urban centers because the necessary transport of food to such centers cannot be organized. Most ancient civilizations were situated on navigable rivers, and until fairly recently the towns in the interior of Africa were in fact large villages drawing their food supplies from surrounding fields.

With growing population density in a region, it becomes possible to construct and maintain a good network of roads linking the town or towns to food-producing areas or it becomes possible to dig canals or to canalize rivers for transport purposes. At this stage of development, it is no longer necessary that specialized craftsmen and persons performing specialized services for society at large live scattered in villages or move frequently from place to place living off the land, as did the European kings and their courts until population density in their kingdoms increased and the transport system improved. When population density increases, and the land-using subsistence systems are replaced by land-saving systems, both rulers and craftsmen can settle permanently in towns with the additional advantages of still more specialization, better organization, and more specialized equipment.

We may define a town as a major population center, the inhabitants of which do not themselves produce the food they consume. This definition brings into focus the fact that urbanization in primitive societies requires either a high density of rural population or particularly favorable opportunities for the transport of food, for instance, by boat.

It is thus inaccurate to say that the appearance of towns depends upon a high level of labor productivity in agriculture or upon a high degree of exploitation of peasants by a social hierarchy. What is needed is a large food surplus in an absolute sense but not necessarily a large food surplus per agricultural producer. Urbanization in Europe made rapid strides in the eleventh and twelfth centuries; we know that population was increasing considerably in this period, but we have no reliable information about any major improvements in agricultural equipment and in the productivity of agricultural labor at that time (Wailes, 1972). However, a large town may be supplied by small marketable surpluses produced by a large number of producers, if settlement patterns and the available means of transport permit the transportation of food surpluses.

Thus, as far as production is concerned, there may be nothing to prevent long-fallow agriculture from making available the surpluses needed for the supply of towns, but the producers fail to do so because transport to towns is uneconomical with this type of agriculture and because the dispersion of populations using long-fallow systems usually prevents them from reaching the stage of specialization and social organization needed for the development of urban centers. Martin Orans has stressed that long-fallow producers have potential surpluses of food that are not actually produced because there is no need for more than what is customarily consumed in their local communities (Orans, 1966). But food is not the only article of consumption, and it could as well be said that such peoples have potential surpluses of specialized crafts and services that do not materialize because the local market is too small to permit specialization of labor.

Many of the ancient urban centers obtained their food supply from intensive irrigated agriculture in the region where they were located, and it is usually suggested that this is because labor productivity is particularly high with irrigated agriculture. It seems more relevant to point out that this type of primitive subsistence system has a particularly high output per unit of land, since crop yields are high and more than one crop may be obtained per year. The high demand for labor per unit of land and the high output per unit of land make it necessary and possible for a large number of families to live within a small area. Therefore, even if the surplus per family is small, the total surplus available within a fairly small distance from the town will be large. In addition, the irrigation canals, or the river used for irrigation, can be used for boat transport of food to the town.

It takes a large labor force, however, to construct and maintain a major irrigation system and to cultivate irrigated crops with primitive technology. Therefore, a major town can be provided with food from this type of agriculture only if the region where it is situated is densely populated or if the military strength of the town forces the outlying population to settle around the town and construct and operate the irrigation system. In any case, it is the total labor force at the disposal of the society that matters and not the size of the surplus that can be extracted per agricultural family. As long as the ancient civilizations had small populations, they used small-scale irrigation; the systems of major irrigation seem to have been created after these societies had grown populous by natural population growth and by immigration of either slaves or free labor from other areas (Adams, 1968).

Effects of Unequal Demographic Growth on Social Organization

There seems to be a fairly close correlation between population size and density, on one hand, and the degree of stratification and complexity of the social system, on the other (see Sanders and Price, 1968; Harner, 1970). Hunting-gathering groups are usually small and scattered, and they have a simple social organization. Long-fallow cultivators usually live in somewhat larger groups and in regions of somewhat higher population density, and they may reach the stage of tribal organization and chiefdoms. But only larger groups, with higher population densities and more land-saving agricultural systems, are likely to reach the next stage, that of preindustrial peasant community with a certain degree of urbanization. Thus when the size and density of population are increasing in a primitive society, the social organization of this society becomes increasingly complex through the interplay of several factors, all of which seem to be related to population density. One of these factors is the gradual development of hierarchical systems of land tenure, in step with the change to more land-saving systems of subsistence. Another is an increasing tendency toward tension and hostility both within each local group and between neighboring groups, when the numbers in each group become larger and the distances between the local groups smaller. This may create or enhance social differentiation and a more centralized organization of society either through warfare or through the appearance of a ritually sanctified social ranking. A number of writers have reviewed specific factors in the relationship of complexity of society to density. Thus Boserup (1965) reviews changing patterns of land ownership. Carneiro (1961, 1970) relates intergroup and intragroup hostility to group density. Netting (1972) discusses ritualistic stratification of society. And Adams (1965b) discusses such stratification as it is brought about by warfare.

Egypt and some "circumscribed areas" in Asia reached fairly high population densities many centuries before the Western Hemisphere or Africa (as far as we know), and this may help to explain why we have found the oldest urban civilizations in the Near East and Asia. Robert Adams has shown that ancient Mesopotamia and Mesoamerica at the time of the Spanish conquest reached strikingly similar stages of civilization. But both the Old World during the height of Mesopotamian culture and America before Columbus seem to have had such small populations that only a few peoples in each continent reached the minimum population density required for urban civilization. The few existing urban civilizations were like small islands in a sea of "barbarian" communities, primitive tribes practicing one of the land-using subsistence systems.

To build an urban civilization with the technology available to the population in such a center required a large labor force occupied in labor-intensive investment work, and, as a rule, the peoples who managed to build such civilizations seem to have used all the means at their disposal to obtain foreign labor from the surrounding barbarian groups. But if the urban civilizations skimmed off the population increase of the surrounding barbarian peoples or even decimated their numbers, the remaining barbarian population were prevented from reaching the minimum density for urbanization. The barbarians continued their land-using subsistence systems, caught in the trap of low population density described above. More recently, the American slave raids in Africa seem to have had similar effects.

Such developments entailed a growing technological and cultural gap between the centers and the surrounding peoples. The high-level technology used in the centers was inapplicable in the sparsely populated regions that separated the centers from each other, and this also hindered the diffusion of technology from one center to another.

Environment and Population Growth

While war casualties and forced migration no doubt helped to keep rates of population growth below or close to zero in many primitive societies, environmental differences also are often important in explaining divergent demographic trends. However, we should avoid the common fallacy of thinking of environment exclusively in terms of potential for gathering and producing food. We must also take account of other factors, especially the different incidence of disease in different environments.

It is well known that most contemporary primitive peoples live in the wet tropics—an environment in which both temperature and humidity allow abundant plant growth in all seasons, but one that also provides particularly good conditions for the growth of bacteria and other parasites that decimate primitive populations. As a consequence, mortality due to disease is likely to be much lower in dry and temperate climates. This positive environmental factor in the latter climates may be more important for rates of population growth than the negative environmental factor: the greater difficulty of providing food because of the interruption of plant growth in the dry or cold seasons. In view of the foregoing discussion of the far-reaching impact of population growth on technological change, the implied demographic differential may help to explain why it was the dry and temperate climates that gave rise to most of the early civilizations.

PART II

Food

[1970]

Present and Potential Food Production in Developing Countries

Technical Potentialities for Additional Food Production

In the recent past, some developing countries achieved spectacular progress in food production by the use of fertilizer for food crops and by the introduction of improved seeds, of which the first was hybrid maize. Moreover, in many countries a shift took place from the cultivation of low-yielding cereals to that of high-yielding food crops such as rice, maize, cassava, sugar, and potatoes. In most developing countries, there is scope for much more progress through these methods. Yields of food crops remain at low levels because little or no chemical fertilizer is applied, and improved seeds are used on only a small part of the sown area. Likewise, there is much scope for accelerating the substitution of high-yielding types of food crops for low-yielding types.

The dramatic increase in crop yields caused by the use of fertilizer and improved seeds has focused attention on these particular ways of increasing food production, and other possibilities have tended to be overlooked. In fact, taking the developing world as a whole, it is true to say that the largest potential for increased food production is in the replacement of extensive systems of land use by more intensive ones, rather than in the achievement of higher yields for a given crop or in the substitution of one crop for another.

It may be useful to begin the discussion of the potential for more intensive use of land for food production by a systematic grouping of the main systems of land use (E. Boserup, 1965). If the land used for nonfood crops and for nonagricultural purposes is disregarded, the main systems of land use are as follows, listed by increasing degree of intensity:

1. Cultivable land in completely uninhabited regions.
2. Land used only for the collection of vegetable foods and for hunting.
3. Land used only for grazing by domestic animals.

4. Land used in long-fallow agriculture (sometimes called shifting cultivation).
5. Land used in short-fallow rotations with grazing on fallow land.
6. Land used for annual cropping without fallow.
7. Land cropped twice a year, without fallow.
8. Land cropped three times or more annually, without fallow.

Many sparsely populated developing countries, as for example in parts of Africa, still have huge areas under the first four types of land use listed above. More densely populated developing countries, among them those of the Indian subcontinent, have relatively little land under the first groups and much under groups 5 and 6. In the most densely populated developing countries, such as Egypt and eastern China, a large share of the cultivated land is under type 7, and in Japan a considerable share of the cultivated land is under type 8.

It is not possible to tell precisely how much of the land in developing countries is under one or other of these systems of land utilization. The classifications found in international statistics of land use are Eurocentric. For instance, bush land used in long fallow rotations, the predominant type of land use in many developing countries, finds no place in international statistics; it is included, or rather hidden, under broader headings such as "arable land," "forest land," or "wasteland" (Clark, 1967).

To be useful in the analysis of food potentials, statistics of land use should distinguish five categories, viz. shifting cultivation with long and medium periods of fallow for regeneration of fertility; land in short-fallow rotations; land cropped annually; and land under multicropping. Preferably, there should be a distinction between rain-fed and irrigated land within each of these groups. Some of the basic information needed for such a classification is available in specialized literature of various types; but more field surveys and a more systematic use of existing information brought up to date at regular intervals would improve the basis for estimates of the potential for additional food production.

The first, spontaneous reaction of tribal or peasant families to population growth within their community is to look for additional land to cultivate by the traditional methods. If no such land is available, they have to use the land at their disposal more intensively, that is to move one or more steps in the list above. Thus, people who have been collecting more food than they produced may see the amount collected per head decline when their numbers are increasing, and this will induce them to produce more. People who have been cultivating their land, for instance, with two years of cultivation after eight years of fallow may change, say, to three years of cultivation after six years of fallow. Peasants who used a short-fallow rotation may put some of their land under annual cultivation, and peasants who previously took one crop a year may begin to sow successive crops on some of their land.

Such intensification of land use may mean that the land gets too little time for recovery, so that yields decline. If the land under more intensive use is sloping, erosion may result, and the reduction of fallow and pasture areas may entail weakened draft animals, and hence poor land preparation and reduced yields.

Since antiquity, several methods have been known whereby such deterioration of land and animals can be avoided: (a) the natural regeneration of the land during the periods of fallow can be replaced by various other methods of fertilization; (b) sloping land can be terraced; and (c) instead of grazing and browsing, the animals can be fed cultivated fodder. In recent decades, technical and scientific progress have much enhanced the efficiency of these methods and thereby increased the possibilities of raising food production under population pressure.

FERTILIZATION AS A FACTOR IN INTENSIVE LAND USE

Where extensive types of long-fallow rotations are used, the burning of the natural vegetation on the ground before sowing may provide sufficient fertilization. With short fallow, or no fallow, one or more of the following types of fertilization must be used: (a) vegetable or mineral matter collected from surrounding land, to be spread on the cultivated area; (b) manuring by droppings from grazing animals or by the spreading of composts with animal manure; (c) manuring by nightsoil, household waste, and crop residue; (d) the use of leguminous crops in the rotation; (e) industrial fertilizer.

In regions where multicropping is practiced without the help of industrial fertilizer, several of the other methods are usually applied simultaneously. Nevertheless, it may be impossible to find enough fertilizer of various kinds to have more than a minor share of the land under multicropping, especially where animal manure is used for fuel. The use of chemical fertilizers removes this limitation to the expansion of the area under multicropping, thereby increasing the food potential considerably in densely populated developing countries.

Progress in soil chemistry and biology are steadily enlarging the potential for food production by making it possible to use land which was previously considered useless and to obtain high yields from land which used to be regarded as poor. With scientific progress, ideas as to what land should be considered good or bad, cultivable or incultivable, are steadily changing. At one time, land in the tropics was considered unsuitable for more intensive cultivation than that by long-fallow techniques. Now the problem is seen as that of finding the suitable methods for intensive land use in particular tropical regions. It is a problem which is far from solved for all tropical regions, but intensive land use is spreading in many parts.

IRRIGATION AS A FACTOR IN INTENSIVE LAND USE

In dry regions the soil may not contain sufficient moisture to allow a crop each year without irrigation. In such regions, population pressure promotes on one hand the more intensive use of rain-fed land and on the other the spread of irrigation (table 1). For instance, crop rotations may change with increasing population, as shown in the table.

TABLE 1. Agricultural effect of increasing population density in a dry region

Population density	Humid land	Dry land	Irrigated land
Low			
A	Wheat/fallow	Grazing only	No land irrigated
B	Wheat/fallow	Wheat/fallow	No land irrigated
Medium			
C	Wheat/fallow	Wheat/fallow	Wheat/fallow
D	Wheat/fallow	Wheat/fallow	Wheat/fodder
High			
E	Wheat/fodder	Wheat/fallow	Wheat/fodder
F	Wheat/fodder	Wheat/fallow	Double cropping

In the end, nearly all humid and dry land may be brought under irrigation. In Egypt virtually all land sown seems to be under perennial irrigation, with about two-thirds of it double cropped. In other parts of the Near East, where population densities are much lower than in Egypt, there is a long way to go before the intensity of land use becomes comparable with that of Egypt. Most of the irrigated land in the Near East is still under a wheat/fallow rotation, and in addition, parts of the region have extensive humid rain-fed areas under wheat/fallow rotations. However, the potential for further expansion of the area under irrigation is much larger than in Egypt (FAO, 1966).

The scope for irrigation has been widened in recent years by technological innovations and in the related activities of terracing and levelling of land. Subterranean water can be brought up from deeper layers; perennial-flow irrigation can be introduced in regions where this would have been impossible or extremely costly with traditional techniques, and sometimes water can be saved and salinity and waterlogging avoided by the use of spraying techniques instead of flow irrigation. Modern equipment makes it possible to reshape sloping land and thus control erosion and prevent the silting up of dams.

FODDER PRODUCTION

The successive stages of land use in a dry region listed above may also serve to illustrate the potentialities for fodder supply with growing population densities in North Africa and West Asia. The transition from a very low population density to a somewhat higher one turns permanent grazing land into cultivated under a wheat/fallow rotation. This reduces the fodder potential. But the introduction of irrigated land with a wheat/fallow rotation with further increases in population enlarges the potential, and so do the succeeding changes from wheat/fallow to wheat/fodder rotations in irrigated and humid land and the final change to double cropping in irrigated land, if some of the additional crops are fodder crops. If there is less demand for fodder, the crops replacing fallow may be leguminous or other crops for human consumption. If a more rapid increase of crops for human consumption is needed, the draft animals may be replaced by tractors. Draft animals are a heavy drain on land resources in dry regions, because each animal can be used only during a short period of the year if the crops are to benefit from the best growing season, and can therefore be utilized for only a small area.

Both in regions with a dry season and in regions with a cold season, the more rapid operations made possible by using tractors instead of animals can help to make room for more than one crop annually. Widespread tractorization was the basis of the recent change from two to three crops per annum in Japan. Also, biological research, producing fast-growing crops, has contributed to increase the potential for multicropping.

Although modern techniques have widened the potential for food production in very densely populated regions, the potentialities are, of course, much larger in more sparsely populated regions. In the Indian subcontinent, population density is very high in some districts, but in others fairly extensive types of land use predominate. Even in the most densely populated districts, multicropping is less widespread than in Egypt or the Far East, and in some of the less densely populated parts of the Indian subcontinent there is much scope for additional irrigation and for more intensive use of rain-fed land. Systematic fodder production for domestic animals is still the exception rather than the rule, and pasture improvement is extremely rare. Little chemical fertilizer is used on food crops, and crop yields can be much improved.

In most of Africa, population is still so sparse that the grazing of natural pastures and long-fallow agriculture in rain-fed land are the predominant systems of land use for food production. But present high rates of population growth make it necessary to find alternatives to the traditional systems, lest the land deteriorate because of reduction of the regeneration periods between the crops. There remain huge untapped food potentials in Africa. River valleys and swamps in Africa—and in Latin America—are as suitable for paddy production as the Asian ones. Chinese advisers in Africa were amazed to discover the unused possibilities of paddy production in that continent. In actual fact, however, there is small reason for amazement; these African potentialities remained largely untapped because the sparse population could be fed without considerable capital investment in land improvement and without the addition to the daily work load which irrigation would entail.

Developing countries, within which there are some very sparsely or completely uninhabited regions, sometimes choose to make the sudden transition from the most extensive to intensive types of land utilization by means of settlement schemes for such regions. This has been done not only in sparsely populated countries in Africa and Latin America, but also in more densely populated countries like Viet Nam and Ceylon, which have seen their potentialities for food production suddenly enlarged by the eradication of malaria from regions which used to be regarded as uninhabitable for settlers from outside. Also, veterinary progress has enlarged the food potential, for instance in regions of Africa where the risk of trypanosomiasis had hitherto prevented the rearing of cattle.

The widespread concern about the population explosion in developing countries has given much stimulus to systematic agricultural research. This has already widened the potential for food production, as mentioned above; but many results of recent research are still in the pipeline, and the number of scientists working with these problems is steadily increasing. In fact, the problem of food supply in developing countries is less one of technical feasibility than of the rapidity with which the technically possible can become actual practice. More precisely, the problem is whether it will be possible, in the period until birth control can markedly slow down rates of population growth, to sustain annual rates of growth of food production which are as high as, or preferably significantly higher than, the rates at which population is growing. The main factors which need to be analyzed in order to answer this question can be grouped under three headings: the capital requirements for agriculture; the ability to organize this investment (i.e., agricultural planning); and the strength of the political and social obstacles to such capital investment. These problems will be dealt with in the following sections.

Capital Requirements for Additional Food Production

As population increases in a given country, the labor force available for agricultural production expands at roughly the same rate and, of course, the area of land per head declines. These changes, naturally, raise the demand for the third factor of production, capital. Production of food for the increasing population requires an increase in the amount of capital (particularly in the public sector), not only in step with the increase of the labor force in agriculture, but beyond that an increase of the amount of capital per head of agricultural worker so as to compensate for the declining area of land at his disposal (including fallow and grazing land). If the purpose is not only to produce food for the increasing population, urban as well as rural, but also to improve nutritional standards, the amount of capital per worker in agriculture must increase even more steeply.

Nobody will object to the statement that the feeding of an increasing population from a given area requires an increase in the amount of capital. It is less generally realized that demand for agricultural labor may also be increasing. In discussion about possibilities of food production, many take for granted that the existing agricultural labor force in developing countries is more than sufficient to produce even a rapidly increasing output.

Two factors help to explain this belief: (a) the large amount of seasonal unemployment in agriculture in many developing countries and the short working hours in some regions of long-fallow cultivation are taken as sufficient proof of the existence of a *general* labor surplus, supposed to be readily available and sufficient for large-scale expansion of agricultural output; (b) as mentioned above, attention is most often focused on the need and the scope for raising crop yields rather than on the transition to more intensive land use—in the sense of more frequent cropping of a given piece of land. This means that labor requirements per unit of additional output are underestimated, since an increase in the area sown each year requires a roughly proportionate increase in the input of labor, while little additional labor is needed in order to apply chemical fertilizer or improved seeds, though additional labor will be needed to harvest a larger crop.

Often the change from extensive to intensive systems of land use brought about by the pressure of population requires, in addition to the increase in capital per worker, an increase in hours of labor per unit of output. Under long-fallow systems, tribal populations may be able to produce their food with a small input of labor per family, a very large land area (including fallow) per family, and virtually no capital. When they change to more intensive use of the land, they need much less land per family and they need to invest considerably in land improvements, in additional implements, and so on; but they also need to work more hours per year in order to obtain the same amount of food per family as before. Available information about labor input in the production of food with long-fallow methods suggests that a family of man, wife, and small children may typically use around 1,000 hours of work per year to produce their food, most of this work being performed by the women (Clark and Haswell, 1964). Peasant families producing food by intensive systems of agriculture, but without mechanized equipment, must work many more hours per year in order to produce the necessary food for subsistence, especially if they must also produce fodder for their draft animals. Hours of work per family spent on food production may be 3,000 to 5,000 per annum in regions with labor-intensive systems of production (J. Buck, 1937). Part of this labor is spent on the maintenance and renewal of the capital investment in irrigation canals, bunds, and terraces.

In view of these large differences between labor input in extensive and intensive systems of agriculture, we cannot exclude the possibility that the realization of the potential for food production under rapid increase of population may sometimes be prevented by an insufficient supply of labor. This, however, occurs in special cases; more generally, the limiting factor is the supply of capital.

For the expansion of food production in response to the increase of population, capital investment is required in the following: (a) land improvement; (b) equipment; (c) infrastructure; and (d) knowledge.

LAND IMPROVEMENT

In this category, heavy investment is required in the clearing of land for permanent cultivation, as compared with the more superficial clearing for shifting cultivation; in leveling, terracing, draining, and bunding of land; in the digging of wells and of irrigation ditches. Major irrigation works and other land improvements undertaken by public authorities on public land are usually classified as infrastructure investment. Land improvement as here defined may be done by the cultivator and his labor force with traditional techniques, or it may be organized by landlords, cooperatives, or public authorities, using either traditional techniques or modern mechanical equipment.

In the past, traditional techniques of land improvement have been used successfully under various types of organization in communities with growing populations. But with the high rates of population growth now prevailing, it would seem desirable to use mechanized equipment for land improvement to a much larger extent than is usual in developing countries. This would make it possible to accelerate the transition to intensive land use and thus to achieve a more rapid increase of employment opportunities for *current* agricultural operations and of food production.

EQUIPMENT AND MATERIALS

In addition to the equipment for land improvement mentioned above, more intensive land use requires additional equipment for current operations, either of the traditional type (hand tools, plows, and draft animals) or mechanized equipment. In densely populated regions, irrigation equipment for use on farms is an important item. Also, a choice is possible between traditional and modern equipment, such as between the *shaduf* and the diesel pump.

Many economists advise against the use of mechanized equipment for current agricultural operations in developing countries, their attitude being motivated by the fear of creating unemployment. They overlook that some types of machinery, such as pumps for watering, may create additional employment because they permit irrigation on land which otherwise would have remained unirrigated. Likewise, the use of tractors may create additional employment by facilitating multicropping, as already mentioned; in some regions, for instance in part of the Near East, it is the number of draft animals and the grazing area required for them that effectively limits the sown area (FAO, 1966). Therefore, it is important that decisions on mechanization in agriculture be made with an open mind, and should be dependent on specific local conditions. A dogmatic denunciation of the use of mechanized equipment may prevent a fuller development of the potential for food production in developing countries.

INFRASTRUCTURE

This category includes, among other things, major irrigation works and public works designed to prevent erosion in catchment areas, floods, and the silting up of dams. Investment in these accounts for a large share of total investment in agriculture in regions with dense population dependent on irrigated agriculture, and many developing countries have invested heavily in this way in recent decades (Clark, 1967).

Development of marketing facilities, provision of grain stores, feeder roads, and other transport investment in settlement areas may conveniently be included in infrastructure investment for agriculture. Some investment of this nature, in particular feeder roads and other transport improvement, may require large amounts of capital in cases where settlements are established in remote regions without any existing facilities. The true costs per additional unit of output may turn out to be extremely high in new settlements based upon capital-intensive irrigation schemes which are so located.

KNOWLEDGE

It seems natural, for our purpose, to define investment in human capital in agriculture rather broadly, so as to include not only the creation of physical assets, such as agriculture schools and research establishments, but also costs of operating such establishments, as well as current expenditure for extension and advisory services. The needs for these developments emerge when population pressure on food resources makes it necessary to change from the traditional methods of cultivation to systems of more intensive land use. It seems pertinent therefore to regard them as investments needed for the introduction of new systems of agriculture.

The classification of agricultural services as investment in agriculture serves to remind us that in a number of developing countries there has been, in the years after independence, a decline in the existing fund of human capital in the form of knowledge of agriculture. Many foreigners employed in agricultural services left without being replaced by similar numbers of the country's own nationals, with similar qualifications as teachers, technicians, or administrators. Where expatriate experts are employed, their service now tends to be for limited periods on contract, so that they are unable to build up a fund of experience, and continuity in development is broken when they are replaced.

Attention is often drawn to the contrast between rapid progress in agriculture in industrialized countries in recent decades and the slow progress in the developing countries, and the corresponding contrast between "burdensome surpluses" on one side and difficulties of financing imports on the other. In considering this widening food gap in developing countries, it must be remembered that far more investment (per unit area and per worker in agriculture) has been undertaken in the industrialized countries than in the majority of the developing countries; and that, for instance, the marketing facilities developed in developing countries were usually limited to nonfood crops. The way to avoid further widening of the food gap between industrialized and developing countries is, therefore, to invest more in the agricultural sectors of developing countries and to invest less in subsidized high-cost food production in industrialized countries. A first step might be to channel a drastically increased share of foreign aid to the agricultural sector in the developing countries.

Apart from the need to invest more in the agricultural sector and in ancillary facilities and services, including marketing facilities, there is also need for much larger investments in industries producing for agriculture—fertilizer, other chemicals, and equipment—and in industries processing agricultural produce.

Agricultural Planning

In the past, adjustment of food production to higher population densities was brought about most often through the spontaneous action of cultivators and of tribal or village authorities. Under the far more rapid increase of population now prevailing in developing countries, agricultural change needs to be more radical and accelerated than in the past. In particular, governments in developing countries are coming to play a more active role in agricultural planning than most colonial or national governments in these countries used to play in the past. The government's role can no longer be limited to the traditional one of financing and organizing major infrastructural investments. The government will have to take the initiative in village planning, provide the cultivator with plans for the intensification of land use adapted to local conditions, and supply the necessary credits and some sort of incentive to undertake the investment. This may involve, for instance, support of food prices or the granting of subsidies to some particularly desirable inputs.

The problems which must be solved by agricultural planning may be discussed under four headings; (a) choice of the regions for the development of intensive land use; (b) choice between short-term and long-term investment; (c) coordination between investment and incentive policies; (d) changes in land tenure related to the changes in land use. A few comments on each of these problems are offered below.

THE CHOICE OF REGIONS FOR DEVELOPMENT

The first problem is to decide whether efforts should be spread evenly over a large area or be concentrated, at least to begin with, in a few places where conditions for more intensive agriculture appear to be particularly promising. Of course, the answer to this question must differ for countries with uniform climate and soil from those with wide regional disparities in conditions for intensive agriculture.

If failures are to be avoided, the choice of development regions must be preceded by systematic studies of the potentialities for food production in the different parts of the country in question. For this, large numbers of specialists of various types are needed, and such personnel are available in few if any of the developing countries. In the next few decades, more and more developing countries will discover the need for systematic research into their agricultural potentialities, and the demand for agricultural planning will increase accordingly. Up to a certain point, the specialist required may be available under existing programs of technical assistance; but the supply is likely to be exhausted in the relatively near future, unless the problem of training of agricultural experts is tackled vigorously and without delay.

THE CHOICE BETWEEN SHORT-TERM AND LONG-TERM INVESTMENT

Some types of investment in agriculture yield results in the form of larger output a few years after the investment decision is implemented, while other types of investment in agriculture contribute to larger output only several decades after the investment plan was first initiated. An example of the latter type of investment is the capital-intensive irrigation projects supplemented by settlement schemes, on which some developing countries are concentrating most of their efforts in the agricultural sector. Such schemes usually take between one and two decades before the first crops are available from the land to which a controlled supply of water has been made available, and it may take half a century before the whole area is bearing crops. The concentration of agricultural investment on this type of development is an important factor which helps to explain the slow growth of food production in some developing countries where large sums have been invested in agriculture in recent years.

The preference for capital-intensive irrigated agriculture and for settlement in "new villages," and the neglect of investment in minor irrigation works and in other land improvements in "old villages," is a legacy from the colonial period. The idea of creating new agricultural units appealed to the colonial administrator, who usually desired to intervene as little as possible with the traditional way of life of the indigenous population. Furthermore, the need for the development of food production in that period was primarily a need to provide food for the growing urban centers, and this could be done by means of surplus production in new villages. Less concern was felt about the development of food production and incomes in the old villages, where population at that time was increasing less rapidly and sometimes was stagnating.

A change of attitude in favor of the expansion of food production in old villages occurred in many areas before the end of the colonial period; and at present governments in many developing countries feel the need for other types of investment than settlement schemes. The two types of development, however, require different types of technicians, and therefore the new policy is likely to come up against difficulties in the supply of adequate manpower.

COORDINATION OF INVESTMENT WITH INCENTIVE POLICIES

Most cultivators in developing countries produce crops for sale in addition to producing food for their own use, and many produce food surpluses by employing hired labor. These cultivators will take up intensive systems of land use only if they can expect what they regard as a sufficient return on expenditure for land improvement and other investment. Therefore, governments may have little success with supplying infrastructure investment, credits, and extension services unless the relationship between prices of inputs (including the cost of employing hired labor) and of outputs are such that they encourage new farming methods. The utilization of the capacity of irrigation facilities often remains low, because governments fail to provide the incentive for growing irrigated crops for which costs per unit of output may be higher than for crops grown by extensive methods.

In other cases, food production may fail to expand, in spite of incentive prices or subsidization of inputs, because insufficient investment has been made in marketing facilities for food crops, in food processing plants, or in the production of agricultural inputs. For instance, if investment or import policies hold down the supply of fertilizer so that it must be distributed by some kind of rationing, the subsidization of its price is a sheer waste of public money and can have no incentive effect. In India, fertilizer is subsidized but often unavailable in the required quantities in the villages.

CHANGE OF LAND TENURE RELATED TO CHANGE OF LAND USE

The systems of land tenure in developing countries are closely connected with systems of land use. Therefore, changes in land use are often thwarted by existing tenure arrangements (E. Boserup, 1965). For instance, long-fallow cultivators have a right to clear land in areas belonging to their community. When long-fallow agriculture is replaced by a system with cultivation of permanent fields, it is necessary to change to another system of tenure, which gives the cultivator more permanent rights to the land he is cultivating. Under land use systems based on the grazing of fallow land, some of the cultivators, or some noncultivating members of the village community, enjoy the right to graze animals on the fallow area for a certain part of the year. In that case, the substitution of a more intensive system for the old one requires the abolition of the grazing rights. In densely populated regions the introduction of multicropping may be impossible without a change of the customary system of rent; for instance, when custom requires that the land owners be paid a certain share of each crop, such as is the case in many parts of India. If, then, the cost of the second crop is higher per unit of output than the cost of the first crop, there may be insufficient incentive for multicropping unless the customary rent system is replaced by a system of fixed annual rent.

Because of this interdependence of land use systems and land tenure systems, tenure reforms must be an integrated part of agricultural planning. The first step in planning local food production must be to choose a region for development and to determine the appropriate system of land use and the type of crops to be grown. The next step is to find out what changes of land tenure and what types of investment are necessary to bring about the intensification of production. The third step would be a decision about the ways and means to convince the cultivator of the advantages to be gained from carrying out the desired changes. If any one of these steps is neglected, the system of land use will fail to change in the desired direction and the planned additions to output will not materialize.

The tenure reforms which are required in order to facilitate the change from extensive to intensive systems of land use are not necessarily identical with the kind of change the cultivators demand in periods of population pressure. When the number of members in his family is increasing, the first reaction of the cultivator will be to look for more land to cultivate with the traditional methods. Hence, in periods of rising rural population there are likely to be demands for the transfer of land from large to small holdings. To avoid this, governments would have to take prompt action to promote changes to systems of more intensive land use.

A redistribution of land from larger to smaller holdings can raise food production and create more employment only to the extent that it may induce the adoption of a more intensive pattern of land use. On the other hand, if more intensive land use is introduced in the larger holdings without a preceding redistribution of land, the increase of employment thus obtained will make redistribution seem less urgent. If governments, for political or other reasons, hesitate to provide sufficient incentive for more intensive land use in larger holdings using hired labor, a vicious circle may develop: the lack of employment opportunities creates strong demand for expropriation of land from larger holdings. The owners of such holdings feel uncertain of their future rights of ownership and therefore hesitate to invest in agriculture. Thus, when the government finally takes action to encourage more intensive land use, the attempts may be unsuccessful; the pattern of land use then remains extensive, and employment opportunities become more and more inadequate in relation to the increasing supply of labor. The result is growing political tension and declining living standards in rural areas.

Political and Social Obstacles to the Utilization of the Potential for Food Production

Many developing countries have quite recently advanced from colonial status to independence. This change of status unavoidably gave a stimulus to administrative and other investment in the new capitals and in other large towns. In addition, many independent governments regarded the establishment of industry as a requirement of highest priority. In these circumstances, as might be expected, most of the domestic investment resources and the major part of foreign aid have been devoted to purposes other than the expansion of food production. Moreover, in some cases the easy terms on which food aid could be obtained acted as a disincentive to either public or private investment in domestic food production. Political and social considerations induced governments to supply the urban population with cheap imported food, rather than raise food prices in order to encourage a more intensive use of the national potential for production.

Governments were not alone in considering food production as less important than industry or other urban activities. The more enterprising members of rural youth in all developing countries, including a large proportion of the literate population of rural origin, have been drawn toward city life with its more attractive employment opportunities in administration or in new industries. The migration from the villages of the most enterprising and best educated young people has done much to delay agricultural change.

Young people at higher levels of education have also tended to regard agriculture as a less desirable occupation. In some developing countries, the few small agricultural schools have difficulty in finding pupils, or else they manage to attract mainly those who have been unable to get access to more desired types of higher education. Even those who have been trained in such institutions afterward apply for and obtain urban jobs unrelated to agriculture.

While there is growing awareness among governments in developing countries of the need to devote more resources to the expansion of food production, there is much less sign, if any, of a change of attitude among the literates in the villages and the applicants for higher education. The difference in living conditions in cities and rural areas in developing countries is so wide that very attractive incomes and careers would have to be offered in agriculture and agricultural services in order to attract sufficient numbers of qualified candidates. In other words, very large income differentials would have to be accepted between government officials posted in the villages and educated farm managers on one hand and the ordinary cultivators on the other. This may be unacceptable for political and social reasons, and thus the lack of qualified manpower is likely to be a serious obstacle to the development of the potential for food production.

Improvement of Food Standards

The need for expansion of food production in developing countries is based partly upon the growth of population and partly on the unsatisfactory levels of nutrition. In some developing countries, calorie intake is deficient for a considerable proportion of the population; in many more countries the intake of animal protein is very low. As long as per capita incomes remain low, the per capita demand for animal food will also remain small, at least in densely populated countries where animal food is expensive as compared with vegetable food.

In recent years much research has been done for the development of cheap vegetable substitutes for animal proteins, based on different crops including maize, groundnuts, soybeans, and pulses. Such substitutes are industrially produced in some developing countries and are used for school meals or sold through ordinary commercial channels. By promoting their use, improvements in nutritional levels can be achieved in developing countries which are unable to secure a rapid increase of per capita incomes.

A similar need to promote the use of suitable vegetable substitutes for animal food may exist in those developing countries which succeed in raising per capita incomes. Experience has shown that when developing countries succeed in raising per capita incomes, a stage is reached where the demand for animal food is increasing rapidly. Some types of domestic animals are quick breeders, and output can be rapidly expanded if fodder is available. But the transformation of fodder into animal food involves a considerable loss of calories, and a rapid expansion of animal production based upon homegrown fodder is possible only if crop productions can be increased rapidly. Therefore, many governments which cannot afford to use foreign exchange for large-scale purchases of fodder or animal food will have to find ways of preventing a major increase in the consumption of animal food. For this purpose, the use of vegetable substitutes may have to be encouraged while, at the same time, measures are taken to restrain the general switch of consumption from vegetable to animal food.

Conclusion

The preceding analysis of the potential for food production suggests the conclusion that in most developing countries competing demands for scarce capital resources, and the lack of qualified agricultural planners, farm managers, and advisors, are major impediments to the utilization of technical potentialities. Therefore, even in countries where technical potentialities for additional food production are considerable, the rate of increase of agricultural incomes may remain relatively slow in the next decade.

This may not prevent rapid economic development in those few developing countries which have particularly rich nonagricultural resources. For instance, countries with rich oil resources or other mineral resources can use foreign exchange earned from nonagricultural production to purchase the required food supplies in countries where the supply elasticity of food is high. In such countries, a rapid rate of growth in the nonagricultural sectors may compensate for a slow rate of growth in the agricultural sector.

Also, developing countries with less favorable conditions for an expansion of exports may be forced to import part of their food supplies until they succeed in stepping up food production or reducing birth rates or both. In such countries the need to use foreign exchange for major imports limits the scope for importing capital equipment. Therefore, the nonagricultural sectors cannot grow at a rate sufficiently high to compensate for a low rate of growth of the agricultural sector which employs a large proportion of total population in nearly all developing countries. Thus, in countries of this type, the over-all rate of growth is likely to remain fairly low. In such cases, food aid may have constructive effects, if it can be supplied on terms that induce farmers and governments in the recipient countries to increase their own efforts. This implies that the price structure in the country which is receiving food aid must be inducive to expansion of food production; and it implies moreover that food aid must be supplemented with other types of aid, aimed at promoting home production of food.

Indian Agriculture from the Perspective of Western Europe

INDIA'S POPULATION DENSITY and area of arable land per inhabitant are similar to western Europe's (table 1). The much smaller Indian agricultural output per head is primarily due to the extremely low level of output per hectare in India. Hayami, Ruttan, and Binswanger have computed comparable statistics for agricultural output of land and labor in many countries, including India and the most important western European countries. The main results of this comparison are shown in table 2. Output per hectare in India in 1970 was only 20–30 percent that of continental western Europe (represented by Denmark, France, and Germany) and was on the same low level as that of these countries a century ago. The much lower level of output per hectare in India is not a result of much poorer natural conditions for agriculture in India than in western Europe. Much land in western Europe was poor before it was improved by agricultural investment and other inputs. India is much more dependent upon irrigation than western Europe, but if irrigation is provided, conditions in India are vastly better for multiple cropping than in western Europe, with its cold winters.

Although output of land was as low in western Europe a century ago as in India today, output of agricultural labor was much higher. Agricultural equipment in western Europe was much better than that of nearly all agricultural regions in India today. Output per male worker in agriculture was four or five times larger than in India today, and one worker cultivated a much larger area. The huge increase in agricultural output between 1880 and 1930 in continental western Europe was obtained mainly by raising output of land. There was little change in the area cultivated per worker. This type of development, with focus on output per hectare rather than a change in man-land ratio, continued to be characteristic of western European agriculture, particularly in Denmark from 1930 to 1960. Only after 1960 did rapid tractorization and other mechanization result in a rapid increase of the area cultivated per worker, accompanied by rapid transfer of agricultural labor to nonagricultural occupations.

"Indian Agriculture from the Perspective of Western Europe." Reprinted from J. S. Sarma, *Growth and Equity: Policies and Implementation in Indian Agriculture.* © International Food Policy Research Institute, Washington; Research Report 28, November 1981.

TABLE 1. Hectares per inhabitant, India and western Europe, around 1970

Country	Total area	Arable land	Permanent pasture	Forest and other land
India	0.61	0.31	0.03	0.27
Denmark	0.85	0.54	0.06	0.25
France	1.08	0.38	0.27	0.43
Germany, Fed. Rep.	0.39	0.13	0.09	0.17
United Kingdom	0.43	0.13	0.21	0.09

Source: FAO statistics.

In contrast to India, multiplication of output in western Europe was obtained by means other than investment in irrigation. It is worth looking at changes in western European agriculture to see what scope there may be for using similar policies to speed up the increase of per hectare output in India and raise the living standards of the rural poor.

Most of the multiplication of output per hectare in Europe was obtained by a huge increase in fertilizer input and the spread of animal husbandry based upon production of labor-intensive fodder crops.

Compared to Europe, fertilizer application in India is extremely small (table 3). Around 1970, fertilizer use per hectare in western Europe was 20–30 times larger than in India, which explains a large part of the differences in per hectare output between these two regions. Sarma mentions that around 1970, 15 percent of the districts in India used 80 percent of all the fertilizer used in the country (Sarma, 1981). This implies that these favored districts used some seventy kilos per hectare, or between one-fifth and one-third of the western European level, whereas the rest of India used some three kilos per hectare, which amounts to saying that is used almost no fertilizer at all.

The districts in India in which large quantities of fertilizer are applied are those best supplied with roads and other rural infrastructure. Distribution of large amounts of fertilizer is possible only in regions with a dense road network. In the absence of such a network, it is either impossible or uneconomical to raise crop yields by using large quantities of fertilizer. Table 3 shows that the Indian road network is very poor for a country with a high population density. Around 1970 the density of the Indian road network was one-fifth that of western Europe. Moreover, in contrast to Europe, most of the roads in India were unsurfaced. Thus, a precondition for intensive fertilizer use in the poor rural areas of India is very large investments in rural roads and other rural infrastructure. It is unfortunate, therefore, that road investment is not included among the components of growth with equity recommended by Sarma.

Although rural public works programs are mentioned as the last of Sarma's six components, they are not recommended as badly needed productive

TABLE 2. Agricultural output of land and labor, India and western Europe, 1880–1970

Country	Output, in wheat units, per hectare[a]				Hectares per male worker				Output, in wheat units, per male worker[a]			
	1880	1930	1960	1970	1880	1930	1960	1970	1880	1930	1960	1970
India				1.2				2				2
Denmark	1.2	3.0	4.7	5.3	9	8	10	18	11	24	48	94
France	1.1	1.5	2.5	3.7	7	9	13	16	7	13	33	60
Germany, Fed. Rep.	1.3	2.5	4.0	5.4	6	6	9	12	8	16	35	65
United Kingdom	1.1	1.2	1.9	2.6	15	17	23	34	16	20	45	88

Sources: Hayami and Ruttan (1971); Binswanger and Ruttan (1978).
[a] A unit of output is equivalent to one ton of wheat; calculation by Hayami and Ruttan (1971).

TABLE 3. Fertilizer use and road networks in India and western Europe, around 1970

Country	Kilograms fertilizer per hectare	Meters of road per km²	Percent of hard surface road
India	13	290	35
Denmark	223	1,490	92
France	241	1,430	
Germany, Fed. Rep.	400	1,670	72
United Kingdom	258	1,450	100

Sources: UN (1976a); International Road Federation (1973).

investments, indispensable for agricultural improvement. They are viewed as ways to "alleviate the immediate problem of rural unemployment, particularly in drought years and in chronically drought-affected areas." This tendency to treat investment in rural infrastructure (and even that in rural industries) as social works and ways of creating employment rather than as productive investments of high priority is an inheritance from the colonial past of India, when the British administration used rural works to provide incomes for famine-stricken peasants and workers. When rural investments are viewed as social works, neither the types of works nor their location and timing are likely to be suitable for agricultural expansion. This may explain Sarma's comment that "experience with the implementation of such programs in India has been mixed."

In addition to abundant use of fertilizer, labor-intensive animal husbandry (including poultry raising) made a large contribution to the increase of per hectare output in western European agriculture. If India succeeds in accelerating the growth of per capita income, demand for milk and milk products, poultry, and other meat will increase rapidly. Sarma mentions increased animal husbandry as especially important for providing better incomes for rural people with little or no land of their own. However, he sees promotion of animal husbandry by special government support schemes primarily as a means of raising rural employment opportunities and contributing to greater equity. The role of these activities is repeatedly described as "subsidiary."

This is very different from the role played by animal husbandry in western Europe from 1880 to 1960. Animal husbandry was not a subsidiary activity by which small peasants and workers supplemented their incomes from the sale of cereals. Small-scale agricultural producers in Europe specialized in production of animal products that provided their main income. Only larger farms derived the bulk of their incomes from the sale of cereals. Producers with little land, whether owned or rented, used all or most of it for production of fodder crops, which they fed to their animals, or they specialized in other labor-intensive crops such as vegetables, fruit, or vines. In many regions, small holders expanded their production of animal husbandry by buying fodder from larger farms or from importers.

In other words, in much of western Europe small producers applied a development model different from that of the larger producers. Small producers were not less efficient and therefore in need of special government support programs. Small and large holdings were not competitive but were complementary. They relied on sales of different products and often purchased inputs from each other, not only labor but also materials.

Small producers could earn a sufficient family income, not only because of their specialization in products particularly suited for small-scale production but also because they made much more extensive use of cheap family labor of both sexes and nearly all ages than did larger producers. Wives and children of small producers not only worked extensively in the family holding, but they also earned supplementary incomes by seasonal wage labor in the larger holdings. Nevertheless, they remained poor compared to larger producers. When comparing European and Indian incomes, it should not be overlooked that minimum subsistence levels are much higher in Europe than in India because of the colder climate. Better housing, clothing, and food are needed for survival.

Because of the specialization of western European small holdings in activities with high output per hectare, redistribution of land did not become a crucial problem in this period. There was little change in the size of holdings, except in the period after World War II when many owners and tenants of small holdings shifted to full-time or part-time employment in nonagricultural activities in rural and urban areas. In some regions, prohibition against amalgamation of holdings and effective control of land sales contributed to security of tenure for both small and large producers.

Sarma regrets that in India "the only language and authority that are understood are directives and vertical lines of command," while horizontal coordination is ineffective. This is another inheritance from the colonial period, when a small number of British administrators tried to control and govern the huge population and area of India. In their homelands, quite different policies were used by the Europeans, both in administration and in agriculture. Private and local initiative rather than government directives and control were responsible for the intensification of small-scale farming. Service cooperatives often played a very important role, but they were voluntary associations ruled by the general assembly of members, which decided on activities and recruited and paid the manager and other staff. These cooperatives were specialized; for instance, cooperative dairies, cooperative slaughterhouses, cooperative centers for collection and sale of eggs, cooperative associations for purchase of fertilizer and other inputs, cooperative credit associations in which the members were collectively responsible for the debts of the association, and cooperatives for purchase of consumer goods.

In some cooperatives, voting rights were in proportion to sales and purchases, and the larger farmers dominated. In other cases, each member family had one vote and smallholders dominated. Sometimes small and large producers had different cooperatives. The important feature is that the members rather than government officials were responsible for their cooperatives and took the initiative in establishing them. If small producers believed the cooperative neglected them, they could break out and establish their own.

This situation changed considerably after 1960, when urban activities increased very rapidly in western Europe and a large share of the small producers and agricultural workers shifted to nonagricultural work. Since 1960 large-scale "poultry and pork factories" using industrial techniques have replaced small-scale production. Small holdings have either been absorbed by larger ones or have become subsidiary activities for families whose main income is from outside agriculture. Moreover, the agricultural policy of the western European Common Market countries has changed radically. This organization has attempted to raise agricultural incomes by means of a large number of bureaucratic directives and special support measures. An enormous bureaucracy has grown up. Large-scale misdirection of resources has resulted in accumulation of large surpluses and in a growing need for government subsidization. As in India, bureaucratic control of agriculture has mainly benefited the large farmers, who have the largest surpluses. Thus, in western European countries the experience with bureaucratic control of agriculture has resulted in less equity and less economic efficiency than in the previous period, when government intervention was less prescriptive and bureaucratic.

In the period of efficient small-scale farming in Europe, the large-scale poultry factories had not yet been invented. Today, such factory production of animal products is often introduced in developing countries and is often subsidized by direct and indirect measures. In a country like India with a rapidly increasing rural population, a shortage of land, and limited possibilities for nonagricultural employment, the European experience suggests that placing ceilings on the size of enterprises engaged in such activities as poultry production might be as important—or even more important—than placing ceilings on land holdings.

[1974]

Food Supply and Population in Developing Countries

Recent Trends in Output and Trade

OUTPUT IN DEVELOPING COUNTRIES

From the middle of the 1930s to the beginning of the 1960s, population in developing countries increased by nearly 50 percent. About three-quarters of the cereal supply for this addition to population came from an expansion of the sown area; only one-quarter was the result of higher crop yields (Brown, 1963; U.S. Department of Agriculture, 1964).[1]

Only a small part of the expansion of area was in the form of settlement in hitherto empty lands. Far more important was the spontaneous expansion of cultivation in the land surrounding existing villages in response to the increasing need for food and the increasing supply of rural labor that accompanied the increase of population. Since the increase of output was provided mainly by area expansion within traditional techniques, employment in agriculture increased *pari passu* with output, with relatively little change in labor productivity.

In the two decades from about 1950 to about 1970, urban income and urban employment opportunities increased fairly rapidly. Most governments gave priority to investment in industry and other nonagricultural activities and did little to encourage expansion of food production. Concerned as they were with labor costs in urban occupations and with living standards of urban low-income groups, governments were mostly disinclined to allow food prices to increase, if this could be prevented by means of food imports. This policy of stabilization of food prices through imports was made more acceptable by the conviction prevailing during most of this period that the supply elasticity of food production in developing countries is inherently inelastic.

Since the change in labor productivity in agriculture was in most cases small, the increasing incomes in urban areas widened the gap between urban and rural incomes, and this must have contributed to the increase of the flow of rural-to-urban migration. Without the possibility of increasing food im-

---

"Food Supply and Population in Developing Countries." Reprinted from *Agricultural Policy in Developing Countries.* Proceedings of a Conference held by the International Economic Association at Bad Godesberg, West Germany. Edited by Nurul Islam. St. Martin's Press; Macmillan, 1974: 164–76.

ports, the gap between the rising urban demand for food and the less rapid increase of food supplies from rural areas would have shifted sectoral terms of trade within food-deficit countries in favor of food producers, and this might have given a fillip to investment in agriculture and output of food, and have restrained the rural-to-urban migration. This did not happen because of easy access to grants of food and to food imports at prices subsidized by the exporting country.

OUTPUT IN INDUSTRIALIZED COUNTRIES

The changes in food supply and population growth in industrialized countries were quite different. Population increased rather slowly, income elasticities for food were low, and policies with regard to agricultural prices were the very opposite of those in the developing countries: most governments in industrialized countries supported agricultural prices as a means of helping the group of small and marginal farmers whose incomes tended to lag behind incomes of other groups of the population.

But this support to the weaker parts of agriculture in industrialized countries stimulated output on intramarginal farms, and since wage labor tended to be in short supply, this was accompanied by the introduction of labor-saving equipment, of new scientific methods, and of industrial inputs to agriculture. Hence, there was in the industrialized countries a marked increase in output per man, per unit of land, and per unit of livestock. In the 1950s and the first half of the 1960s per hectare yields of the twelve most important crops increased by 2.2 percent per annum in industrialized countries, as against 1.2 per cent per annum in developing countries (FAO, 1970). Thus, in spite of area restrictions in the United States and stagnant areas under crops in other industrialized countries, food production tended to grow faster than the demand for food.[2]

FOOD TRADE BETWEEN INDUSTRIALIZED AND DEVELOPING COUNTRIES

In order to prevent or limit the accumulation of food surpluses, many industrialized countries, among them countries of the European Common Market, sharpened their import restrictions for food, and both European countries and the United States introduced or increased subsidies to food exports, including deliveries of food on concessional terms to developing countries. Indeed, such a policy was recommended to member governments of the OECD as a means to reduce the need for other farm-support measures (Kristensen, 1969).

Net exports of food from industrialized to developing countries increased not only because developing countries became more, and industrialized countries less, dependent on food imports, but also because subsidized food exports from industrialized countries reduced the market for commercial food exports from developing countries. Thus, among the developing countries two groups must be distinguished: those countries which relied on food imports in a form which tended to reduce farmers' or governments' incentive to apply measures which might expand output; and on the other hand, the traditional food exporting countries, which suffered from the competition in export markets with subsidized food exports from industrialized countries.

Thus, the tendency for net imports of food to developing countries to increase in the 1950s and the first half of the 1960s cannot be explained solely as the result of increasing population pressure in these countries; factors wholly unrelated to this population pressure, in the form of policies of farm income support, of import restrictions for food, and of export promotion of food in industrialized countries helped to produce the large changes in the world trade in food products.

THE ADVENT OF THE GREEN REVOLUTION

During the two decades beginning about 1950 a gradual change of methods of food production began to occur in a number of developing countries.

While population growth continued unabated, or even accelerated, the rate of increase of sown area slowed down. In the developing countries as a whole, the annual rate of increase of the area under cereals seems to have been 1.5 percent in the 1950s, but less than 1 percent in the 1960s. On the other hand, the improvement of crop yields became more pronounced, particularly towards the end of the 1960s when the new high-yielding varieties of rice and wheat began to be used in Asia.

This new development, the so-called Green Revolution, may be seen as the accentuated continuation of a trend toward improving yields which has been going on for some time. As already mentioned, crop yields of cereals in developing countries had been increasing by a little over 1 percent per year during the 1950s and the first half of the 1960s. This reflected the spread of irrigation, more extensive use of improved varieties, and increasing use of fertilizer and other chemicals on food crops. Fertilizer consumption increased by about 12 percent per annum in developing countries from the beginning of the 1950s to the late 1960s, when the rate of increase in the major rice-producing countries rose to over 15 percent per annum (UN, 1971).

The technological changes in the two decades from 1950 to 1970 were most pronounced in some of the densely populated countries of Asia, where governments were more concerned than elsewhere with the problem of food supplies to the increasing populations and took steps to promote additional irrigation, new methods, and agricultural extension services. As a result, before the advent of the Green Revolution the rate of increase of crop yields in Asia was higher than in other developing regions. Indeed, it is somewhat arbitrary to date the Green Revolution in Asia from the time when the new varieties of wheat and rice were first introduced. In India, Pakistan, and some other Asian countries the technological revolution had started long before, under the pressure of the rapid population increase, which induced Asian governments to make available and subsidize modern inputs in production of food. This technological change in food production in densely populated countries must be considered a response to the challenge of rapid population growth.

TABLE 1. Land use in developing countries, by region

Type of land	China	South and Southeast Asia	Near East and North Africa	Africa south of Sahara	Latin America
Percentage of total land area					
Arable land	11	24	7	7	6
Permanent pasture	18	11	17	32	24
Forestland	8	35	5	27	48
Other	63	30	71	34	22
Potentially cultivable land as percentage of total		2	4	3	3
Irrigated land as percentage of arable land	68	21	24	1	8
Area sown as percentage of arable land					
Irrigated	147	110	75	100	75
Nonirrigated		95	50	40	50

Source: FAO (1970, 1971a).

Land Resources of Developing Countries

Until recently, most economists took a pessimistic view of the developing countries' abilities to produce within their own borders the food needed for the increasing populations. There were several reasons for this pessimism: the scope for increase of crop yields by means of modern inputs was underestimated before the results of the Green Revolution became known; it was generally assumed that uncultivated land in developing countries was of poor quality; and the possibilities for intensification of land use by more frequent cropping were overlooked or assumed to be small.

This section deals with the problem of land resources, while the possibilities for intensification of land use are examined in the following section.

THE QUALITY OF PASTURELAND AND FORESTED AREAS

Table 1 gives an impression of the large differences in land use in developing countries and in China. It can be seen that arable land accounted for 10 percent or less of total land area in all regions except for the region of South and Southeast Asia. On the other hand, only China reached high rates of irrigation and multiple cropping in its arable area.

In most developing countries, forest and pastureland occupies much larger proportions of total area than land which bears a crop. There is a widespread belief among economists that nearly all forest and pastureland is submarginal and not suited for cultivation. Those who hold this view sometimes make calculations of the resource endowment of various regions by means of arbitrary reduction of the areas classified as pasture and forest, before these are added to the area classified as arable land. For instance, Hollis Chenery calculated land resources by adding 5 percent of meadow and pastureland and 1 percent of forestland to arable land (Chenery, 1964).

In densely populated countries—for instance in Europe—it may be reasonable, for the purpose of making an estimate of the agricultural potential, to make a rough reduction in the figures for pasture and forestland, so as to take account of the fact that such areas are likely to be less well suited for cultivation than arable land in the same country, but it is misleading to apply this procedure when dealing with sparsely populated developing countries.

First, in such countries much grassland and forested land which does not bear crops at a given time serves as fallow in long-fallow systems, and there is no reason whatever to believe that land which happens to be unused in any given year is of a quality inferior to that of land which happens to bear a crop in that year.[3] In such regions, if long-fallow agriculture is being replaced by a system of more frequent cropping with a suitable system of fertilization, the additional area thus gained will be as good as the existing one, and there is no need to make any reduction when calculating the potential for area expansion.

Second, much land in sparsely populated developing countries is used permanently for pasture and forest, not because it is less suited for bearing crops than the land actually cropped, but because the population is too small or too primitive to make use of more than a small proportion of the land which is suitable for cultivation. Many economists fail to distinguish between land which *is* used, and land which *could be* used if the population was larger or if it used modern equipment. To take just one example, R. K. Som says: "Since Africa is predominantly an agricultural continent, population pressure can best be measured by overall population density and density of rural population per square kilometre of arable land." (Som, 1968). In a table purporting to measure population pressure by this method, Som, by leaving out pasture and forestland, implicitly assumes that these types of land cannot be used for cultivation. The failure to distinguish clearly between cultivated and cultivable land probably reflects a belief that the potential for food production is generally the effective barrier to population growth in preindustrial communities, and therefore that all suitable land is being used for cultivation.

FAO ESTIMATES OF LAND RESOURCES

An apparent confirmation of the belief that land resources are small could be found in Food and Agriculture Organization statistics, which until recently included a category of unused but potentially cultivable land. Those countries which provided such information placed very small areas in this category, as can be seen from table 1. However, the criteria used to determine the amount of potentially cultivable land necessarily vary with the existing density of settlement and the need for additional land within a near future. Countries with considerable population pressure on land may be prepared to

TABLE 2. Agricultural inputs and land use in developing countries, by region, 1962 and FAO targets for 1985

Item	South and Southeast Asia	Near East and North Africa	Africa south of Sahara	Latin America
Percentage increase of arable area, 1962–85	6	11	24	30
Area sown within a year as percentage of arable land				
1962	100	56	42	54
1985	121	64	52	60
Irrigated land as percentage of arable land				
1962	21	24	1	8
1985	31	26	1	10
Kilos of fertilizer per hectare sown (nutritive content)				
1962	6	11	1	12
1985	80	51	7	64
Number of tractors per 1,000 hectares sown (adjusted for differences in size)				
1962	0.4	1.7	0.3	5.0
1985	4.1	3.6	0.6	8.0

Source: FAO (1970).

include under this category land which would require large investment in land improvement or in roads to make it accessible. On the other hand, countries where land resources seem abundant in the light of foreseeable demand for it would never include such areas. They usually include only good but unused land in private holdings or good public land which is particularly well located for the purpose of settlement.

Consequently, sparsely populated developing countries, or sparsely populated regions within more densely populated countries, may have large areas which could be brought under cultivation after investment in land improvement and infrastructure, even though little or no land is officially recorded as "unused but potentially productive."

A study by Thorkil Kristensen for the OECD provides an extreme example of pessimistic evaluation of land resources in developing countries. In this study it is suggested that between 1965 and the year 2000 arable area in developing countries will increase less than 15 percent, although the agricultural population is expected to become nearly twice as large (Kristensen, 1969). By contrast, the FAO suggests that in 1985 the arable area in developing countries will be 17 percent above that of 1962 (see table 2), and it is explicitly stated that in many countries it is not shortage of cultivable land, but high costs of land improvement and settlement, which will limit the rate of expansion of area (FAO, 1970). It is assumed that in 1985 only half of the area which is cultivable in developing countries will be used for cultivation.

The area which can be considered cultivable is of course larger, the more remote is the date considered. Walter Pawley has suggested that a century from now most of the land area in developing countries may have become cultivable if the aridity constraint is eliminated by suitable techniques for desalinization of sea water, and if suitable techniques are developed for intensive cultivation of tropical land (Pawley, 1971).

The Scope for Intensification of Land Use

It was pointed out above that in the region of South and Southeast Asia the share of total area that is under cultivation is much larger than in other developing regions. Moreover, the use of the arable land is more intensive. But even in this region there is still considerable scope for an even more intensive utilization of both cultivated and uncultivated land:

1. *Expansion of the sown area by the introduction of multiple cropping.* Since antiquity, multiple cropping has been used as a means of increasing food production in many regions with a dense population. In recent decades the practice has spread widely in various parts of China and other parts of Asia in response to increasing population pressure on land. Many economists have overlooked this possibility of expansion of the sown area, and some governments have failed to take account of the spread of multiple cropping in their statistics of food production, thus underestimating the rate of increase of output. Dana Dalrymple has made the first systematic survey of multiple cropping in developing countries (Dalrymple, 1971). The development of quickly maturing varieties, the spread of the use of chemical fertilizer in developing countries, and the increasing rural labor force all facilitate the spread of multiple-cropping techniques in densely populated regions. The FAO assumes that by 1985 it should be possible (if necessary) to use multiple cropping with high-yielding varieties on one-third of the world's arable land (FAO, 1970).

2. *Elimination of fallow.* The amount of fallow land in dry regions can be much reduced if the increasing labor force is used to build irrigation facilities, and if the system of rotation is changed. Much land in other regions can be cropped more frequently with an increasing labor force. New techniques in irrigation and new results of agronomic research steadily enlarge the possibilities for these types of intensification of land use.

3. *Change from natural grazing to produced fodder.* Most domestic animals in developing countries are left to find their own food in unimproved pastures and forests, as was the case in Europe before the eighteenth century. Very large areas can be brought under cultivation if part of the increasing labor force in developing countries is used to improve pastures and produce

fodder in intensive rotations. The next step in the Green Revolution in densely populated developing countries is likely to be a complete change in the system for providing fodder to domestic animals together with a continued change from land-using to more land-saving species of domestic animals. The conditions for such a change are provided by the continued population increase and the increase of per capita incomes together with the high income elasticity of demand for animal food. The rapid increase of demand for animal products will raise relative prices, thus inducing labor-intensive fodder production and expanding output at higher marginal costs.[4]

4. *Change from timber collection to planting of forests.* In nearly all developing countries the use of forestland is as wasteful as the use of pastures. If a part of the increasing labor force is used for planting forest instead of continuing with the usual collection of self-grown timber and wood, the number and quality of trees per hectare would increase, the land would become better protected, and much additional land could be transferred to cultivation of crops for human consumption or for consumption by domestic animals.

Many warnings are given by experts concerning damage to arable, pasture, and forestland by more intensive use, but such damage can usually be avoided if governments initiate a systematic planning of land use. Damage to the environment occurs mainly when increasing rural populations are left to undertake an uncontrolled expansion of cultivation and animal husbandry without any guidance from public authorities or other experts. Even in regions where the limit for uncontrolled expansion without damage to the land is exceeded, there may still be large scope for further intensification of land use provided that it is accompanied by suitable measures of land preservation and fertilization.

Reasons Why the Rate of Increase of Sown Area Has Diminished

Since there is much scope for further expansion of sown area in developing countries, it is pertinent to ask why the rate of expansion has gradually slowed down, as stated earlier in this essay.

1. The tendency towards *increasing costs* for preparation and improvement of land with continued expansion is usually invoked as the explanation. But this is only one of the factors which may motivate governments and cultivators to avoid area expansion and give preference to other means of increasing food supplies.

2. Continuing expansion of sown area will usually create more and more acute need for various adjustments of *land tenure.* Ownership rights or customary rights in forest and pastureland can prevent more intensive use, regardless of whether the owners and users are central or local governments, village or tribal authorities, feudal landlords, or other owners of land. Grazing rights, land fragmentation, and sharecropping are among the obstacles which have prevented more frequent cropping of arable land in many parts of the world. Sharecropping systems often stand in the way of the introduction of

multiple cropping (M. Boserup, 1963). Governments often shun the political problems which they would have to face if they were to change systems of land use and land tenure, and prefer either to support measures to improve crop yields or to rely on food imports.

3. Continuing expansion of sown area may end by causing tension between cultivating and *pastoral tribes,* another cause of political difficulties which governments may avoid by avoiding area expansion.

4. More and more governments grant *subsidies to fertilizers and other Green Revolution* technologies, and agricultural extension services are usually instructed to recommend increase of crop yields rather than expansion of sown area. Therefore, cultivators are likely more and more often to choose this type of change and to become less and less inclined to invest family labor and wage labor in expansion of area.

5. In many developing countries the alternative which has been preferred to area expansion has not been subsidies to improvement of crop yields, but *food imports on concessional terms.* By accepting such imports governments have not only avoided the political difficulties mentioned above; they have also saved the costs of subsidizing food production and investing in infrastructure, such as rural transport and irrigation. Massive food imports on concessional terms have sometimes discouraged expansion of the sown area. For instance, in some Near East countries expansion of area under food crops had kept well ahead of the rate of population growth until the end of the 1950s. From that time, imports under P.L. 480 rose to high levels, and the area under food crops ceased to expand (FAO, 1966; 1970).

6. Other countries in which expansion of sown area has slowed down or stopped are the group of food exporting countries, which suffer from *export difficulties,* as already mentioned, because of the accentuation of import restrictions in industrialized countries, their inability to compete with subsidized food exports and food grants, and the reduction of their market in those developing countries which are more nearly self-sufficient as a result of the application of Green Revolution technologies.

Industrial Input and Foreign Aid to Food Production

The modernization of food production which is now taking place, particularly in Asian countries, has reduced the dependence on food imports, and the FAO expects that food imports into developing countries will decline further in the near future, when India has finished building up its emergency stocks (FAO, 1971b). But the cost of the modernization in terms of imports of industrial inputs to food production is high. The Indicative Plan of the FAO expects that commercial inputs into agriculture in developing countries will be three times larger in constant prices in 1985 than in 1962, which implies that their value as a percentage of gross output will increase from 15 to 22 percent. The expected increase in the use of fertilizer in this period is dramatic: a twelvefold increase in twenty-three years, from 1962 to 1985. The proportion of fertilizer in total commercial inputs would as a result increase from 8 to 34 percent (FAO, 1970). Most of this fertilizer is expected to be used in Asia, where also most of the investment in irrigation is expected to take place (see table 2).

In view of these figures, it is understandable that the Indicative Plan makes a plea for financial aid to the agricultural sector in developing countries. It is explicitly stated that the further agricultural modernization proceeds, the more necessary will it be to supplement internal savings by foreign aid (FAO, 1970). FAO expects that, in the end year of the plan, import needs for current inputs will amount to US$7 billion (at 1962 prices) and that, in addition, 40 percent of the investment outlays of that year will need to be covered by imports.

Experts in the United States administration (in a report to the president in April 1970) suggested that the developing countries may be able, by the year 2000, to provide their expected populations with nutritionally adequate diets with unchanged levels of per capita food imports from developed countries, but only on the condition that foreign aid to agriculture can be raised to more than ten times its present level (U.S. Department of State, 1970). The report points out that the degree of self-sufficiency mentioned would fall far short of disposing of the surplus grain capacity in the developed countries (estimated at 30 million tons per annum after 1980), and that from the exporters' point of view the high-cost self-sufficiency policy of developing countries seems incompatible with a prospective abundance of exportable supplies (U.S. Department of State, 1970).

Since the food exporters among developed countries are among the largest donor countries, it is perhaps somewhat unrealistic to plan for very large amounts of aid to inputs in agriculture in developing countries as a means of preventing food imports. It is true that the small and marginal farmers in industrialized countries, who have hitherto played an important role in decisions concerning aid to exports, are slowly disappearing, but a new feature, the international farm corporations, is emerging, and they too are likely to exert pressure for access to markets in developing countries and for favorable export conditions. In view of this, it would seem desirable to aim at factor combinations in food production in developing countries which put more emphasis on the use of labor-intensive techniques, including extension of the sown area, as substitutes for some of the imported inputs.

Labor-intensive techniques can be used both to extend cultivation into hitherto uncultivated regions and for each of the types of intensification of land use set out in a previous section of this paper. There is much more scope in agriculture (including animal husbandry and forestry) than in industry for choice between techniques that require large amounts of imported materials and equipment and techniques that use large amounts of unskilled labor. In view of the rapid increase of the rural labor force in developing countries and of the need to avoid heavy reliance on foreign aid, the choice of techniques in the future expansion of food production needs to be carefully considered and adapted to local conditions.

Notes

1. If not specifically mentioned, China is not included in "developing countries." The term *sown area* is taken in the sense of total area sown within a year—that is, areas under multiple cropping are counted more than once.

2. With the major exception of the Soviet Union.

3. International statistics of land use distinguish the traditional types of land use in industrialized countries, such as arable land, pastures, and forest, but they fail to make provision for such categories as bush, grass, or forestland used in long-fallow systems of agriculture. These categories of land, which are the dominant types of agricultural land in many developing countries, are usually classified, or rather hidden, under one of the groups mentioned above or under "other land."

4. In the Indicative World Plan, the FAO suggests covering the increasing demand for animal products by special efforts to promote modern large-scale production of poultry and pork in order to keep marginal costs as low as possible (FAO, 1969). This policy seems debatable, since in all circumstances the loss of calories in the transformation of feed to animal products will keep prices of poultry and pork at levels that will prevent more than a small proportion of the output from being consumed by low-income groups. Moreover, by encouraging large-scale production, governments discriminate against poultry and pig raising by small farmers, activities that are well suited to provide the increasing labor force in small holdings with additional employment and income. Development of vegetable substitutes for animal protein and development of protein-rich strains of cereals seem better suited methods to combat malnutrition among the poor than low-cost production of animal products.

Population and Agricultural Productivity

It is generally agreed that the way to obtain a rapid increase in output per worker in agriculture is to replace the traditional systems by systems based on scientific and industrial inputs into agriculture. However, it would be wrong to jump to the conclusion that this is the only way in which to obtain a substantial increase in total agricultural output during periods of rapid increases in population and in the labor force. When population growth and economic development raise the demand for agricultural products, there are two ways to raise the total output of the agricultural sector. One is to apply more agricultural labor to the available land resources: (a) by bringing forest and wasteland into cultivation; (b) by turning fallow land and natural grazing land into cultivated land, producing fodder for animals currently in the fields; (c) by reducing the fallow period; and (d) by the expanded use of multiple-cropping systems. The other method is to apply increasing amounts of industrial and scientific inputs, such as improved seeds, chemical fertilizer, insecticides and mechanized equipment. It is characteristic of the first approach that it increases the area harvested per year, but with relatively small changes in productivity per hectare harvested and in productivity per man-hour in agriculture, while it is characteristic of the other approach that it raises gross output per man-hour of agricultural labor and per hectare harvested, with little change in the size of the area under cultivation.

In this essay, the two methods are set against each other as if they were alternative strategies; but this is, of course, an oversimplification. The conditions for achieving more intensive land utilization, especially multicropping, are much better if use is made of chemical fertilizer, insecticides, and mechanized equipment. The choice is not to apply one or the other of these methods, but the problem is to choose a combination of the two methods, which is suitable in a region at a given stage of development and with a given set of factor proportions.

It is not possible to deal with all aspects of this problem in a short essay, but some light can be thrown upon it by comparing the targets in the Indicative World Plan for Agricultural Development issued by the Food and Agri-

"Population and Agricultural Productivity." Reprinted from *The Population Debate: Dimensions and Perspectives.* Papers of the World Population Conference, Bucharest, 1974. Volume 1. United Nations 1975: 498–501.

TABLE 1. Industrial inputs and land use in developing countries, by region, 1962 and FAO targets for 1985

Item	Asia and Far East[a]	Latin America	Africa south of Sahara
Fertilizer, kilos per hectare harvested (nutritive content)			
1962	6	12	1
1985	80	64	7
Pesticides, US$ per hectare harvested (in constant prices)			
1962	0.10	2.00	0.20
1985	4.50	5.20	3.10
Tractors per 100 hectares harvested (adjusted for differences in size)			
1962	0.4	5.0	0.3
1985	4.1	8.0	0.6
Arable land as percentage of total land area, 1970	24	6	7
Percentage increase of arable land, 1962–85	6	30	24
Intensity of cropping on arable land (harvested area divided by arable area)			
1962	1.00	0.54	0.42
1985	1.21	0.60	0.52
Percentage of arable land under irrigation			
1962	21	8	1
1985	31	10	1

Source: FAO (1969).
[a]Region covered by the UN Economic Commission for Asia and the Far East, now designated Economic and Social Commission for Asia and the Pacific.

culture Organization of the United Nations (FAO) with actual events in the 1960s. Some papers prepared by the United Nations and FAO contain information which makes it possible to assess the changes in agricultural productivity during the period of rapid population growth in the 1960s. The purpose of the present essay is to combine this information, to examine it critically, and to draw some tentative conclusions from it.

The Indicative World Plan (FAO, 1969) covers the period 1961–85. The available information about major inputs according to the plan is reproduced in table 1. The information in the table is given for major geographical regions, because the availability of land varies so much from region to region that overall figures for all developing regions are of little interest. Population density is much higher in the Asian region than in Latin America and Africa.

Some 24 percent of total land area is under cultivation in the Asian region, against 6–7 percent in the others, and both the intensity of cropping on arable land (i.e., the ratio of harvested area to arable land) and the percentage of arable land under irrigation is much higher in Asia than in the other regions.

It can be seen from table 1 that the Indicative Plan puts the main emphasis on the use of industrial inputs, as illustrated by the rapidly rising inputs of fertilizer, pesticides, and tractors. In contrast with the very rapid increase in use of these inputs, the planned increases in arable land and in cropping intensity are of modest dimensions. Arable land in the Asian region is assumed to increase by only 6 percent in a period of twenty-three years, although considerable land reserves still remain in some parts of this region and although very little progress has yet been made in shifting over from the grazing of animals on common pastures to fodder production. In those parts of the world where as little as 6–7 percent of the land is used in cultivation, FAO assumes that the area of arable land will increase moderately by 25–30 percent, that is, to some 8–9 percent of the land area. The targets for the increase in cropping intensity are very modest in all regions.

The Indicative Plan contains specific targets for the period 1961–75. An FAO publication compared these targets with actual performance in the period from 1961–63 to 1969–71, with specification for the output of major products and for the area harvested of major cereals (FAO, 1973). This makes it possible to derive figures for yields per crop hectare.

In evaluating the figures for crop yields per hectare in table 2, it must be taken into account that two of the three years, 1969–71, were years of unusually unfavorable weather over large parts of the world. Nevertheless, the shortfall in relation to the targets is so large in both Asia and Latin America that it is unlikely that the 1975 targets for crop yields of cereals will be met. In the Asian region, FAO had expected crop yields per hectare harvested to increase by no less than 3 percent per annum, but the increase has been only 2 percent per annum. It is important to note that this is mainly due to overestimation of the effect rather than of the amount of industrial inputs. Fertilizer inputs in the Asian region increased by 16 percent as against a target of 17 percent; two-wheel tractors increased by 28 percent against a target of 19 percent; and four-wheel tractors to 16 percent against a target of 13 percent. Irrigation seems to be the only input which has fallen short of expectation. The main reason for the shortfall in cereal yields in the Asian region is that the Green Revolution has hitherto affected paddy production far less than wheat production.

Fortunately, some part of the shortfall in yields was offset by a substantially larger expansion of area sown than was foreseen. An increase of 0.7 percent per annum had been expected by FAO, while actual performance was 1.1 percent per annum. This is of the same order of magnitude as the increase of the agricultural labor force, so that the area of cereals harvested per worker in agriculture was roughly unchanged. It is not known to what extent the increase in area is due to more double cropping, to the reduction of fallow land, and to an increase in arable land.

TABLE 2. Agricultural progress, actual and target, 1961–1975, developing countries, by region

| | Annual percentage increase | | | | | |
| | Asia and Far East[a] | | Latin America | | Africa south of Sahara | |
Indicator	Actual	Target	Actual	Target	Actual	Target
Population	2.7	2.5	2.9	2.9	2.4	2.6
Labor force	2.0		2.3		2.0	
Agricultural labor force	1.0		0.9		1.3	
Area of cereals harvested per worker	0.1		1.6		−0.1[b]	
Area of cereals harvested	1.1	0.7	2.5	2.1	1.2[b]	2.1
Yield of cereals per hectare harvested	2.0	3.0	0.8	1.4	1.3	1.0
Output of cereals	3.1	3.7	3.3	3.5	2.5[b]	3.1
Output of starchy roots	5.5	3.9	4.7	2.5	2.7	2.5
Output of livestock products	2.3	2.7	2.8	3.0	2.7	3.3
Total output of agriculture	2.7	3.6	2.9	3.0	2.6[b]	3.2
Gross national product per capita	2.2	3.4	2.4	2.5	2.2[b]	2.3
Agricultural output per capita	0.0	1.1	0.0	0.1	0.2[b]	0.6
Output of cereals per capita	0.4	1.2	0.4	0.6	0.1[b]	0.5
Output of starchy roots per capita	2.8	1.4	1.8	−0.4	0.3	−0.1
Output of livestock products per capita	−0.4	0.2	−0.1	0.1	0.3	0.7
Output per worker in agriculture	1.7		2.0		1.3[b]	
Gross national product per worker in total labor force	2.9		3.2		2.5[b]	
Ratio of increase of agricultural output per worker to ratio of increase of output per worker in total labor force	0.6		0.6		0.5[b]	

Sources: FAO (1973); UN (1973).
[a]Region covered by the UN Economic Commission for Asia and the Far East, now designated Economic and Social Commission for Asia and the Pacific.
[b]Figures underestimated by either national or FAO statisticians.

In contrast with Asia, cereal production in Latin America came close to the FAO targets, but there also with more expansion of area and much less increase of productivity per hectare harvested than was foreseen by the FAO. In Latin America, the shortfall in yields increase goes together with a lower increase of the input of fertilizer than expected (14 percent increase per annum against an FAO target of 22 percent per annum). It is natural that in Latin America, with its large availability of uncultivated land, the area under cultivation should increase rather than productivity per hectare. The only surprising fact is that FAO had not foreseen that Latin American agriculturalists, with an increasing labor force and large amounts of uncultivated land, would make this choice.

In contrast with the other regions, Africa had a larger increase of productivity per hectare harvested than the target set by FAO, which was as low a 1 percent per annum. It might seem that Africa is exceptional also in having a lower rate of increase of area harvested than the FAO target, but here the figure shown in the table is spurious. The large shortfall in area harvested in Africa is in subsistence crops, for which hardly any statistics are available. For instance, the FAO target for area harvested under millet and sorghum is a 2 percent increase per annum, but the actual increase is given by FAO as 0.8 percent per annum, that is less than two-thirds of the increase in the African agricultural labor force. This is almost certainly due to considerable underestimation by either national statistical offices or by FAO statisticians or both. The underestimate of the increase of area under subsistence crops affects most of the figures for Africa.

In comments on developments during the 1960s, FAO emphasized that agricultural output increased only in step with overall population increase, so that per capita availabilities remained unchanged, as shown in table 2. It must be taken into account, however, that this is due to a less than proportionate increase of some export crops which suffer from marketing problems and to a relatively slow increase of some livestock products. Output of cereals per head of population did, in fact, increase by 0.4 percent per annum and output of starchy roots much more, while output of livestock products *per capita* increased little or declined. What happens, apparently, is that under population pressure consumption is shifted from land-using products like mutton, beef, and milk to cereals and starchy roots. Similar changes of consumption apparently took place during the nineteenth-century demographic transition in Europe.

With agricultural output increasing by a little less than 3 percent per annum and with the agricultural labor force increasing by about 1 percent, gross output per worker increased between 1.7 and 2 percent per annum in the regions in question. Part of the expansion of output per worker was probably due to a larger number of hours of work per year and worker, brought about by greater use of multicropping and more intensive methods of animal husbandry, which provided more work outside the traditional peak seasons. In view of the rapid population increase, this development in agricultural productivity cannot be described as unsatisfactory, although it must be noted that the increase of net income was smaller, since the rapid increase in total output was obtained by means of increasing amounts of industrial inputs. It must, however, also be noted that the increase in agricultural labor productivity is considerably lower than the increase of productivity per worker in the economy as a whole, as can be seen from table 2. The result is that the already wide gap between agricultural and nonagricultural incomes is steadily widening, except for cases where sectoral terms of trade move in favor of agriculture.

There is much concern that rural-to-urban migration in most parts of the world will be greater than can be absorbed by the labor market in urban economies. This trend is likely to continue while the productivity gap is widening, unless support is given to agricultural income from other sectors of national economies, since it is unlikely that the solution will come about as a result of improvements in the terms of trade for agricultural exports.

PART III

Women's Employment and Fertility

[1990]

Economic Change and the Roles of Women

Women's work, women's fertility, and women's role in the family and in society at large are radically changed by economic development. To understand this it is important to view these changes in women's position not as isolated factors but rather as part of general changes that come about as human societies slowly develop from subsistence economies to high-technology societies. Economic development is a gradual change from family production of goods and services to specialized production. This specialization of production makes it possible to use better technologies, scientific methods, and a more and more elaborate economic and social infrastructure (E. Boserup, 1981a).

As economic development proceeds, family production for its own use diminishes, and a larger and larger share of goods for family consumption is produced outside the family in specialized enterprises. Moreover, most of the services, which in subsistence economies are produced by the family members for each other (including physical protection, health care, and education), are taken over by public institutions or specialized private enterprises. During this process, the family gradually becomes stripped of most of its original functions. This causes radical changes both in the relation of family members to the outside world and in the relations between family members. All contemporary societies are in transition between subsistence economies and fully specialized economies. Even in highly industrialized countries, production of goods and services in the family, mainly by women, accounts for a considerable share of total work hours. In developing countries, family production is much more important, and in the least developed countries it accounts for the major part of total production of goods and services.

Family Organization in Subsistence Economies

Pure subsistence-producing families are rare today, but the traditional attitudes in many rural areas of the least developed countries continue to be those typical of subsistence economies. The family head has extensive, if not absolute, power over other family members. Older people have power over younger people, adults over children, and men over women of the same age group. The extensive power of the family head, and the whole hierarchical organization by age and sex, may have secured the discipline necessary for family survival in difficult circumstances and situations, but it usually results in discrimination in favor of the dominant groups (Sen, 1985). However, under this system women are not the only subservient group. Although they are subservient to husbands, fathers, and brothers, older women have extensive power over younger women and girls, and sometimes over boys and younger men. Old men constitute the top of the power hierarchy, and girls occupy the bottom position, but other age and sex groups are dominating in some relations and subservient in others.

Privileges and obligations are usually distributed according to this ranking. The members of dominating groups enjoy more leisure, perform the most interesting and pleasurable jobs, and pass on onerous and tedious jobs to the persons over whom they have power. Other privileges for groups in power are access to the best food and other consumer goods and to sufficient food in times of scarcity, when members of the dominated groups may starve. Groups in power also have the right to control the movements and the sexual relations of the members of subservient groups. Under this system, the prime obligation of young men is to secure the physical protection of the family group, and they are trained in weapon use. Young women must do hard work, while delegating lighter tasks to children.

The need for self-protection is a strong incentive for rearing large families. This, together with the large work burden carried by women and children, makes subsistence families pronatalist (E. Boserup, 1985). So all women are married off at puberty, and since long periods of breast-feeding are important determinants of fertility, women spend their childbearing period under a permanent stress of hard work, pregnancy, or breast-feeding, except for peoples who impose periods of postpartum abstinence even longer than the periods of breast-feeding. Under these conditions, female morbidity and mortality, spontaneous abortion, and child mortality reach such high levels that few women succeed in rearing large families, although some family heads obtain this by marrying many women. In this type of society, young women and children serve as family investment and providers of social security for the privileged groups of old people. Children belong to the father, and men and women are usually eager to adopt children.

Discrimination in Access to Resources

Primitive subsistence producers usually live as hunters, herders, or food producers using long-fallow methods in regions of low population density and with free access to the natural resources of the tribal area. When population density increases in such a region, competition among tribes over land, water, and other natural resources becomes more acute, and warfare among pastoral and cultivating tribes becomes more frequent. The result may be the dominance of one tribe over another. Either the militarily strongest tribe establishes itself as an upper class, imposing tribute or labor services on members of the vanquished tribe, or the latter become servants or slaves in the households of the members of the stronger tribe, excluded from access to natural resources, and forced to till the land or perform other services. In both cases, family heads of the weaker tribe lose their autonomy, and both male and female members must work harder than before. But the members of the stronger tribe, including the women and children, are likely to be relieved of a large part of their work burden, which is passed on to the members of the vanquished tribe. So the inequality between women (and men) belonging to the same age group, but to different ethnic groups, increases sharply.

Another result of increasing population density is the need to intensify the use of land for food production. With permanent instead of incipient use of the land, the system of tribal ownership of land is usually transformed into a system of peasant production, with private ownership of land and with use of animals for cultivation and transport (E. Boserup, 1965). In addition, these changes are accompanied by important changes in women's position (E. Boserup, 1970a; Ahmed, 1985). The favored male group becomes owner of the land and usurps the use of the new and more efficient equipment. Men are taught to operate the animal-driven equipment, while women continue to prepare the land with hand tools. Men use pack animals and wagons for transport, while women carry head loads. The discriminatory use of technology continues even when the stage of mechanized equipment is reached. In Asian regions of the Green Revolution, where land preparation for paddy production has been mechanized, men ride tractors while women continue to work with hand tools or without any tools, performing the backbreaking, tedious work of weeding and transplanting. But owing to inequality in landholdings between families of the same, or of different, ethnic groups, some women can escape work in the fields, while others must work hard, either on family land, or for wages, or both.

Marriage systems tend to differ in regions of peasant production from those typical for tribal areas with common land. In the former, marriages arranged by the parents are used as a means to secure and, if possible, to add to the family landholding, and girls and boys may be married off long before puberty. Women who do not work in the fields are felt to be an economic burden for the husband's family, who insist on payment of a dowry, while bride prices are usual in regions, and among tribes, in which women do most of the work in the fields (E. Boserup, 1970a). The attitudes toward childbirth are also different (Schutjer and Stokes, 1984). In regions of private landownership, late marriage and celibacy, as well as precautionary spacing and termination of childbearing by traditional methods, may be applied as means to avoid subdivision of land, and the number of daughters may be limited by discriminatory treatment or infanticide.

From Family Enterprises to Large-Scale Enterprises

In the change from family subsistence production to large capitalist enterprises based upon wage labor, small family enterprises producing for the market are often an intermediary step. A family producing only for its own use, and perhaps in order to pay taxes or tribute, may increase its production of one or more crops, or other products, and offer them for sale to traders or directly in local markets while continuing to be subsistence producers of other items. If the production for sale becomes important, the household is transformed into a family enterprise with specialized production, in which all or some of the family members take part. If the goods or services produced for sale are some traditionally produced by male family members, the oldest male will become the manager, with younger family members and servants as assistants; but, if women are traditionally producers of the items offered for sale, the housewife may become the manager, assisted by younger women, children, and servants. Often such female-managed enterprises are created by widows and divorced women, who in this way provide for themselves and their children and other dependents (Dauber and Cain, 1981; Buvinic, Lycette, and McGreevey, 1983).

The creation of such enterprises can be a means to liberate women from family obligations and unhappy marriages, but in most societies there are many obstacles to such a process. Whether the traditional family hierarchy is imposed by custom or is confirmed by formal legislation, men's customary right to dispose of women's labor usually becomes extended into a right to dispose of their income-earning activities ("Symposium on Law and the Status of Women," 1977). Women are not allowed to undertake money transactions or to engage in outside work without permission from their male family guardian, whether he is father, husband, brother, or perhaps son. And even if a woman gets such permission, the guardian remains the master of the woman's activities, with right to the money earned by her, and is thus able to prevent her from investing in and expanding her enterprise. Moreover, women's household obligations, pregnancies, and breast-feeding are powerful obstacles to business activities on any large scale. Usually, all or nearly all the family enterprises that succeed in growing into more productive and remunerative capitalist enterprises are the ones managed by men, with women and other men as assistants. When the transformation of some family enterprises into large-scale capitalist enterprises creates an increasing economic gap between persons belonging to different families, the traditional age, sex, and race hierarchy is transformed into an age, sex, race, and class hierarchy, with positive results for some women and negative results for other women.

Family enterprises may be located either in rural areas or in towns. Until fairly recently, health conditions in towns were so poor that urban populations did not reproduce themselves by natural growth, but had to rely on migration from the countryside to preserve and expand their population base. Townspeople who could afford it might send their children to rural areas to reduce the risk of early death, and married migrants might leave wife and children in the countryside, especially in regions where women were accustomed to doing most of the agricultural work with the help of the children. Often, towns have a large surplus of adult men over women, and prostitution flourishes. Such circumstances are conducive to attitudes that exalt female chastity and the mother role and that seclude women in their homes, if it is at all possible for the family to subsist without allowing women to work outside the home. It is no coincidence that regions with the longest urban experience are the ones where traditional culture is most oppressive to women (E. Boserup, 1970a).

In spite of the cultural objections to female labor market participation, women from poor families are forced by economic necessity to work in family or large-scale enterprises. But the female-managed enterprises suffer from severe handicaps, partly because of the lack of economic autonomy of their managers, as mentioned above, and partly because women from the less poor or well-off families (who could better provide the resources needed for business than the poorest ones) may be unavailable for work in such enterprises due to cultural prejudices against female labor market participation, to their unwillingness to do double work, and to their desire to take good care of their children. Therefore, economic development often results in the gradual disappearance of female-managed enterprises, even in countries where such enterprises are tolerated. The large majority of female labor market participants are working as low-paid or unpaid assistants to male managers and supervisors. In all countries, the typical organization in both private enterprises and public service mirrors the typical hierarchical organization in subsistence economies, with old men at the top, younger men at middle levels, and women at the bottom. But for women, there is an important difference: old women have lost their preferential status and are now in the bottom group, if they are not fired before they grow old.

Investment in Human Capital

Human capital investment in subsistence economies consists of two elements: one, training the young generation in the necessary technical skills and, two, the transmission of traditional cultural features, including knowledge of and respect for the existing hierarchical order relating to age and sex and to foreigners. From a young age, children of both sexes are socialized to accept their present and future roles, not only without protest but also without resentment. Boys learn to fight, girls to obey.

Since the use of improved techniques is usually monopolized by the men, economic development gradually creates a widening gap between the skill levels of men and women. Boys get systematic training as apprentices in family enterprises, while girls continue to be taught only simple household and agricultural operations by their mothers. When large-scale enterprises appear, these recruit male craftsmen and apprentices for skilled and supervisory jobs, while women and foreigners are excluded from learning other than routine skills in simple, specialized operations. By preventing women from getting training, men prevent them from getting access to better jobs and higher incomes, supervisory work, and management jobs. Much job discrimination in recruitment and advancement is made inevitable by the traditional sex discrimination in training.

The transfer of the education of children and youth from the family to private and public schools is another change that has far-reaching effects on the position of women and other disadvantaged groups. School education is a means of supplying the next generation with the superior skills that become necessary as the national economy evolves, or that are recognized as necessary to make further development of the economy possible. Educational systems have started everywhere with the education of male children from the most privileged family groups, thus widening the gap in opportunities between dominant and subservient groups. However, development requires that a larger and larger share of the population be provided with more and more knowledge and skills of the types that are taught in schools and higher educational institutions. Education, therefore, is extended gradually to disadvantaged groups, by making it obligatory and free. As a result, the gap between men and women in education first widens and later narrows. Similarly, the gap between women belonging to racially and economically favored and disfavored families first widens and then narrows. Nowhere in the world have these gaps completely closed.

School systems have not only the purpose of teaching intellectual skills and scientific knowledge, but also of indoctrinating pupils with the dominant cultural values. However, cultural education for both girls and boys is usually (whether deliberately or unintentionally) a teaching of traditional prejudices, not only against foreigners, but also against members of the female sex. Not only the early socialization of girls by parents and brothers, but also the later experience in schools, contributes to the development of superiority feelings in boys and inferiority feelings in girls.

In developing societies, education will gradually replace physical strength and ability in weapon use as male status symbols. When this change coincides with rapidly increasing education of women, it may be felt as a potential threat to male domination, both in the labor market and within the family. This threat may be reduced by educating women to lower levels or in less prestigious fields than men. So, a number of middle-level educations may be arranged mainly or exclusively for women, thus pushing women into fields where they will become assistants to better educated men, belonging to the economically and racially dominant groups. The female occupations that require middle-level education are mainly in shops, offices, schools, hospitals, and other social services, and for educated women, they provide escapes from the traditional, unskilled, female jobs.

Decline in Birth Rates

Until the middle of this century, the societal changes brought about by economic development had gradually increased the differences in the lifestyle of adult men and women. In the industrialized countries, virtually all adult men were full-time labor market participants, while a large share of adult women were fully occupied with child care and domestic duties. Nearly all the women who participated in the labor market worked in unskilled, low-wage occupations specially reserved for female labor. It is true that the functions of the family household had been much reduced by gradual specialization of goods and services, but this had been compensated for by transfer of children, adolescents, adult men, and female servants from work within the family household to schools and specialized work in the labor market (Tilly and Scott, 1978). This process gradually transformed most housewives from small-scale managers of younger family members and servants to lonely performers of routine manual domestic work, confined to the household by child care.

The reduction in the number of tasks performed in the family is accompanied by a reduction in the autonomy of the family, which becomes dependent not only upon the market but upon the government and other public institutions. These changes also influence the power of the family head over other family members. While his exercise of physical power over other family members most often becomes restricted by law, both obligatory schooling and the institutionalization of religion may serve either to limit or to reinforce the influence of the family head and the older generation. Moreover, the economic requirements of a developed society induce changes in the legal and factual position of younger family members and of those women who are drawn into the labor market as monetization of the economy proceeds. When the individual household is stripped of more and more functions due to increasing supply of public services and purchase of goods from outside, it becomes in the economic interest of the male head of household and the tax authorities that the participation of female family members in money-earning activities be facilitated. Thus in the course of European development, adult status in economic affairs was granted to more and more groups of women—first to widows, who, by entering into market trade and small-scale production, could support themselves and their offspring, thus avoiding becoming economic burdens to male family members and public relief systems. Later, for the same reason, adult status in economic affairs was granted to adult unmarried women, while married women continued to be "nonadults" until recently ("Symposium," 1977).

The transfer of functions from the family to the labor market and the public sector has important effects on birth rates (E. Boserup, 1986). No longer valuable contributors to the family labor force, school-age children become an economic burden. Parents' reliance on adult children in emergencies and old age is reduced when the public sector or private institutions take over both physical protection and economic support. The number of surviving children increases when child mortality declines due to public health measures and medical progress, and this provides additional incentive for application of traditional or modern means of birth control within marriage.

The gradual reduction of birth rates to reproduction level or less inaugurates a period of rapid change in marital relations. Married women return to the labor market when their children reach school age, or they continue without interruption in the labor market, leaving preschool children to public or private care outside the home, and modernizing the household by purchase of mechanized household equipment and semiprepared food. Nevertheless, the inequality in access to leisure between male wage earners and wives with child care, domestic duties, and full-time participation in the labor market, leads increasing numbers of women to take the initiative to divorce, or to avoid formal marriage and further reduce births. As a result, public opinion in industrialized countries is more and more preoccupied with the prospects for population decline and for decay of the traditional authoritarian marriage institution.

Determinants of Wage Differentials

In subsistence economies, the age-sex-race hierarchy is reflected in the type of work a person performs; in monetized societies, the hierarchy is, moreover, reflected in the differentials between the wages paid to young and old, indigenous and foreigners, men and women (E. Boserup, 1970a). Although age differentials in wages have become less important, and are sometimes reversed due to increasing education and technical dynamism, wage systems which in effect increase wages by age have by no means disappeared. In multiracial societies, wages for similar work are usually higher for persons belonging to the dominant ethnic group, and usually the higher status of men is underlined by paying them higher wages than women for similar work, both in public service and in private enterprises. Only in periods of acute labor shortages, for instance during wars or extreme seasonal labor peaks in agriculture, may wages paid to women and minorities temporarily approach those paid to male labor of the dominant ethnic group. As soon as the specific shortage is over, however, the customary wage differentials tend to be reestablished.

Relative prices of products and services adapt to the traditional wage differentials. Products made mainly or exclusively by female labor can be sold more cheaply than products made by male labor. An employer of male labor who has difficulty selling his products may reduce his costs by changing from male to female labor if his workers and their unions allow him to do so, but he will not attempt to eliminate the wage differential of his male workers by paying them female wages. If legislation or public opinion exerts pressure to eliminate traditional wage differentials by sex, the employer is most likely to react by making all operations sex-specific and continue to pay lower wages to women. As a result of such behavior, the trades with the weakest trade unions gradually become female, low-wage trades, while stronger unions are able to preserve a number of occupations as male, high-wage monopolies.

In the period in Europe in which a large share of the female labor force consisted of young, unmarried girls living with their parents, sex discrimination in wages was usually explained not by status considerations but by the need to pay adult male labor a wage on which they could support a family. But permanent female breadwinners, whether single or with dependents, were never paid breadwinner wages, and single men without dependents were paid more than females. Because female labor market participants were either young or from very poor families and were socialized by family and school education to feel inferior to men, the system was never seriously challenged until recently. Even men who had full-time working wives supported the system because it secured them the status of main breadwinner, which reinforced their marital authority and their general social status. Moreover, since economists taught that wage differences reflected differentials in labor productivity, it was easy to draw the conclusion that their existence everywhere was proof of female inferiority in the labor market. The use of female labor in inferior jobs, therefore, seemed economically rational (Becker, 1981).

The increasing replacement of male by female labor in office trades and other white collar services changes the traditional wage differences between white collar and manual work. White collar work at the higher supervisory stages remains predominantly male, and continues to be well paid. At lower levels, however, wage differentials between white collar and manual work often become reversed. With increasing numbers of women in white collar jobs which require middle-level education, more and more manual workers have wives with more formal education and sometimes with a higher income than they. In such cases, the increase in the wife's prestige and in her earning power strengthens her marital position considerably, and this contributes no doubt to the increasing frequency of divorce, which was mentioned earlier. Women's position also improves in the labor market with the entry of women with more education and belonging to other age classes and other social classes than those that earlier were predominant in the female labor market.

The Concept of Westernization

It was underlined in the previous sections of this essay that, at certain stages of economic development, women's position is likely to improve, while at other stages it may deteriorate. It was also underlined that development often improves the position of certain groups of women but causes deterioration for other groups of women, and that such changes are likely when there is increasing economic inequality or a shift of power relations between national or ethnic groups. The period of overseas colonization by Western powers and the later shift to national sovereignty provide important examples.

During the colonial period, colonial administrators and white settlers recruited indigenous male workers for plantations, mines, and transport, and they taught indigenous male producers to produce cash crops for export to European and North American markets. As a result, the work burden of the women increased. More of the subsistence production was pushed onto women and children when the men got other work to do, and often the women also had to help with the cash crops. Because a large share of the additional agricultural work was taken over by women without pay, the costs of agricultural and mining products and the costs of transport investment could be kept low, and the male workers in these activities could be paid wages that only covered the immediate subsistence needs of the worker, but not the cost of supporting dependents (E. Boserup, 1970a; Pala Okeyo, 1984). In other cases, colonial plantations recruited the whole family, which obtained a subsistence income through full-time work by men, women, and children on the plantation, thus forcing the women to perform the domestic work on top of a full day of hard plantation work.

In the colonial period, married European women, and often unmarried ones too, were denied adult status, and the official ideal of a woman was the faithful, domestic housewife and mother, devoting her work and interest exclusively to husband and children. If administrators and missionaries discovered indigenous women with more sexual and economic freedom than corresponded to this ideal, they did their best to change the customs by legislation and education. This meant that change, from common cultivation rights for both men and women to private property, usually became a change to male property rights, with the result that women's possibility for independent self-support was reduced or eliminated (Ahmed, 1985). Where she had been an independent producer with free access to land, she became an unpaid family aide on her husband's farm, or she became a wage laborer if local agriculture used female wage labor. If not, her fate might be prostitution or begging, if her husband died or left her. In most colonies, girls' possibility for formal education was limited to attendance in missionary schools, which focused on religious instruction and teaching of domestic skills and elementary literacy.

Independence brought radical changes in the traditional hierarchy for men, but much less change for women. The small elite of young men who received Western education in missionary schools and sometimes in schools and universities in Western countries moved into top jobs in administration and business, bypassing the older, uneducated or less educated traditional elites. For women, the most important change was the rapid spread of public, female education. Moreover, in countries with rapid industrialization, urban wage employment for unmarried women increased, resulting in later marriages for women and more freedom for women to refuse undesired marriage partners. But these changes were the results of industrialization and only related to independence to the extent that decolonization led to acceleration of the rate of industrialization.

It is also true for rural women that economic changes are more important than political independence. If national governments neglect rural development, women's traditional toil in agriculture continues, or becomes worse due to acceleration of male migration from the villages. If independence results in promotion and modernization of agriculture, as has happened in some countries, mainly in Asia, the reduction of the work burden made possible by new equipment and methods benefits mainly the men and the children who are sent to school (Tinker & Cho, 1981). Women continue to perform their traditional hand operations, unless they belong to families with so much increase in income that the female family members can pass all or some of their agricultural work on to women or men from less well-off families (Ahmed, 1985).

Industrialization has opposing effects on different groups of women. While young women are drawn into industrial employment, and increasing numbers of educated women obtain white collar jobs in social and other services, the situation of older, uneducated women may deteriorate because the family enterprises in which they work may suffer from competition with the growing modern sector (Dauber and Cain, 1981; Buvinic, Lycette, and McGreevey, 1983). There are similar opposing changes within the family sphere. Young women, especially educated ones, achieve a stronger position in relation to both male family members and older women, and the older women lose whatever authority they had in the family, especially if they are the only illiterate family members.

When development is rapid, it is inevitable that these changes create tension between sexes and generations, and that pressure groups appear that seek to preserve or reintroduce the traditional, hierarchical cultural pattern. The tension is most acute and the pressure groups become strongest if development is rapid in societies that have long had particularly oppressive age-sex hierarchies. This is the case in oil countries in the Arab world, which have attempted to preserve the family system of domesticated and secluded women by mass importation of foreign male labor, and in which mass movements of Moslem revival pursue the same aim.

Active pressure groups of men and women aiming at preservation or revival of traditional systems of age-sex discrimination are not limited to the Arab world. In most previous colonies, nationalist feeling is accompanied by hostile feelings toward remaining Western influence in the cultural field. Groups that are against changes in the traditional age-sex hierarchy gain strength by describing such changes as results of Western influence, undisturbed by the fact that, first, white rule and, later, Western experts most often strengthened male positions and weakened those of women by their interventions. It is often overlooked in developing countries that Western culture was strongly antifeminist in the colonial period, and that it is only as a result of recent economic and demographic changes in the Western countries that the traditional sex hierarchy is beginning to be undermined in those societies.

Employment of Women in Developing Countries

The Effects of Differences in Classification of Women

ORIGINALLY, THE CRITERION for the distinction between members and non-members of the national labor force were laid down using statistics of industrialized countries, and the applicability of this labor force concept to developing countries is highly questionable. In particular, the category of housewife is unsuitable when applied to women in rural areas of developing countries. In most of these areas, women would spend little time on domestic work in the narrow sense of cooking, house cleaning, and child care, and much more on providing the types of goods and services which are bought for money in industrialized countries, such as food production, food gathering, crude processing of food, and provision of water and fuel.

Many developing countries choose to consider women who perform such activities for family use as subsistence producers and members of the national labor force. In such countries, the agricultural labor force includes approximately the same number of women and men, and when, in the process of urbanization, the agricultural labor force is declining as a share of the total labor force, female activity rates necessarily decline, unless all wives and daughters of urban immigrants happen to become active members of the urban labor force after migration.

However, other developing countries follow the alternative rule and classify women in farm families as housewives. In developing countries which follow this system of classification, the female labor force, as shown by the statistics, will remain extremely small, as long as the bulk of the population is rural and market trade and home industries little developed. But female activity rates will increase with economic development, when women become relieved of some of their subsistence work and feel the need to earn a money income which can be used to purchase the food and other necessities which they no longer produce.

Thus, official statistics in a developing country may show female activity

"Employment of Women in Developing Countries," reprinted from *International Population Conference 1973* (Liege: IUSSP), is a shortened version of "Employment of Women in Developing Countries" in Leon Tabah, editor, *Population Growth and Economic Development in the Third World*. 1975. Liege: Ordina.

rates as increasing or decreasing over time depending on which of the two systems that country happens to use for the classifications of its female labor force. Likewise, the levels of female activity rates shown at any given time may differ radically among countries using one or the other statistical system, without any real difference in the work performed by women being involved.

In most developing countries, more persons are occupied in agriculture than in all other occupations taken together. Hence, the choice as to whether all women in farm families or only very few of them are to be counted as members of the labor force strongly affects the apparent size of the total labor force. By the same token, attempts to describe the labor market structure by showing a particular group, say persons occupied in industry or in agriculture or all wage and salary earners, as a percentage of the total labor force tend to become misleading.

It seems to me that the only acceptable solution to this very real problem is to disregard the concept of total labor force as denominator in computations of percentage shares and to use instead the figure for total population of working age. Thus, instead of measuring, for instance, employment in industry or total wage and salary earners as a percentage of a labor force defined by widely varying methods, such fairly well-defined groups could better be measured as a percentage of another well defined category, that is, all persons in certain age groups.

A New Method to Measure Female Employment

Difficulties in the classification of women are not confined to agriculture. Since women in all countries carry a larger burden of domestic work than men, they naturally have part-time work much more often than men. Part-time work is an important source of statistical error, because in census reports a person is classified either as working full time or not working at all. However, in certain occupations part-time work is far more frequent than in others, and it is therefore possible considerably to reduce the error due to this factor by basing the calculations on those types of work which are least likely to be part-time work—wage labor in modern occupations. This means the exclusion primarily of self-employment and domestic services, where part-time work is particularly widespread.

If we select within nonagricultural activities wage and salary earners in modern-type occupations who are likely to be full-time workers and, on the other hand, exclude persons performing small-scale services and other self-employment, distortions due to differences of classification are minimized and an index is provided showing the amount of employment in those kinds of occupations which are likely to have increasing employment with increasing per capita incomes and stage of development. In other words, we are provided with an index which can be of help in the ranking of countries according to stage of development, as is done in the tables below.

In these tables, the international standard classification of occupations

TABLE 1. Percentage of adult population in each occupational sector, by country group

Country group	Modern sector	Mining and transport	Other nonagricultural sectors	Agricultural sector	Unspecified	Outside labor force	Total adults
1	5	2	7	45	2	39	100
2	7	1	8	51	3	29	100
3	9	2	10	32	2	46	100
4	11	1	10	31	2	45	100
5	16	2	10	27	3	42	100
6	20	2	12	18	2	46	100
7	31	4	10	10	2	43	100
8	36	3	7	6	2	45	100

Note: Adult population is all people fifteen years and over.

was used for the calculations, and the groups which were selected for inclusion in the modern sector are all persons in professional, administrative, and clerical occupations, together with wage and salary earners in industrial and sales occupations. The calculations were made by expressing employment in this modern sector as a percentage of all persons of fifteen years and more. A total of thirty developing countries and nine industrialized countries were included. Censuses taken as close as possible to the year 1960 were used. The countries were ranked by the percentage of persons of both sexes occupied in the modern sector and were grouped in six groups of developing countries, with five countries in each group, and two groups of industrialized countries. A summary of the results of the calculations is shown in table 1 for the labor force of both sexes and in table 2 for the female labor force separately.[1]

The first column in table 1 is the ranking order for the countries, as mentioned above. As was to be expected, the higher the employment in the modern sector as a percentage of the total number of adults, the lower the corresponding percentage for the agricultural sector, but this is not true for groups 1 and 2, and it can be seen from table 2 that it is the large differences in the figures for the female labor force in agriculture which explain the abnormalities in the figures for total labor force. There happen to be more countries in group 2, which classifies all women in farm families as members of the agricultural labor force, than in either group 1 or group 3, and the result of these differences in classification are mirrored in the column for persons outside the labor force in both tables.

The other nonagricultural sectors include the self-employed in production and services, and wage labor in domestic and other services. These are the activities which women are able to enter, if neither they themselves nor the members of their family have major objections to female work outside the household. This is true of self-employment in small-scale production, trade, and other services, and it is also true of domestic services, an occupation which poor parents are likely to push their young daughters into, unless the attitude in their community makes it difficult for a girl with such work to find a suitable marriage partner. It can be seen from table 2 that in countries at early stages of development there are many more women in these occupations than in the modern sector. In group 1, which includes the least developed countries, only 1 percent of adult women are employed in the modern sector, and even in group 6 less than 10 percent of adult women are in modern sector employment. Only in the two groups of industrialized countries does the modern sector employ a higher percentage of adult women than the sectors of self-employed and domestic and other services.

The sex distribution of the labor force within a given country reflects partly the stage of development reached by that country and partly the cultural pattern, which influences attitudes to employment of women. Because it is easy for women to enter other nonagricultural sectors in countries without prejudices against working women, the sex distribution in these occupations is a mirror which reflects the cultural pattern. In table 3, the thirty-nine countries are grouped horizontally according to sex distribution in other

TABLE 2. Percentage of adult women in each occupational sector, by country group

Country group	Modern sector	Mining and transport	Other nonagricultural sectors	Agricultural sector	Unspecified	Outside labor force	Total adult women
1	1		3	30		66	100
2	3		7	38	1	52	100
3	2		9	8	1	80	100
4	4		8	2		85	100
5	7		8	8	1	76	100
6	9		11	3	2	75	100
7	18	1	11	5		65	100
8	22	1	8	1		68	100

Note: Adult women are all women fifteen years and over.

TABLE 3. Women as percentage of the modern sector labor force by national acceptance of women in the traditional, nonagricultural labor force and country group, thirty-nine countries

Country group	Women as percentage of traditional, nonagricultural labor force								Average for country group
	6–9	10–19	20–29	30–39	40–49	50–59	60–69	70–79	
1		3	10						
			9						
			15						
			8						9
2	12		9			26	29		
						25			21
3	7	6			20		9		
							25		14
4	5		15		21	25	25		18
5			12		25	32			
			14		22				21
6				11	30	22		29	
				19					22
7					26	25			
					32	32			
					32				30
8					29	30			
					29				
					33				30
Average	8	5	12	15	27	27	22	29	

nonagricultural sectors and vertically in the eight groups which represent economic development. The table shows the sex distribution in the modern sector in each country. Thus, it presents a broad picture of the way the two different factors, cultural pattern and economic development, influence sex distribution in the modern sector of the labor market.

Let us first look at the horizontal position of the thirty-nine countries. Five have less than 20 percent women in the sectors of self-employed and service employment. These are all countries in North Africa and West and South Asia with ancient urban civilizations and strong traditions for keeping women out of the urban labor market. By contrast, all the developing countries with more than 50 percent women in these occupations are countries with Negro or American Indian populations, or they are Southeast Asian

TABLE 4. Women as percentage of modern sector labor force, by occupational group and country group

Country group	Wage labor		Salary labor			
	Industry	Trade	Clerical	Administrative	Professional	Average
1	6	11	10	3	17	9
2	16	25	18	7	37	21
3	7	19	16	3	35	14
4	14	27	20	4	39	18
5	11	18	30	7	47	21
6	14	21	33	11	50	22
7	19	45	51	11	42	30
8	15	42	62	11	42	30

countries which have no ancient traditions for keeping urban women at home.

Let us now turn to the percentages of women in the modern-sector labor force. They illustrate the interaction between cultural and economic forces. There is a clear trend for countries where the two factors combine to limit the share of women within the modern sector. All industrialized countries have at least 25 percent women in their modern sector, and all countries which have 25 percent or more women in their modern sector have either reached stage 5 in economic development or more, or they are countries with more women than men in their other nonagricultural sectors—that is, they are countries with little prejudice against female employment.

It can be seen from table 4 that industry seems to be the occupation where prejudices against employment of women are most important. The sex distribution among wage labor in industry shows wide variations from country group to country group, but with little relation to the stage of economic development. In many countries, the disinclination of employers to recruit women for industrial work and prejudice among women and their relatives against industrial employment of women reinforce each other. By contrast, even countries with very restrictive attitudes toward employment of women need female nurses and teachers to cater to the needs of the female population. Therefore, there is a high share of women among the professional staff in nearly all countries.

Female Employment and Family Obligations

It was mentioned above that the percentage of women in the labor force in other nonagricultural sectors of developing countries is much higher than in the modern sector. When as a result of economic development the modern sector expands while other nonagricultural sectors stagnate or decline, women may be unable to find employment in the modern sector, and the share of women within total nonagricultural occupations may decline, although the share of women within modern sector employment may increase. Statistics of changes in the sex distribution in nonagricultural occupations confirm that such a change took place in many developing countries in the period 1950–60 (E. Boserup, 1975b).

However, we cannot be sure that an observed decline in the share of women in nonagricultural employment is due to difficulty in finding a job and not to voluntary withdrawal, either because of increasing family incomes or because family obligations prevent women from working full time in modern sector occupations.

The old conflict between woman's work outside the family and their role within the family has taken new forms with the sharp increase in family size resulting from the decline in infant and child mortality with roughly unchanged rates of fertility. As long as infant and child mortality was very high, there was a conflict between the need for help from the women in economic support of the family on the one hand and on the other hand the desire that rates of abortion and child mortality should be reduced by sparing women too high a burden of work and allowing them to stay at home and take care of the children. Families who could afford it attempted to increase the number of surviving children by keeping women at home.

This motive has lost much of its force with the decline in rates of mortality. Increasing family size may have given women more incentive to contribute to the money income of the family, but with the larger number of children in the homes, it becomes more difficult for women to accept wage employment. Also, employers may hesitate to recruit women because of their large family responsibilities. Moreover, in many countries the rule is to give priority in recruitment to the rapidly increasing numbers of young male school leavers who wish to be employed in the modern sector and to avoid the kind of manual jobs which do not require education and which are therefore held in low esteem.

All these factors combine to restrain the movement of women from self-employment to the modern sector. Self-employment allows flexible work hours and can often be done in the woman's home or another place where she can bring the children. Therefore, self-employment, more easily than modern sector employment, can be combined with domestic duties and responsibility for supervision of children. Women are therefore both pushed and pulled into self-employment, and often they prefer self-employment and domestic service although they are low-income jobs, because they can have shorter hours than is usual in the modern sector, and thus limit their total work load.

One might think that the wide differences between earnings in full-time jobs in the modern sector and earnings in typical female self-employment occupations and services would help to motivate women to control their birth rates as a precondition for obtaining and retaining employment in the modern sector. But employment opportunities for women in the modern sector are far too limited in most developing countries to provide a realistic alternative to the rearing of a large family. The present occupational pattern with most working women in self-employment or agricultural work offers little inducement to control births. In some cases, women working hard in such activities are positively motivated to rear a large family in order to get children to help them. This is true particularly in countries where school attendance for girls is not obligatory.

Rural-to-Urban Migration and Female Employment

Census returns usually distinguish between female employment in rural and in urban areas, but since the size of the female labor force in rural areas reflects the classification used for agricultural work, such rural-urban distinctions of activity rates can be highly misleading. But even though statistics may be misleading, the broad picture is reasonably clear: in countries at low stages of development, where rural women take a very active part in subsistence activities, their migration to urban areas is likely to reduce their participation in economic activities. They can no longer provide the goods and services in kind which they provided for family consumption in the village, and they are not likely to find employment opportunities in the town. Nonagricultural sectors are small in the least developed countries, and at the early stage they employ mainly men.

Even if there are some modern sector jobs open to women in countries at an early stage of development, the wives and daughters of migrants from rural areas are not likely to be qualified for such work. Whether they can find some employment or must remain idle depends therefore on whether the country has restrictive attitudes toward self-employment for married women and domestic service for young girls. If the dominating attitude is restrictive, female work will be sharply reduced after migration. But this need not be the case if the country has a tradition of female self-employment in nonagricultural activities in urban as well as rural areas. In this connection, the pattern of female employment in nonagricultural activities in rural areas is important for the employment opportunities of migrant women, because a woman who was employed in nonagricultural activities in a village is much more likely to continue to work outside the home after she has migrated to a town than a woman who did only agricultural work before she migrated to the town (E. Boserup, 1970a).

These differences in patterns of female employment and attitudes to female employment are often reflected in the sex pattern of migration, because men may migrate without their female relatives if they know that the town offers no employment opportunities for women.

In developing countries at a more advanced stage, rural-to-urban migrations are less likely to reduce the female work input. The villages the women leave are likely to have preserved fewer subsistence activities, and these women may therefore have been less hardworking in the village than women who leave more primitive villages in the least developed countries. Moreover, in towns in developing countries at more advanced stages of development, the modern sector offers more employment and is likely to employ a larger share of female labor than in the least developed countries. Migrant women are also more likely to have attended village schools and thus be more qualified for modern sector employment. Thus, there is a better chance that female employment opportunities in the town are more ample than in the village and, in countries at this stage, sex distribution among migrants is radically different from that of the least developed countries.

In countries where women migrate more than men, a stage may be reached where a shortage of young marriageable women in the villages push more and more men to towns. Therefore, in developing countries of this type, steps to improve employment opportunities for young female school leavers in rural areas may be a means to slow down rural-to-urban migrations.

Note

1. Additional tables and more information about the composition of the tables are given in E. Boserup, 1975a. Tables for the female labor force in each of the developing countries included in the calculations are available in the statistical appendix to E. Boserup, 1970a.

Women in the Labor Market

IT IS A CHARACTERISTIC feature of labor markets all over the world that certain jobs are performed only by men, while others are performed only by women. In most societies, there is some work which may be done by both men and women, but this is somewhat exceptional. The general rule is that a particular operation is either a male or a female task. This is true of virtually all agricultural tasks, and it is equally true of a great majority of the jobs in urban industries and service establishments.

This division of labor according to sex is often explained as a natural result of physiological and psychic differences between men and women. But apart from the obvious case of childbearing, there are extremely few convincing examples of sex division of labor being truly explainable in terms of natural differences between men and women. This is apparent when the sex patterns of work in different parts of the world are compared: in different human communities, quite different tasks are labelled as male and female work.

To be an independent farmer is a male role in India and in Europe, but in many other regions it is a normal occupation for a woman. In African agriculture, more hours of work are performed by women than by men, and these women own and sell the crops they have produced in local markets. A similar system exists in some Indian tribes and in some other Asian countries. Indian and African sex patterns are quite different in market trade and other retail trade. In many African countries, most retail trade is in female hands. Here again, there is a similarity between Africa and tribal peoples in India, while the typical Hindu pattern of male tradesmen is a characteristic not only of India but of North Africa and many other parts of the world.

But if men in India perform tasks that women do in other countries, Indian women undertake work performed by men in other parts of the world. For instance, very few countries have a parallel to women in the building trade, a characteristic feature of the Indian scene. While women in most countries outside India would think it unsuitable to be an assistant to a male bricklayer, men in most European countries would find it unsuitable to be a typist and stenographer, as is customary for men in India. In other words, the

---

"Women in the Labor Market." Reprinted from *Indian Women*, edited by Devaki Jain. Publications Division, Government of India, 1975: 99–111.

idea that the specialization of male and female tasks is related to natural differences between the sexes is proved wrong when we compare labor markets in different parts of the world. If it were true that the specialization is rooted in physiological and psychic differences between the sexes, we should expect to find the same tasks were male or female all over the world. Clearly, the key to understanding these patterns is in the culture rather than in human physiology or anatomy.

Division of Labor within the Family

If specialization of male and female tasks is unrelated to special physical or psychic differences between the sexes, why then do we find a sharp division of labor between men and women in all countries in the world? In order to understand this division of labor, it is necessary to consider the division of labor within the family in primitive communities with subsistence production.

Even in the most primitive society, the members of a family use a multitude of different products: They eat many types of food, they use jars, pots, and baskets for storing, preparation, and transport of food, they use many different tools as well as clothing and dwellings. They have also many services to perform: to prepare the food, to clean the dwelling, to take care of the sick, to bury the dead, to play music and dance at tribal feasts. This means that young people have much to learn before they are able to care for themselves and that much time spent on teaching the next generation can be saved if men teach the boys half the tasks and women teach the girls the other half.

However, within intermarrying groups, it is necessary that all boys are taught to perform the same tasks, and that all girls are taught all the tasks which boys are not taught. Otherwise, the system cannot work. It must be avoided in a married couple that both can spin but neither can weave. Thus in a community where each family produces all the goods and services consumed by that family, the sharp distinction between male and female tasks is a necessary result of the simple fact that families are formed by the union of men and women. When the fathers teach their sons to perform half the jobs and the mothers teach their daughters to perform the other half, everybody needs to teach and to learn half as much as would be necessary without such a rigid division of labor between men and women. It is customary in all primitive communities to ridicule and despise men who perform female tasks and women who perform male tasks, and this custom can be seen as a social sanction by which the sex division of labor is enforced and perpetuated.

This obedient attitude to economic sex roles is preserved in all higher civilizations, where boys and girls are taught, both in their homes and in schools, that decency requires them to stick to traditionally male and female jobs. This ingrained custom dates back to a distant primitive past, where it had an obvious productive function. It is worth noting that only within groups who intermarry is it necessary that the same tasks be male or female. When human groups with a different division of labor between the sexes live close together, the different customs create a lack of sympathy and a disinclination to intermarriage. Intermarriage is then seen not primarily as impractical but as undesirable, because people with different customs are ridiculed and despised. This attitude contributes to preserving rules of exogamy and to preserving a certain amount of hostility among ethnic groups living in the same region, even in cases where their members have come to work closely together in the labor market.

The rationale of a sharp division of tasks gradually disappears as economic development moves some tasks out of the home and transforms them into specialized occupations. But the idea that men and women should avoid doing work which by custom belongs to the domain of the other sex is so firmly rooted in the national culture in all countries that male occupations usually continue to be male and female occupations continue to be female. In India, where spinning and weaving for own use were suitable jobs for men, textile industries have mainly male workers. But in Europe, where home spinning and weaving were female occupations, men regard spinning and weaving as proper for women only, and all textile industries are female industries, with few male workers except for supervisory work, repair of machines, and so on. Some Indian textile industries started with recruitment of large numbers of women, because their first owners were Europeans or under European cultural influence.

Economic development does not only move certain activities away from the household to specialized workshops and industries—it also affects the amount of work done in the home. Some activities which used to be subsistence production become a source of money income, as larger quantities are produced for sale. For instance, some crops become cash crops and some home crafts and services may be performed for other households in the local community. Such changes must necessarily interfere with the customary divisions of labor within the family. If the cash crop (or the craft) which is now performed for sale was hitherto produced by men (or women), the work load will be heavier for men (or women), and they may need help from the other sex.

In such cases, men or women may agree to undertake new tasks and change the traditional division of labor; but often they refuse to do work which is not considered appropriate for their sex. The result may be that men (or women) accept a disproportionate share of the work load, or else that the introduction of the new money-earning activity is given up or retarded because of the prejudice concerning sex roles. Many attempts to foster agricultural development have failed because men refused to weed a crop which women had no time to weed. Or the introduction of cash crops was retarded because women refused to help with a new crop and insisted on cultivating only the usual food crops, which were considered proper work for women. Such refusal to change traditional sex roles in the labor market occurs in all parts of the world. African men are often unwilling to cultivate food crops as cash crops, because food production is supposed to be a female task, and men in many parts of Latin America are unwilling to engage in commercial poultry production, because it is traditionally a female task.

However, tradition alone does not prevent or delay a change of sex roles in the process of economic development. In addition, there is the employer's interest in maintaining a sharp line of demarcation between male and female tasks, since this enables him to have female tasks done more cheaply. In some countries, women are paid less than men for equal work, but in countries where this is not allowed, a situation of de facto unequal pay can be maintained by classifying particular tasks as female and placing these tasks in a lower wage category than male tasks. The interest of the employers and the prejudices of the employees against a change of sex roles tend to reinforce each other; therefore, the distinction between male and female work encounters little resistance either in developing or in industrialized countries. It is only in recent years that discussion has begun in some industrialized countries about the need to change this ancient custom in order to obtain more flexibility and more equality in the labor market.

Hierarchy of Work between Men and Women

In the labor markets of industrialized countries, the distinction between male and female tasks goes together with a hierarchical ordering. Women perform the least qualified jobs, which require supervision, while nearly all more qualified jobs, and supervisory jobs, are filled by men. This feature is not, like the distinction between male and female jobs, an inheritance from the division of work within the families in a distant past. Quite the opposite, in primitive family production we never find such a hierarchical division of labor, with men as supervisors and women as supervised. There is a hierarchy of supervisors and supervised in primitive family production, but the distinction is not by sex, but by age. Older men supervise the young men, and older women supervise the young women. Older men and women have different tasks, but each of them works independently, without supervision, and all the young and less experienced are supervised by older persons of their own sex. Thus there is no hierarchy between men and women in the performance of productive work within the household, even though in other walks of life women may be under the control of the men.

This age-determined hierarchy of work continues to prevail in domestic work, for instance in India, where young women are supervised first by their mothers and later by their mothers-in-law. By contrast in the modern Indian labor market, the European custom of men as supervisors and women as supervised is introduced in step with the entrance of Indian women into employment in the modern sector—except, of course, in fields like schools for girls, where the whole staff is female.

It is pertinent to ask, at what stage in economic development does a change take place from age hierarchy to sex hierarchy? In agriculture, it seems to happen when the plow and plow animals are introduced. At this stage, men usually leave hand labor to women, while they perform the operations with the animals. For nonagricultural activities, the decisive moment when the change takes place seems to be when productive activities move from the premises where the family is living to a specialized workshop or shop. As long as an activity is carried out as a home industry located in the dwelling of the family, women usually continue to work independently, if the activity is traditionally a female occupation. But when the production or service is established in special premises, married women with children tend to drop out, because it becomes more difficult to combine job and family obligations.

When this happens, only young women are available for this kind of employment, and these inexperienced workers are now—like the young boys—trained and supervised by the older men. These may be inclined to be more careful with the training of the boys, since the girls are expected to work only a short span of years on the job. Thus, a new pattern for the division of labor gradually emerges: older men supervise young men and young women, while the older women stay at home with the children. This stage is intermediate between the original age hierarchy and the modern sex hierarchy. Young girls are likely to accept this division of labor, partly because it is customary that older people supervise younger people and partly because young girls often consider their time in the labor market as somewhat transitory and unimportant compared to their later roles as wives and mothers.

In India and other countries of old civilization, where specialized crafts were developed in ancient times, it is considered normal and natural that independent business and supervision of labor is the preserve of men. But not so in countries which never developed specialized groups of craftsmen and traders but passed directly from the stage of family production for subsistence to the purchase of imported products from foreign tradesmen. In such countries, women continue to be independent producers, and large numbers of women earn their living by crafts, trade, and services. In many countries in Africa, Southeast Asia, and Latin America, the number of women working as independent producers is much higher than the number of female wage earners. By contrast, in Europe and other countries with an older urban tradition, there are few women among independent producers and large numbers among the wage and salary earners.

From Family Education to Vocational Training

The transfer of production from the home to specialized premises is not the only explanation for the change in women's status in the labor market by which they became the subordinates of male supervisors. Another factor explaining the deterioration of the female role in the labor market is the inferior position of girls and young women in the educational system in general, and especially in the vocational training system.

School education is prestigious in all countries where only a part of the population is literate. It is, therefore, a serious handicap to women that they have less school education than men. In those income groups where more boys than girls go to school, the boy comes to look down upon the girl who stays at home under the instruction of her illiterate mother, while the boy enjoys the prestige of being an "educated" person. In the old times when neither boys nor girls went to school, ignorance and superstition was a characteristic of both sexes, and the girls had less reason to feel inferior.

School teaches the pupils more than to read and write. It also teaches how to organize one's thinking and how to express one's ideas clearly and logically. Persons who have been to school have an advantage in a discussion over persons who have not been to school, just as a person with many years of schooling has an advantage in oral disputes over persons who dropped out of school at an early stage. Since the average girl goes to school for a shorter span of years than the average boy, and since more girls than boys never go to school, the school system contributes to creating and upholding the idea that men are spiritually and intellectually superior to women. This in turn makes women inclined to accept being treated as inferior in the labor market, even in cases where the vocational qualifications of men and women are similar. It thus becomes acceptable to women and natural to men that the latter should hold the supervisory and well-paid jobs and the former the jobs as assistants at low pay.

In communities where girls receive an education and training which makes them feel inferior to men in the labor market, it is inevitable that young women who enter the labor market will suffer from a deep feeling of insecurity and insufficiency. It is not surprising, therefore, that they seek security by sticking to jobs and occupations traditionally regarded as female, while only a small minority want to enter into open competition with men in the fields considered unsuitable or at least unusual for women. Therefore, the crowding of women in certain occupations would seem to be primarily due to their own desire to be employed in supposedly feminine professions, while men's wariness of accepting women in the masculine occupations may be a less important factor.

When women feel that they are inferior to men in the traditional male occupations, they are inclined to seek compensation by claiming special competence and superiority to men in a small number of occupations, which are related to the traditional female role. The teaching of children in primary schools is an important example of this. In some countries in Europe, primary schools prefer to have children taught by persons of both sexes, while in other countries, mainly America, the agreed assumption is that by nature women are better teachers for young children than men. This prejudice against men as teachers at preschool and primary levels is likely to have the effect that teaching at these levels attracts many able women but few able men. And this skewed selection of applicants, in turn, provides a spurious confirmation of the prejudice. This kind of selection in special fields, combined with better vocational training of men than of women and a basic belief in male superiority in the labor market, must inevitably reinforce the conviction about the innate differences in the abilities of the two sexes.

The gap in formal school education between boys and girls is now narrowing in most countries. But in the field of vocational training, the gap appears to be widening, since more and more young men receive vocational training in school and on the job, while few girls in developing countries get any vocational training, except for the small numbers who attend a university. A vicious circle is developing: ordinary girls are supposed to need no special training because they are thought to be eligible only for jobs which require little qualification; and without any vocational training, they can take only jobs which require no particular qualifications.

In many cases, young women attempt to escape from this vicious circle by keeping away from the labor market and doing only domestic work in their own home. The result is a perpetuation of the traditional pattern of one-earner, poor families with many children instead of the desired shift to a pattern of two-earner, less poor families with few children.

The absence of female vocational training is both an effect and a cause of high birth rates. The increase of the labor force resulting from high birth rates detracts from their competitive position in the labor market. And untrained women marry earlier and have more children than vocationally trained and working women. This vicious circle cannot be broken by a retreat of women from training and work, but only by speeding up economic development, so that both male and female youth can be absorbed into the labor market.

[1990]

Population, the Status of Women, and Rural Development

MAJOR INCREASES IN population modify the man-land ratio, facilitate specialization and communication, and provide other economies of scale. Whether the impact of these changes on rural development is positive or negative, and the likely feedback effects on demographic trends, depend in the first instance on macroeconomic factors, notably including government policy. But, microeconomic factors enter the picture as well. This essay deals with one of these microeconomic factors, namely the subordinate status of rural women as compared with men of the same age and social group. I consider how women's status varies under three types of family organization and land tenure arrangements prevalent in rural areas, and argue that the response of rural populations to economic and demographic change is more or less flexible depending on the type of family organization.

The status of women varies between rural communities and sometimes between families in the same village. The roles of women are also strikingly different. Christine Oppong (1980) distinguishes between seven roles that compete for women's time and energy, but here I shall focus only on those that are most relevant to my subject.

Of course, it is impossible to discuss the multitude of local patterns in a brief review. Nevertheless, family organization and the status of women are related to the agricultural system, which in turn is related to population density and technological levels. Therefore, it is possible to simplify the analysis by distinguishing between a few major patterns of interrelationships between population, status of women, and rural development that together describe most rural communities in the Third World.

The Conflict between Motherhood and Work

Rural communities at low levels of economic development usually have high levels of fertility. Young children can substitute for adults in many forms

"Population, the Status of Women, and Rural Development." Reprinted with permission from Population and Rural Development: Institutions and Policy, edited by Geoffrey McNicoll and Mead Cain. New York: The Population Council, 1990. A supplement to Population and Development Review, vol. 15. © 1990 The Population Council.

of agricultural and domestic work, including child care, animal husbandry, and gathering and transport of food and fuel wood. Therefore, children are likely to contribute more to family production of goods and services than they consume, at least if they are not sent to school.

Moreover, child mortality continues to be high in rural areas of most Third World countries in spite of the spread of modern medicine and improvements in sanitation. In the recent past, mortality was often so high that many families had few surviving children in spite of high fertility, and many women died before the end of their childbearing years. In regions with low levels of economic development, a sufficient reproduction of the population was a condition of survival both of the parents and of the community. The young generation had to support their elders, and in communities where the maintenance of law and order was left largely to members of the family or the village, adult sons had to defend family and village against enemies.

Until recent times, the need for defense against enemies motivated not only parents, but also governments, local and national, to be pronatalist. The social pressure on parents to maximize family size was bolstered by granting a high status to fathers and mothers of large families, and a low status to the unmarried and infertile, especially women. Under these circumstances, family organization was based on the institution of early and universal marriage for girls, with men tending to divorce or abandon infertile and subfecund women.

Families were organized as autocratic age-sex hierarchies. Younger family members owed obedience to older persons, and the oldest man in the family was the decision maker. In daily life, men and women could dispose of the labor power of younger members of their own sex according to the customary distribution of labor, but when a change in the distribution of labor became necessary—because of changes in the method of production or in the availability of resources, for example—the family head decided on the new distribution of labor. By assigning as much work as possible to women and younger family members, he could increase family income while reducing his own work burden.

Either custom or the marriage contract stipulated that the wife must do the work that was needed to serve male family members and children. This obligation included not only child care and domestic duties, but also carrying water, gathering fuel, and often caring for domestic animals and processing crops. In most rural communities, women were obliged to work in the fields, and in some communities women and children did nearly all the agricultural work.

Frequent pregnancies and prolonged breast-feeding tax a woman's health. If a woman married early and spent the entire period between puberty and menopause being either pregnant or breast-feeding, and if she also worked hard at multiple tasks in the household and in agriculture, the strain on her health was heavy. Maternal and infant morbidity and mortality and the frequency of involuntary abortion were attributable to or aggravated by such patterns of childbearing and work. Thus, a conflict existed between the family's interest in a large number of surviving children and the family head's interest in obtaining as much work as possible from the adult women.

Rural societies have dealt with this problem in a variety of ways. One is spacing of births, another is polygyny, and a third is customary strictures on women's work in agriculture.

In communities where modern contraception is not practiced, a family can prolong the period in which the wife can recover strength between the end of breast-feeding and the onset of a new pregnancy by abstinence or other traditional means of fertility restriction. Traditionally, most African societies had enforced periods of abstinence after each birth, and in many parts of India women moved back to their parents' household after childbirth.

The custom of marital abstinence after childbirth provides an inducement to polygyny. Moreover, the conflict between motherhood and work is attenuated when a number of wives share the burden of serving the husband and performing tasks related to domestic duties, child care, and agricultural labor. In sparsely populated regions with free access to cultivation of common land, polygyny is highly advantageous to the family head, because he can combine large family size with a negligible work burden, all the work being done by his wives and children. Where market access is available for surplus products, he can expand the area under cultivation in step with the increase in the family labor force and become rich by means of unpaid family labor. In other words, polygyny is a means to create family wealth in regions without land shortage and without the availability of labor for hire. A likely outcome for the society as a whole is increased income inequality.

The sexual division of labor is different in rural areas where increasing population density has led to the replacement of long-fallow production on common land with more intensive systems of agriculture using animal draft power. The use of animals for land preparation and transport is always a male monopoly. Men perform the operations for which animals are employed, while women and children perform some or all of the tasks for which only human muscle power is used. In this system of agriculture, women and children contribute a smaller share of total agricultural work and animals and men a larger one. Moreover, since additional land can be obtained only by purchase, if at all, women's agricultural work is less of an economic asset than under common land tenure. There is less economic motivation for polygyny, which at most is practiced only by a small number of rich men.

In many rural communities, men exercise control over women to such an extent that they prevent them from working outside the home. Women who do no work in the fields can devote all their time to child care, domestic work, and other activities that can be performed in or close to the home. With this type of family organization, as well, only a small minority of rich men can afford to be polygynous.

The interrelationship between demographic and economic change differs in these various rural settings. The sections that follow describe the relationship between population change, female status, and rural development under each of the three basic patterns of rural organization: first, men

and women farming common land; second, men farming with women assisting on private land; and third, men farming while women remain secluded.
The last section deals with the interrelationship between the status of wom-
en and economic and social services available in rural areas.

Men and Women Farming Common Land

In regions where land is held in common, a large increase in the local
population results in a major expansion in the cultivated area. If market
access is available for cash crops, a share of the increase in the rural labor force
will be absorbed in expanding production of cash crops for urban use or for
export. Since men have the right of decision, they leave the production of food
crops for family consumption to the women and devote their own labor to
cash-crop production. When women are obliged to feed men and children,
men can earn money by cash cropping or wage labor. Thus, the first pattern is
characterized by a division of labor, with men as producers of cash crops and
women as producers of subsistence crops.

Although cash crops are produced mainly by men, who in turn reap the
income from sales, men in most cases require their female family members
and children to do some of the manual work in production and processing.
Many cash crops are produced with the help of large amounts of family labor
provided by women and children. Even in cases where women do all the work
on a cash crop, men often sell the crop and pocket the income or oblige the
women to hand over the money to them.

This organization of family labor, in which male farmers require women
and children to do a large share of the work without pay, provides a strong
inducement to the expansion of commercial agriculture, but it is a handicap
to the production of food crops. When the population in a village increases,
some of the surrounding pasture and other uncultivated land are brought
under cultivation. The men appropriate the best land for their cash crops,
while the women's food crops must be grown on poorer land or land at a
greater distance from the village. As the cultivated area is expanded, fuel,
wild food, and fodder must be gathered further away from the village. All the
additional work is usually the responsibility of women and children. In these
circumstances women may be unable to produce enough food for the family;
either the diet deteriorates or imported food is purchased.

Men are unlikely to fill the gap in food production, because this low-
status activity is women's work and depends on primitive techniques, which
the men avoid using whenever possible. Thus, the unequal burden of family
labor contributes to the shift from subsistence production to commercialized
agriculture and to increased dependency on imported food. Although the
main cause of this shift to cash-crop production for export is the distortion of
world market prices, due to the farm support policies in the industrialized
countries, the subordinate status of women in the exporting countries also
contributes to the change in the production pattern.

As population growth and increases in cash-crop production make good land scarce, some family heads migrate to find wage labor on plantations or large farms or in urban areas, leaving the women behind to support the rest of the family. In many villages, such deserted wives account for a large share of the agricultural population. A low-status group without male support, female heads of households are usually discriminated against in access to land, agricultural inputs, and credit. The female-headed families become a village proletariat with too few resources to produce sufficient food.

Growing population density and increasing cash-crop production cause a gradual change from common land tenure to private ownership of land. Men who plant trees or intensive cash crops on common land are likely to register this land as their property as the amount of uncultivated land in the area is reduced. When the reduction in uncultivated land shortens fallow periods, a family cultivating the same piece of land with only short interruptions comes to consider the land their own, even when no formal registration of property is undertaken. With few exceptions, privatization of land leads to a deterioration in the status of rural women. Under the system of common tenure, both male and female community members had the right to use the land for cultivation either by simply farming it or by having it assigned to them by the village chief. But only in exceptional cases is land registered as the property of female cultivators. The right of ownership becomes vested in the husband, as head of the family.

As mentioned earlier, common land tenure encourages large family size, because women and children represent free labor; the more of them a man has, the more land his family can cultivate. This advantage disappears, of course, when women lose their cultivation rights through privatization. A larger family no longer confers a right to additional land. Moreover, a private landowner can mortgage or sell land to weather emergencies and support his old age, while cultivators of common land have no such recourse, but must rely on help from adult children. Thus, private tenure provides less inducement to large family size than does common tenure.

However, if privatization makes men less dependent on help from adult children, it renders women more dependent on both adult children and spouses. This has wide implications, especially for women who live under the marriage systems that are traditional in Africa. Most African men have no legal obligation to support a wife and children, even while the marriage lasts, and they are free to terminate the marriage at will. The age difference between spouses is large—around eight years in first marriages and much greater when a married man takes additional wives. In a family system based on the principle of an autocratic age-sex hierarchy, a large age difference implies a low status for the wife, especially the youngest wife. A wife's lack of adult status makes her extremely vulnerable, particularly if the husband exercises his right to abandon her.

Because men are the decision makers, African societies tend to make progress in modernization through routes such as privatization of land, where men win and women lose, but they avoid forms of modernization that would be to the advantage of women—as demonstrated by the nearly total failure to modernize family legislation. Thus, rural African women are more than ever dependent upon adult children for help in old age and in case of abandonment by the husband. For such women, voluntary restriction of fertility is a risky affair, given the persistence of high child mortality and widespread subfecundity in many regions (the latter due to a variety of sexually transmitted diseases).

Men Farming with Women Assisting on Private Land

The second pattern of rural organization is one of private property in land and use of animal draft power. The male family head and other male workers use the animals, while female family members perform some or all of the operations for which only human muscle power is used. In communities of this type, the main means of accommodating population increase is by intensification of agriculture. Continued population increase in an area with no unutilized land leads to reduction in farm size with subdivision among heirs, and the smaller farm size leads to intensification of land use. High-yielding crops are introduced, and short-fallow agriculture is replaced by annual cropping. When this reduces the area available for pasture, fodder crops may be introduced in the rotation. In the most densely populated areas, annual cropping may be replaced by multicropping.

When extensive systems of agriculture are applied and animals gather their own feed, most of the work is concentrated in the sowing and harvesting seasons, with long periods in between without any work in the fields. Women's participation is limited to the relatively short peak seasons. But, when population growth results in intensification of agriculture, many traditional operations require more labor, and additional operations that were unnecessary with more extensive production must be introduced in order to obtain high yields or to avoid declines in yields and damage to the land.

When both cultivation and animal husbandry become intensive, many operations must be performed in the dry season, and the growing season may be prolonged by means of irrigation and by cultivation of crops with overlapping growing seasons. Much of the additional work involves hand operations of the type usually done by women, so that women perform agricultural work for a much longer part of the year. Many of the female operations, like weeding and transplanting rice to permit multicropping, are onerous, highly labor-intensive tasks. When intensification results in high crop yields, the work involved in harvesting and processing of crops increases. Usually, women are obliged to do all the additional work.

When infant and child mortality declines, more children survive to an age at which they can produce more than they consume. If children do not attend school, the male head of the household can freely deploy the labor force of several family members and reap considerable benefit from labor-intensive agricultural production with relatively little additional work on his part. The extensive use of women and children for the additional operations required by labor-intensive production provides a greater inducement to intensification than would be the case if the adult male labor force had to do all the additional work or to hire agricultural workers.

If the availability of female family labor promotes labor intensification of agriculture, it also retards industrial inputs. In some cases, the potential for increasing yields and speeding up seasonal operations that such inputs offer makes them economical, notwithstanding the availability of unpaid female family labor. But in other cases, such changes are prevented or delayed because wives and children work without pay.

Use of mechanized equipment is a status symbol reserved for males. When tools and other techniques are upgraded, female labor is systematically replaced by male labor. The application of chemical inputs is considered high-status work reserved for men. This helps to explain why chemicals are used mainly on cash crops, although such inputs would also raise the yields of subsistence crops, thus saving both land and female labor.

The Green Revolution in Asia combined labor-intensive and modern inputs. Chemical inputs raised crop yields, and tractors speeded up the operations to allow multicropping; but once Green Revolution techniques were introduced in rice farming areas, women had to do much more hand weeding and transplanting. The availability of female family labor may help to explain why herbicides were little used while hand weeding was extensively employed in many regions. In their choice of techniques, the decision makers, be they male farmers or male agricultural experts and advisors, take little account of the disutility of backbreaking work for the women in the family, and the women themselves have no say in the choice of technique.

Use of tractors, pumps, and other machinery is spreading rapidly in many developing countries. As soon as an operation becomes mechanized, men take over, while women continue to use only hand tools. Examples of this abound in the development literature. In Korea, even transplanting, once exclusively performed by females, became a male operation with the introduction of a rice planting tractor. A man drives the tractor, while women follow after and hand plant seedlings. In other agricultural tasks, the same trend is seen: with the introduction of hand tractors and threshing machines, women became assistants to the male operators. Their work burden was not necessarily reduced by this type of mechanization; it even increased in some cases, because the machine could cover a much larger area than could the old techniques.

In villages where land is held privately, those with small holdings and the landless work for large landholders in the peak seasons. Female family members of these laborers also often work for wages in the peak seasons, still performing traditional female jobs. Because of their inferior status, traditional female jobs command much lower wages than traditional male jobs, although the former are often the most unpleasant.

As mentioned above, when population increase leads to intensification of agriculture, the demand for additional female labor is large. The same is true for diversification of the cropping pattern, because most secondary crops rely on hand labor while the basic crops use animal-drawn or mechanized equipment, at least for some operations. Low female wages help to make labor-intensive crops profitable even on larger farms, but since the small farms have access to unpaid female family labor, while large farms must pay for their marginal labor, small farms are usually more intensively cultivated and have a more diversified cropping pattern. Specialization in labor-intensive crops helps the small farms to survive the competition from larger farms. Female family members on small farms are usually prevented by male heads from accepting employment as wage labor on large farms.

When farms are subdivided among heirs, some small farmers survive on reduced landholdings by intensification of land use, while others change from full-time to part-time farming supplemented by wage labor on larger farms. Increasing pressure on agricultural land can lead to land concentration. Larger farmers or persons in nonagricultural occupations buy up small farms, and the former owners become full-time wage laborers. These alternative responses to the problem of increasing man-land ratios have different effects upon demographic trends, because the attitudes of landowning farmers and full-time agricultural workers toward family size are likely to differ.

As mentioned in the previous section, privatization of land weakens motivations for large family size because land ownership provides security against destitution in old age and emergencies, thus making the landowner less dependent on help from adult children. Moreover, if a family has too many male heirs, it risks losing status through subdivision or sale of the farm. Therefore, in communities where landownership is long established, attitudes toward family size are likely to differ from those in communities that have—or until recently had—common land tenure. Among landowning farmers, the parents of a large family are held in high esteem only if the landholding is large enough to support the family. There is evidence in many societies of customary family limitation among landowning farmers, the means ranging from late marriage, celibacy, and prohibition of remarriage of widows to induced abortion and infanticide. Voluntary family planning programs in rural areas are most successful in such societies.

The increasing incomes and monetization in rural areas during the spread of Green Revolution technologies in recent decades permitted a growing share of the population to count on property income and access to credit as security, instead of relying on help from adult children. In Japan, the decline of family size accompanied very high rates of private saving. Where private landownership is the norm, marriages typically are more stable and the wife's right to support from her husband is better secured by legislation than is the case where land is commonly held. In these circumstances, fathers assume greater responsibility for their families, and both men and women are more inclined to practice contraception.

Agricultural workers have less motivation for fertility limitation than landowners in the same community: workers experience higher child mortality; having no property and less access to credit, they are much more dependent upon adult children as economic support; and they command more help from young children, who rarely go to school. Children of agricultural workers help their parents both by engaging in wage labor for land-owning farmers and by assisting in subsistence farming. If population growth results in increasing landlessness, this may retard the fertility decline, unless the harder labor performed by wives substantially increases the number of involuntary abortions.

The relative numbers of landowning farmers and landless workers vary widely among developing countries. In most of Latin America, the share of landless or nearly landless workers in the rural population is high; in most Asian countries it is much lower. This may help to explain why rural fertility is lower in Asia than in Latin America. Another feature that may help to explain the slow pace of fertility decline in much of rural Latin America is the marriage system. Most lower class Latin American women, like African women, live in unstable marriages, and many of them cannot count on much, if any, support from the fathers of their children. Therefore, they must rely on their young children for income support and on adult children for old-age support. Men who feel no obligation to support either their children or the mothers of these children lack motivation to practice contraception, and most rural women in Latin America have recourse to no better means of fertility control than illegally induced abortion.

Men Farming while Women Remain Secluded

The main purpose of the seclusion of women, or purdah, is to ensure the fidelity of wives and the chastity of daughters and other unmarried women. But this institution is also a radical means of giving priority to motherhood over field work by women. Women who avoid outdoor activities devote their time to child care, domestic work, processing of crops, care of stabled animals, and home crafts. When women are secluded, small farms forgo free labor in the fields—a serious impediment to intensification of agriculture and diversification of the cropping pattern. Agricultural production is usually less intensive in regions without a supply of female labor than in regions with similar conditions in which women do participate in field work. Moreover, where female seclusion is practiced, farmers plant mainly crops that use animal draft power, avoiding crops that require the manual labor performed only by women.

When population in a densely settled rural region increases without concomitant intensification of agriculture, the population becomes poorer in the absence of employment opportunities for men on large farms, in rural industries, or through migration. Bangladesh is one such region with severe restrictions on female labor force participation. In spite of the very high population density, agriculture is less intensive in Bangladesh than in many other parts of Asia. There is more broadcasting and less transplanting of rice, and the cropping pattern is little diversified, being concentrated on rice and jute. Rural poverty is extreme, and the country is heavily dependent upon food imports. India also has regions where the cultivator's wife and other female relatives do not participate in outdoor work. But where these are multiethnic communities, the negative effects of lack of female family labor are less severe. Women from landless families belonging to an ethnic group in which both men and women do field work find employment as day laborers for the cultivator families with secluded women.

When women only work indoors, there is little motivation to introduce changes to raise their labor productivity. Food preparation and crop processing are done with primitive equipment and highly labor-intensive methods. Women continue to make clothing and other household items even after the region has reached a stage of development at which such activities are usually replaced by purchases. In some cases, women in seclusion add to family incomes by engaging in domestic production of, for instance, textile or tobacco products, which are sold in the market by male family members or children. Or such women perform services like handweaving or sewing for customers. But, if seclusion is widely prevalent in a region, there will be an oversupply of such products and services. Extremely low prices will yield derisory hourly pay, and women's work will contribute little to family income, even though they work exceedingly long hours.

A more profitable solution, much used in rural communities where women are secluded, is for men to migrate to seek work. If the husband migrates and leaves a secluded wife and children behind, he appoints another male family member as guardian for the wife and sends remittances to support the family. Under seclusion, family organization is highly autocratic and the age hierarchy is pronounced. The status of the wife usually deteriorates, and she is subjected to even stricter supervision when she is left under the charge of other family members instead of her own husband.

Owners of larger farms can in theory compensate for the lack of female family labor by recruiting male wage labor to do the work done by women in other regions. But in fact, men are often unwilling to do these jobs. Men not only support their higher status by monopolizing the use of mechanized equipment; they also defend their status by refusing to do jobs that are usually performed by women. Here again, multiethnic societies may provide a solution. In some regions of India, male wage workers belonging to ethnic minority groups perform the hand weeding that neither the men nor the secluded women from the landowning majority groups will do.

Men who perform work that is also done by women receive substantially higher wages than the women. The large differences between male and female wages arise from the higher status of men rather than from lower female productivity: it is generally agreed that for many operations, such as transplanting and cotton plucking, female labor is more efficient than male. In communities where seclusion is practiced, a competitive labor market between the sexes, which equalizes male and female wages, appears only under particularly acute shortages of labor. Statistics from North India and Egypt reveal that when female labor is crucial for agricultural operations, yet scarce because of widespread seclusion, female wages may be equal to male wages. Because the higher male earnings are status wages and not efficiency wages, female seclusion is a handicap to intensification and diversification of production, not only on small farms relying on family labor but also on large farms relying on wage labor.

When women are secluded, girls are considered an economic burden, because dowries tend to be high and adult daughters cannot provide economic assistance to their parents. Therefore, in communities with restrictive attitudes to use of female labor, preference for sons is strong and in many cases girls are neglected by their parents. Poor nutrition and health care for girls, if not open infanticide, limit family size.

In communities where prejudices concerning women's work are strong, women must rely either on property income or on help from adult sons or other male family members in case of divorce and widowhood. Because of son preference, the risk of divorce is larger, the fewer living sons a woman has. Moreover, the earlier a woman begins childbearing, the more likely she is to have a son old enough to support her in case of widowhood or divorce. So, both parents and daughters have an interest in early marriage. Age differences between spouses are large, thus increasing the risk of early widowhood. School attendance is low for girls in such settings. When women are allowed to work only in the house, education is a luxury that only rich parents may choose for family prestige.

For these reasons, there has usually been little if any decline in rural fertility in those Arab and Asian countries in which the secluded wife continues to be the ideal.

Status of Women and Access to Rural Services

The extent to which national and local governments provide services to rural areas varies widely between and within countries. Some governments supply mainly health and educational services; others make large investments in rural transport and communications, large-scale water control, and major land improvement schemes. Some governments have established extensive networks of agricultural services, including research, training, and extension facilities. Of course, agricultural development is much more successful where government investment is higher, with the result that private services and private investment in ancillary rural crafts and industries are also larger in these areas.

Rural women benefit indirectly from agricultural investments and services because of improved family incomes, but the direct benefits of the research, training, and extension facilities have virtually all accrued to men. In this field, as in many others, the lower status of women has been the main cause of the uneven distribution of resources. Male extension agents address themselves only to male heads of households; neither female producers nor female family workers benefit from their advice. Research activities focus on the cash crops produced by men; the secondary crops and subsistence food produced by women are neglected. Finally, trainees have virtually all been men.

The passing on of skills from parents to children is an important part of agricultural training in most developing countries, but when women are bypassed by the extension agents and the recruiters to training courses, they have no knowledge of modern methods to pass on to their daughters, while the sons learn readily from their fathers. Everywhere, the male status in agriculture is enhanced by reserving formal training for men and male youth; women are refused access, or only a token number are admitted. In many countries, agricultural work has little prestige among young men, and attendance at agricultural schools and courses is often low. In spite of this, the concern for male status among local personnel and foreign advisors prevents women from obtaining agricultural training, even in countries where they do most of the agricultural work. Where courses for rural women exist, they provide instruction in health, nutrition, family planning, and domestic skills, not in agricultural or other income-earning skills.

The exclusion of women from agricultural training and extension has been discussed and lamented at numerous international conferences and meetings. As a result, some national governments and multinational and bilateral donors have set up rural projects aimed at better integration of women in agricultural modernization. Some of these projects have been directed at "women only"; others have been "general" projects meant to take special account of women. Some projects have been sabotaged by local communities or by governments or donors. In other cases, there has been no open resistance, but women have hardly benefited. Few "women only" projects have been outstandingly successful, and in most of the "general" projects the benefits accrued mainly to men.

It is difficult to avoid the conclusion that these projects failed either because the male decision makers were convinced that women were unable to learn, or because they wanted to preserve the gap in status and prestige between men and women. The projects were unable to stem the general trend toward a widening distance between male and female agricultural qualifications, resulting from the sex discrimination in training in modern methods and in access to modern equipment and other inputs. It seems that general improvement in female status by means of political action, legal reform of family organization, and female education are preconditions for substantial changes in women's position in the agricultural sector.

If women have reaped few benefits from agricultural services, the situation is quite different with respect to social services. The most important improvement in the lives of rural women was the decline in maternal and child mortality resulting from the spread of medical and sanitation services. The physical and psychological strain on women is reduced when they produce fewer children for the graveyard. Also, access to modern means of birth control in rural areas of many developing countries reduces the strain of frequent motherhood and of induced abortion.

Health improvements and mortality decline for women and girls have been large nearly everywhere, and girls' use of educational services has increased rapidly. In some countries, boys still represent a large majority of students at rural schools, but the gap between the rates of school attendance for boys and girls has been narrowing everywhere. In regions where women do much of the agricultural work, however, they pay a high price in terms of labor input forgone for the education of their children, especially girls.

Many African mothers have been willing to forgo help from their school-age daughters and to pay their school fees in order to improve the girls' future earnings. Under the optimism prevailing in Africa in the period immediately following independence, parents did not view a large family and education of children as incompatible. Only later did economic crisis radically change the prospects for the growing numbers of educated young people. It remains to be seen whether the shortage of jobs for the educated will influence the attitude of rural parents toward education or toward fertility control.

As a result of the rapid spread of education, age-power relations between women are changing. Illiterate mothers and mothers-in-law have less authority over literate daughters and daughters-in-law than they did over illiterate ones. But it is uncertain to what extent increasing school attendance of girls contributes to greater equality between the sexes. Most of the development literature concerning female education focuses on the quantitative aspects: how many girls go to school, and for how many years? It is tacitly assumed that school attendance helps to improve women's status whatever the ideological content of the curriculum. But indoctrination in national culture is usually an important element in the curriculum of rural schools, and if the principle of female inferiority is an important feature of the national culture, the influence of school attendance on the attitudes of boys and girls to the status of women is not what might be hoped for. Young women may be more inclined to use their educated status to justify withdrawing from agricultural work than to compete with educated young men for more prestigious employment on farms or in rural services. And women who want to improve their position may be more inclined to migrate to towns than to face the rural community's opposition to changes in the status of women.

The occupational choice of female rural school leavers depends not only on the national ideology but also on the opportunities for female non-agricultural employment in rural areas. Development of rural services and small-scale industries provides possibilities for accommodating a large family on a small landholding. In parts of Asia, many girls add to family income by means of nonagricultural work in rural areas. They earn money to pay their own dowry, and this may give them more say in the choice of a marriage partner as well as contribute to a rise in the age at marriage, thus reducing fertility.

Conclusion

Autocratic methods of family organization, with men as decision makers and women obliged to obey them, promote adaptation to population growth by labor-intensive methods, and they help small farms to survive the competition with large farms that must pay for their marginal labor supply. The exception is regions in which women are prevented from working in agriculture for status reasons. In these regions, the need to pay male wages for marginal labor provides a disincentive for agricultural intensification. The subsistence crops that are grown by women are likely to be neglected in efforts to improve productivity, with serious effects on nutrition and family welfare in many countries.

Because women in most underdeveloped rural settings are forbidden to use mechanized equipment and other modern inputs, low (or zero) female wages for labor-intensive operations compete with much higher wages for male use of modern inputs, and the resulting distortion of cost calculations is a deterrent to agricultural modernization. Under these conditions, agricultural work has even less attraction for female than for male school leavers, and the former are likely either to migrate to towns, to become housewives without agricultural work, or, in areas where there are such opportunities, to seek local employment in service or processing industries. The incentives to male migration are strongest in areas where women are secluded and where women produce the family food without male help.

The subordinate status of women is conducive to large family size. Women's dependence upon the good will of their husbands and older family members makes them hesitant to practice contraception, and, because their opportunities for self-support in case of divorce and widowhood are limited by labor market restrictions and wage discrimination, they run a great risk of becoming dependent upon help from their children. However, when rural development raises men's interest in family limitation, the inferior status of women may actually serve to reduce fertility, because it is usually the husband who decides on family size.

[1987]

Inequality between the Sexes

ECONOMIC THEORY CONCERNING inequality between the sexes focuses upon inequality in wages, job recruitment, and promotion and dismissal for women and men with similar qualifications and availability. Neoclassical theory explains these inequalities as a result of free and rational choice, based upon the biological differences between the sexes. According to Becker (1981), women's role in reproduction makes it rational for women to specialize more in family skills and men more in labor market skills, and parents make a rational choice for their children by preparing them for different careers. When women's reproductive role is reduced due to the decline in birth rates, women's availability for the labor market increases, and they begin to invest more in labor market skills than is the case in countries with continued high fertility. So sex-related differences in level and types of human investment and availability provide the explanation for the differences in wages, types of work, and promotion.

By focusing upon the biological differences between the sexes, neoclassical theory selects the features which distinguish inequality between sexes from inequality between other discriminated groups, that is the young versus the old, or foreigners versus members of the dominant ethnic or national group. All these inequalities have been characteristic features of human societies since prehistoric times. The basic principle in the organization of societies is that only members of the superior group have adult status or civic rights, while the members of the inferior groups depend upon the benevolence of the "adults." In most societies, economic and social development have reduced these inequalities, but nowhere have they been completely eliminated, and the traditional power of the superior male group over the inferior female group cannot be ignored in the economic analysis of inequality between sexes. The power of the male group over the female one is supported by access to the best technology and a monopoly in learning how to use it (E. Boserup, 1970a). Men's monopoly in the use of weapons, superior hunting equipment, and animal-drawn agricultural equipment is of ancient origin. But even in societies where men have shifted to tractors and other

---

"Inequality between the Sexes." Reprinted with permission from *The New Palgrave: A Dictionary of Economics*, edited by John Eatwell, Murray Milgate, and Peter Newman. London: Macmillan Press, New York: Stockton Press, 1987.

industrial inputs, women often continue to use primitive hand tools for the operations assigned to them, and even in modern mechanized industries, men distribute the tasks and assign the unskilled, routine operations to the female workers.

In primitive subsistence economies, woman's reproductive role does not prevent her being assigned the most onerous tasks with incessant daily toil, and if the mother's work prevents her from taking care of young children, these are cared for by older sisters or other members of the group. At a later stage of development, when specialization of labor leads to the transfer of an increasing share of the labor power of the family to outside work, the reproductive role of women contributes to explaining why more women than men continue to work in the family and for the family, either as unpaid family members or as domestic servants. However, due to their superior status, men have the right to dispose of money incomes earned by female family members within or outside the family enterprise. There may be regional and local differences in women's status, but in most traditional societies women cannot dispose of money or undertake monetary transactions, accept employment or move away from the locality where they live and work, without the permission of a male guardian who decides all these matters, as well as family matters, like marriage, divorce, and the fate of the children. The right to take part in decisions on public matters is reserved for members of the male sex.

Gradually, as technological development transfers an increasing number of products and services from family production to production in specialized enterprises and institutions, private or public, there is no need for the full labor power of all female family members in the household. Through the same process, the family economy becomes more and more dependent upon money income to purchase the products and services which the family no longer produces, and to pay the taxes which finance the growing public sector. As a result, increasing numbers of women become money earners. At this stage, women's inability to engage independently in economic and other transactions and their lack of responsibility become handicaps not only to themselves but also to their employers, creditors, customers, and guardians, as well as to public authorities and male family members, who must support them if they are unable to support themselves.

In some European countries, "market women," often middle-aged women with dependents, attained adult status many centuries ago. Later, when it became customary for young women to work for wages before their marriage and for other single, divorced, and widowed women to support themselves and their dependents by wage labor or by self-employment, these categories of women were granted adult status in economic affairs; but married women continued to be denied adult status. In most industrialized countries, married women first attained adult status when further reduction of the domestic sector, together with the decline of birth rates, radically increased their participation in the labor market and made their work in the labor market an important part of the national economy. In most developing countries, women, whether married or not, are still denied adult status in economic affairs; in some countries, it severely limits their labor market participation; in other cases, it limits their business activities.

Human capital investment in market skills becomes more and more important with economic and social development, while investment in family skills loses in importance when more and more activities are transferred from the family setting to private enterprises or public institutions. When the responsibility for physical protection is transferred from the family to the government, and formal education is introduced, educational level may replace the ability to use weapons as a status symbol for male youth. The priority given to boys over girls in formal education is not only a result of their larger labor market participation, as suggested by Becker, but also a means to preserve a higher male status, by letting men reach higher educational levels than women.

The status of parents may require that their daughters be educated as well, but that boys should not lose status by receiving less schooling than their sisters, while to preserve the superior status of the husband, the wife must not be more educated than he is. Universities were long closed to women, and in many countries the difficulties of obtaining marriage partners for educated women make both parents and daughters afraid of continuing their education. The low marriage age for girls, another means to preserve male status in the family, may also prevent continuation of the education of girls. The differences between the sexes in educational levels serve to reinforce inequality not only in the family but also in the labor market. With economic development, the difference becomes limited to the highest educational levels, but it has not disappeared even in countries with very high and uninterrupted female labor force participation.

Usually, differences in access to technical training for girls are much larger than differences in access to formal education. From the day women began to work for wages in urban activities, men have insisted on their priority right to skilled, supervisory, and other better paid work. Both in guilds, and later in industries and public service, men became apprentices and skilled workers, while women remained assistants to the male workers, unskilled or semiskilled, working under male supervision. In most cases, male trade unions continued the fight of the guild members against rights for women to training, and even to membership in the organization and the right to work in the trade. The inferior position of women was defended by the short stay in the labor market of young women before they married, with no account taken of the large number of spinsters, poor married women, and female heads of households who were permanent members of the labor force both in European and in many non-European countries.

In addition to the lower position of women in the job hierarchy, female wage rates are usually much lower than male wage rates for similar work. Only in periods of great shortage of labor, for instance in wartime or in agricultural peak seasons, may female wages temporarily rise to the level of male wages. The fact that these wage differences are related to sex and not to the burden of dependency belies the usual explanation for them. They are a result of the principle of male superiority, and neoclassical theory has helped to make the principle acceptable. Since the theory assumes that differentials in wages equal differentials in marginal productivity of labor, the lower wage rates for women could be taken as a confirmation of the general assumption of female inferiority, which also applied to women as workers.

The superior status of men is supported when women doing similar work get lower wages; when a wife is prevented from earning as much as her husband, he preserves his superior status as principal breadwinner, even if he is too poor to enjoy the even higher status of being the only breadwinner in the family. Training girls in low-wage occupations and discriminating against women in recruitment for on-the-job training or access to learning-by-doing supervisory work reduce the risk that male staff will lose status by being supervised by women.

When employers in private enterprises and public service pay males higher wages than females for similar work, they include the higher male wages in their production costs, even if that reduces the demand for products made primarily by male labor. If an enterprise or a trade has difficulties in competing due to the payment of high male wages, employers will not reduce the wage differential, but will instead try to get the workers and the trade unions to accept the recruitment, or additional recruitment, of women. If they succeed, the trade will become less attractive to men, and the labor force will gradually become female, as has happened to many trades in which trade unions were weak. The separation of the labor market into masculine and feminine trades and jobs becomes even more pronounced if the principle of equal pay for equal work is introduced by law or labor contract, since sex specialization makes it more difficult to prove that the work paid at different rates is "equal."

Inequalities between men and women in the labor market and in the family reinforce each other. While Becker assumes a harmony of interests between the marriage partners and an equal distribution of consumption and leisure between them, Sen (1985) uses bargaining theory to explain the observed inequalities in consumption and leisure, which in some countries include differences in calorie consumption and in access to health care between husband and wife and between boys and girls. The wife's bargaining position is directly related to her access to the labor market and position in it, but her bargaining position is also weakened because women are likely to perceive inequalities as natural, and make no objections against them. This feature is due to the family socialization of girls from a young age. In many societies, girls are taught that they are less valuable human beings than their brothers, and virtually everywhere, girls must help their mothers provide domestic and personal services for their brothers, who are allowed much more freedom and leisure.

Even in countries with high and perpetual labor force participation by women, girls' education and training within the family focus on child care and domestic activities and on beautifying themselves to be able to make a good match and reduce the risk of divorce and abandonment, while boys' interests are stimulated in all other fields. Usually, girls are taught to be obedient, to be modest, and to do routine jobs without protest, while boys are encouraged to be enterprising, even aggressive, and self-confident. The inferiority feelings of the girls may induce them to invest less in education and training than boys, as suggested by Arrow (1973), but even if they have the same formal education and training as male competitors, women are likely to lose in competition with males in the labor market. Girls who are socialized to accept routine jobs and to be modest and obedient are unlikely to demand good jobs and advancement or in other ways to fight actively for their interests in the labor market, even when there are few prejudices against them. Much female aptitude for routine and precision work, unsuitability for leadership, and unwillingness to take responsibility results from family socialization in the first years of life. Most often, the schools continue in the same vein, but even when schools aim at abolishing inequality between the sexes, teachers may be powerless, due to family socialization of pupils of both sexes.

In industrialized countries, the last few decades have seen an acceleration of related and mutually reinforcing changes in technology, labor participation by married women with small children, and birth rates. Decline in birth rates to below replacement level and increasing female labor force participation provide an inducement to the improvement of household technologies and the introduction of new products and services as substitutes for women's traditional activities and child care. These technological and social changes further induce increasing female labor force participation. A rapidly increasing proportion of married women continue their money-earning activities without reducing work hours during the period when they have small children. But the traditional sex hierarchy is dying very slowly, and although birth rates are low, female levels of education and professional training fairly high, and labor market participation high and continuous, reductions in sex differentials in earnings, if any, have been moderate. Earnings in female occupations, including those requiring professional training, are lower than in male occupations with similar requirements. Except for a small female elite, women continue to occupy the positions at the bottom of the labor market within each occupation, as assistants to men and often supervised by men even in otherwise female occupations.

Married women with full-time work and young children have much longer working hours than men. Male patterns of work have changed very little, in spite of reduced working hours and the increasing amount of money wives contribute to family expenditure. In addition, many countries lack child care facilities. However, in spite of the differences between male and female earnings, most women in the industrialized countries have become less dependent upon male support because of the general increase of all wages and the reduction of working hours in the labor market. Therefore, women can support themselves by work in the labor market if they choose to. And with the aid of obligatory contributions from the father and public support to female-headed households, they can support children, although the living standards of female-headed households are usually much lower than those of male-headed households. Consequently, many young women react against unequal work burdens by demanding divorce or leaving the home, or by not entering into a formal marriage or cohabitation. Others react by reducing birth rates even further. Contrary to earlier patterns, female applications for divorce have become more numerous than male ones in some industrialized countries. These social and demographic changes serve to make young men, and public opinion in general, more inclined to consider women's demands for more equality.

In many developing countries, economic and social development are producing changes in female labor force participation and birth rates, which resemble earlier changes in industrialized countries. Family legislation has been modernized, there is legal equality or less legal inequality between the sexes, access to divorce has become less easy for men and easier for women, and better access to the labor market provides women with some possibilities for self-support in case of divorce and widowhood. Age differences between spouses are declining due to higher female marriage age, birth rates are declining, and women's position is gradually improving.

But in many other developing countries, either economic changes are few or male resistance to changes in the traditional status of women is strong. Except for voting rights for parliaments with little influence, women continue to be legally minor, and in many cases their situation has deteriorated because technological changes, or changes in land tenure, have deprived them of traditional means of self-support. In some countries, the labor market continues to be closed not only to married women but also to deserted women, divorcees, and widows, and if labor market shortages occur, they are met by large-scale imports of male labor. In these countries, birth rates remain high in spite of economic development. For women, economic support from sons is the only alternative to destitution when their husbands die or cease to support them.

Technical Change and Human Fertility in Rural Areas of Developing Countries

FERTILITY LEVELS VARY from one rural area to another both within and between countries. In countries in which both urban and rural fertility has declined, there has been variation in the timing of declines in both urban and rural fertility. Since the population in rural areas of most developing countries consists primarily of agricultural producers and their family members, it is pertinent to ask: to what extent can the differences in fertility levels, and in the timing of urban and rural fertility declines, be explained by differences in the techniques used in agricultural production? Access to land, tools, and methods, annual working hours, and the distribution of family labor are different in various systems of agriculture, and these differences are likely to have an influence on fertility in agricultural families. Therefore, it is necessary to begin with a brief description of the main agricultural production systems prevalent in developing countries.

It is important that these systems be viewed as adaptations to different population densities and environmental conditions (E. Boserup, 1965). In sparsely populated regions, land may be used for pasturing of herds and flocks, or it may be used for long-fallow agriculture. Since there is more cultivable land than the small local population can cultivate, small plots are cleared and used only until they become infested by weeds, or until crop yields decline for other reasons. When either of these occur, another plot is cleared and brought under cultivation. The result is a system characterized by long-term rotation of productive activity.

In areas of higher population density, the amount of land per inhabitant is insufficient to use in long rotations. The cultivators need to use more of the land for crop production and can leave less as grazing land or fallow for long periods. Thus in regions of medium population density, say twenty to fifty persons per square kilometer, the land is used in rotation in permanent fields in which periods of cultivation alternate with short periods of fallow. During the fallow period, domestic animals may feed on the fallows and other uncultivated land. In regions with still higher population density, there is too little land to permit any of it to lie fallow for years. Here the fields bear a crop

---

"Technical Change and Human Fertility in Rural Areas of Developing Countries." Reprinted from *Rural Development and Human Fertility*, edited by Wayne A. Schutjer and C. Shannon Stokes. Macmillan 1984: 23–31.

each year, and domestic animals have no fallow land on which to feed. If the animals cannot support themselves in areas unsuitable for cultivation, such as mountains or semideserts, owners of animals must produce fodder crops on a portion of their cultivated area. But some regions are too densely populated even for that system. In very densely settled regions, each cultivating family has only a very small area at their disposal, and a system of multicropping must be used. Under a multicropping system, if at all feasible, two or three successive crops must be sown or planted each year in each field.

If the population in rural communities continues to increase, as is the case in most developing countries, local food production must be steadily expanded, and food must be transported between regions or brought in from other countries. This brief description indicates how continuous expansion of food production is likely to come about. In areas with long-fallow systems, cultivators must increase the number of plots which are cleared for cultivation each year, and they must recultivate plots more frequently than was required when the total population was smaller. The long-fallow system develops into a short-fallow system. If population growth occurs in communities which already have adopted the short-fallow system, the area cultivated each year must expand by eliminating fallow and transforming pastures and forested land into fields, some of which will be used to produce fodder. In communities already using annual cropping, land must be improved so that it can be used for multicropping, or fodder production must be given up and the number of domestic animals decreased.

The Organization of Production

The organization of agricultural production within each of these systems will determine how this process of intensification is likely to influence fertility. The important elements in the organization are land tenure, the use of child labor, and the existence of possibilities for the use of industrial inputs. Long-fallow systems may be used as a beginning point. In this type of agriculture, many operations can be done by small children. In thinly populated areas, consistent with a long-fallow system, the numbers of birds and animals are large, and children perform the time-consuming task of supervising the scattered plots and scaring birds and animals away from ripening crops. Children also gather fruit and other noncultivated food, which provide an important supplement to nutrition in sparsely populated areas. Under the long-fallow system, most of the work with vegetable crops is performed by women (E. Boserup, 1970a). Children help their mother carry crops from the widely scattered impermanent plots, often far from the habitations, and with harvesting. Children also help women provide fuel and water for the household, assist with domestic work, and care for younger siblings. Large boys help in felling trees and in preparation of new plots, a task generally reserved for male members of the family.

Child labor is neither the only, nor the most important, motivation for desiring a large family in long-fallow agricultural systems. Members of a large family, and of a large local group, provide protection against outsiders, and adult children help parents to survive in old age. The land used for fallow and cultivation may be tribally owned; and a family can clear and cultivate the number of plots which they need (E. Boserup, 1965). If land use is controlled by the local chief, he usually assigns land to a family in proportion to its size, so a man with several wives and a large number of children gains the use of a large area for cultivation (E. Boserup, 1970a). In addition, children contribute to family status, since large families are both powerful and respected and the status of the head of the family is often directly related to its size. In spite of the multiple advantages of large families in many long-fallow communities, family size is relatively small, because health facilities are poor and morbidity and mortality high. In systems of long-fallow agriculture, most families are unable to rear the number of children they would like to have.

The picture is different in communities employing short-fallow agricultural systems. Some of these communities have recently changed from long fallow as a result of population pressure, but most communities with short-fallow systems have employed these systems for centuries or millennia. In the latter group of communities, attitudes toward family size may be different from those of long-fallow communities. With greater population density, childrens' work with wild crops and with animal and bird scaring becomes less useful, or disappears. Similarly, while the tools used in long-fallow agriculture are hand tools, in most communities which have utilized short-fallow systems for a long period, plows are used for land preparation, and pack animals or animal-driven carts are used instead of head transport. The plows and carts used in the short-fallow system are nearly always used by men, thus women in short-fallow systems have less to do and have less need of help from children. Thus, unless the crop rotation includes cotton or other crops particularly well suited for child labor, such labor is not so widely used that it is likely to provide a motive for large family size.

When fallow is shortened, the cultivated land passes into private property, in some cases by legal reforms but elsewhere by a gradual change of customs. Therefore, the head of a large family cannot obtain additional land for cultivation without cost, but must buy or rent the additional land. Not only is the acquisition of land to accommodate a large family difficult, but a peasant family with many children may be forced to sell land to provide a dowry for daughters. It may also be necessary either to subdivide the holding or to accept a decline in social status, as some of the sons become wage laborers or tenants for families with fewer children and more land. In peasant communities with private ownership of land, parents in a poor family with more children than they can provide for without losing status are regarded as irresponsible parents. It is the size of the landholding and not the size of the family which matters for social esteem. In addition to this, landowning peasants can lease out land or engage wage labor in old age, so they are less dependent upon support from adult children.

Many peasant families in different parts of the world have avoided land shortage by means of induced abortion, female infanticide, or other traditional means of fertility control. One example of the adjustment to land scarcity and other economic pressure is Japan. In Japan, female infanticide had disappeared toward the end of the nineteenth century, when economic development made girls useful in silk production and money earners in textile industries. However, after the Second World War, when large numbers of settlers returned from former colonies, increasing pressure on land and other employment opportunities induced a sharp increase in illegal abortions and eventually led to the legalization of abortion. The decline of fertility in Japan would probably not have been so rapid nor have set in so early after the economic motivation was provided, if a restrictive attitude to family size had not been a traditional custom in Japanese villages.

Concern about land shortage in settled peasant communities with private ownership of land may result not only in deliberate, but also in unintended, reduction in fertility through delayed marriage. If the population is increasing, it becomes more difficult for peasants with many children to arrange favorable marriages for their children, raising the average marriage age, especially if late-marrying daughters are able to earn money to pay their dowry, as was the case in Japan.

The Japanese example should remind us that settled peasant communities with very high population density and intensive agriculture, such as prevailed in Japan in the nineteenth century, may have attitudes toward family size which differ from those of less densely populated peasant communities. The smaller land area available per family enhances the motivation for restriction of family size, but with increasing intensification of agriculture, the need for child labor becomes much greater. To understand this, it is necessary to look at the different functions of fallowing. Some of the most important functions of fallowing are to prevent exhaustion of soil fertility, reduce weed growth, and limit the spread of plant disease. These purposes can, however, also be served by use of chemical fertilizer, herbicides, and pesticides. In other words, industrial inputs to agriculture can substitute for fallowing, as they do in industrialized countries, where fallowing is seldom used. However, chemical inputs are not the only substitutes for fallowing. Soil fertility can be preserved by applying manure, night soil, or vegetable matter gathered in uncultivated areas or at the bottom of rivers and lakes. Use of such fertilizing matter is the chief means of preserving soil fertility in densely populated areas in which neither fallowing nor chemical inputs can be used. In such areas, proliferation of weeds must be prevented by repeated hand weeding, and parasites must be removed by hand, or infested plants must be removed. Each of these functions is highly intensive of the type of labor which children can provide.

Use of intensive agricultural systems with frequent cropping not only requires that problems of fertilization, weed control, and pest control be tackled by one of the means mentioned above; it also often necessitates the regulation of the agricultural water supply. Fallowing is sometimes used to preserve moisture in land which is too dry to bear a crop each year. If annual cropping is introduced, the fields must be irrigated. If multicropping is introduced, the second and third crop must be grown outside the most favorable season, requiring irrigation even in areas with a relatively wet climate. Like the operations mentioned above, irrigation can be undertaken either by means of industrial inputs or by labor-intensive means. Finally, the control of soil erosion can also be accomplished with a range of techniques. If population density is too high to use the forest-fallow system to prevent erosion created by cultivation of hillsides, erosion can be prevented by means of terracing, which can be done either with mechanized equipment or by labor-intensive methods.

In other words, use of intensive agricultural systems requires that problems of soil fertility, weeds, plant disease, water control, and erosion be solved. These problems cannot be overcome by fallowing because of high population density, but a choice remains between industrial inputs and labor-intensive methods. When the latter are used, the demand for labor rises steeply with increased growth of population and increasing cropping frequency. Each additional hectare brought under cultivation, instead of being fallowed, adds to the labor requirement, and the labor input per hectare sown or planted becomes much greater. Women and children gather fertilizing matter, often far from the village, carry it to the fields, and spread it. Women and children are usually the ones who weed, transplant, and try to cope with plant disease. Japanese statistics reveal an extremely high labor input in intensive paddy production as late as the middle of this century, when the use of purchased inputs was already substantial (Ishikawa, 1967).

The need to dig and maintain terraces and irrigation facilities in intensive agricultural systems can also increase the demand for female and child labor because men often compensate for time spent in these activities by making maximum use of female and child labor in the fields. Many densely populated areas with intensive agriculture are often more developed than sparsely populated areas, are closer to urban centers, and have better transport systems. Consequently, they are better able to have labor-intensive commercial crops suited for child labor in the crop rotation. In short, in intensive agricultural systems, children are likely to contribute more than they cost, not only in families of landowning peasants, but also in landless families, especially if children work for wages in agriculture, separately or together with their parents. Landless workers also depend upon support from children in old age.

Technical Change and the Green Revolution

In intensification of agriculture, the choice between labor-intensive methods and chemical and mechanized inputs is of crucial importance for the use of child labor and thus may provide motivation for or against restriction of fertility. It is important, therefore, to note that Green Revolution techniques, which have spread in many densely populated regions, are a mixture of labor-intensive and modern-input methods for the intensification of agriculture. The Green Revolution introduced chemical inputs and certain types of mechanization, but at the same time, land use was shifted to a much more intensive system using irrigation, multicropping, fodder production, labor-intensive commercial crops, and various types of land improvement. Thus labor input increased, and female and child labor continued to be important. Moreover, there was a sudden, and large, increase in total family income, which perhaps made parents feel that they now could afford additional children.

The use of Green Revolution techniques is limited to areas with good infrastructure. Purchased inputs, including chemical fertilizers, must be transported from urban areas, traded, and stocked. In that process, good long-distance transport and local roads to villages and isolated farms are necessary, as are local warehouses. The introduction and use of mechanized equipment require that fueling and repair services be available locally. An extension network may also be a precondition for the introduction and effective utilization of modern methods, especially if the agricultural structure is one of many small producers. Sometimes large-scale, controlled irrigation must be available, or service facilities and equipment for tube wells and other small-scale irrigation systems. The areas where the Green Revolution has had most success, for instance, Korea, Taiwan, and the Indian state of Punjab, were supplied with basic infrastructure by Japanese and British rulers in the colonial period. These areas now have far better rural infrastructure than is typical for developing countries and, in the case of India, other parts of the nation.

When rural infrastructure is very poor, it may not even be possible to produce commercial crops for export by means of hand labor and animal draft power. Because transport of perishable crops may be impossible and transport of nonperishable products so costly, local prices are so low that production is not profitable. Infrastructural obstacles to agricultural development are likely to be worse in sparsely populated regions than in densely populated regions, because it is uneconomic to supply a small and scattered population of agricultural producers with transport facilities and other infrastructure (Simon, 1977; E. Boserup, 1970a). In such a region, the multiplication of population would in the long run improve the possibilities for development by providing an expanded population base for markets and other rural infrastructure. However, for the people living in the region, labor migration by selected family members may be the best, or even the only, way to improve incomes in the short term. If possibilities for employment or other income-earning opportunities are also poor in other regions of a nation, migrants from labor surplus regions may go to foreign countries that offer better prospects.

The local system of agriculture also influences the sex distribution of migrants, which reflects the demand for female and male labor in the local system of agriculture. Similarly, the demand for female and male labor in the areas of destination also affects the sex composition of migrant streams. For example, the migration of women is greater than that of men in regions of Latin America where women's labor input in agriculture is relatively small and urban demand for female wage labor, especially domestic servants, is large. By contrast, in most of Africa, where women do most of the agricultural work and where demand for female wage labor in urban areas is small, male migration is much greater than female migration (E. Boserup, 1970a).

Migration may also be large from regions with better agricultural opportunities, especially if there is a possibility for getting stable, urban employment. To have adult children with urban incomes is often regarded as insurance against both fluctuations in harvests and poverty in old age. Therefore, parents are eager to invest in the education of their children, and the migration of school leavers to urban areas is large. Where prospects are good that adult children may get urban jobs and send money to the family in the village, migration may contribute to delaying a fertility decline. Sex-selective migration to the United States may have contributed to a delayed fertility decline in rural areas of Mexico.

The large-scale male migration from rural to urban areas in Africa has forced many rural women to provide for their children without male help. However, African women are usually able to obtain a subsistence income for themselves and their children by work in agriculture, small-scale trading, and small informal production and services. These income-producing activities are not available to women who belong to cultures which confine women to the household and to work which can only be done in the home. In rural communities of this type, women are completely dependent upon male family members for their own support and that of children below working age. All jobs in such communities are male jobs, and there are very few possibilities for divorced, abandoned, and widowed women to earn income. Under these conditions, the alternatives available to support such women are often limited to prostitution and begging, unless the women are helped by adult or young children.

In many communities of this type, only men inherit land and other property, while in others, men can freely divorce their wives, and are likely to do so if their wives fail to give birth to the desired number of boys. Women have a very strong motive in such situations for bearing many children as quickly as possible (Youssef, 1974). If the age difference between spouses is large and only men inherit, it is important for women to have several sons as soon as possible to assure support should they become widowed or abandoned at an early age. Fertility restriction would likely be more acceptable to such women, if legal reforms gave equal rights to own and inherit land and other property to both men and women, and obliged men to support divorced wives and their children. In order to have a major effect on fertility, however, such reforms need to be accompanied by radical changes in labor market access for women and the modernization of traditional attitudes. The communities discussed here are the ones in which sex differentials in rural schools are the largest, because only a minority of progressive parents send their daughters to school. Such sex bias contributes to attitudes conducive to high fertility, as well as limiting access to modern employment by women.

In some rural communities, women have considerable liberty to decide their own reproductive behavior, but in most cases, decisions about school attendance, marriage age, use of contraception, and even length of breast-feeding may be taken by the husband, elder family members, or the village priest. Under such circumstances, young women have little influence on their own reproductive behavior, and dropout rates for acceptors of family planning services are often quite high. Part of the explanation for the latter phenomenon may be that the person first approached by family planning personnel was not the real decision maker, and this decision maker later sabotaged the effort by not using the services or by putting pressure on the acceptor to discontinue use.

Government Policy

There is a final category of decision makers relevant to fertility: governments and local government administrations. Some governments, mainly in densely populated countries, make family planning services available in rural areas, but if the general attitude of the rural population is hostile to fertility restriction they are little used, and an ambivalent attitude by the local staff providing the services contributes to this result. Other governments, mainly in sparsely populated countries, make more or less successful efforts to prevent the population from restricting fertility. In addition, and more important, many types of government policy designed for other purposes contribute either to preventing or promoting a fertility decline in rural areas. Important examples are the alternative strategies of development for urban and rural areas pursued by governments.

Historically, most governments in developing countries focused upon development of industry and the provision of modern services in urban areas, mainly the metropolitan areas, while they did little or nothing to promote rural development. As a result, before the huge migration to metropolitan areas in developing countries began, these areas nearly always had much better economic and social infrastructure than the rest of the country. Therefore, when industrialization started or accelerated, nearly all new industries and modern services chose metropolitan locations, and both the increasing demand for labor and the better service facilities attracted high-level, skilled, and unskilled labor to these areas. The rapid expansion of economic activities, including government administration, and the rapid increase of population in metropolitan areas made it necessary to give priority to expansion and qualitative improvement of urban infrastructure, an effort which continued to be frustrated by further concentration of population in these areas. In the meantime, few government resources were left for expansion and qualitative improvement of infrastructure in rural areas and smaller towns. Some of the governments that neglected rural development assumed that, because there was no shortage of land resources in the country, market forces would take care of agricultural and rural development. Other governments listened to economic advisors who believed in the now-outmoded theory that agricultural production in developing countries was inelastic, so development could best be pursued by transferring the "rural surplus" of labor to urban areas for employment in industry and modern services.

Because of the neglect of rural infrastructure investment by both central and local governments, the expansion of export crop production and food deliveries to urban areas could occur only in rural areas which already had the necessary infrastructure. The existing infrastructure had been developed to facilitate urban deliveries of food and export crops. But these areas could not supply the rapidly increasing urban demand for food. As a result, the increased demand was met to a considerable extent by imports from industrialized countries.

If rapid increases in the share of total population living in urban areas are to be accomplished without increasing food imports, not only must total food production increase, but labor productivity in food production must also increase. Rising labor productivity will not occur if producers can only expand the output of food by means of labor inputs and reduced fallow periods, and are unable to use modern inputs. Such conditions were characteristic of most rural communities in most developing countries in which governments neglected rural development. In Africa, huge, sparsely populated areas had virtually no economic infrastructure, and women who produced the local food supply had no possibilities for using modern inputs, and could at best expand production proportionate to their increase in numbers. In rural African communities which had somewhat better infrastructure, and in which family incomes increased because of increasing production of cash crops or favorable prices for such crops, women would often give up agricultural work, or reduce it, and purchase imported food for family consumption.

Reliance on imported food to supply urban areas had many attractions for governments that were most concerned with financial problems and the welfare of the urban, especially the metropolitan, population. But the reliance on imports made conditions in the already neglected rural areas even worse, because it discouraged food production for the towns, even in areas which hitherto had commercial production for the purpose. Consequently, in many developing countries national production of cereals declined and was replaced by imports. If surplus production of food in the industrialized countries and the need to dispose of the surpluses by means of subsidized exports, or gifts of food, had not made food imports so attractive for many governments in developing countries, many more would have been forced to devote more of their resources to development of their own rural areas. Landowning peasants would have improved their incomes, and landless labor would have had more employment. There would have been less rural-to-urban migration and less urban congestion. Moreover, if subsidized exports from the industrialized countries, and their restrictions on food imports, had not discouraged developing countries from developing exports for new markets, some of them, including some of the poorest ones, might have been able to finance rural development by means of food exports.

In rural areas lacking improved infrastructure and modernization of agricultural production, fertility rates have usually remained high, and if urban fertility declined due to industrialization, a gap appeared between urban and rural fertility, or the existing gap became larger. In some of the countries which pursued a balanced policy of industrial and agricultural development, fertility rates declined in both rural and urban areas. However, there were also countries that experienced both rural development and continued high fertility. In some cases, this was probably due to cultural obstacles to fertility decline, but it also seems likely that the short-term effect of increases in rural incomes may have caused parents to become less inclined to restrict family size.

Conclusions

It has been suggested that the choice of agricultural policy with radical substitution of mechanized and chemical inputs for traditional labor-intensive techniques could provide motivation for fertility control in peasant families. However, it is not desirable that governments give priority to the likely effects on human fertility in their choice of agricultural policies. Whether fertility rates in rural areas begin to decline rapidly or remain at high levels, rural population increase will continue to be rapid for many decades, because of the increase in the number of young families. To avoid further deterioration of conditions in congested urban areas, a larger share than hitherto of the young families must be able to make a living in rural areas and smaller towns. The creation of economic opportunities in rural areas is more important than a rapid decline in rural fertility. Therefore, the promotion of technological change in rural areas cannot be by means of rapid mechanization of agriculture, even if that might reduce fertility. Rural policy must be designed as a compromise between the labor-intensive pattern and the modern-input pattern, thus ensuring that both employment opportunities and rural per capita incomes increase. In most developing countries, this seems the only way to improve levels of living both in urban and rural areas.

[1986]
Shifts in the Determinants of Fertility in the Developing World: Environmental, Technical, Economic, and Cultural Factors

IN ALL SOCIETIES IN which they were strongly motivated to do so, parents and rulers have attempted to influence fertility. Because child mortality was high until recently, the desire was often to obtain higher fertility by prayers and sacrifices, social pressure, early and universal marriage, tax advantages for large families, and so on. But in many societies there were periods in which large population groups attempted to limit family size or to space births by folk methods of fertility control or infanticide. The idea that parents in preindustrial societies always aimed at maximum family size is unrealistic. In the developing countries, in which fertility has been declining rapidly, family control by folk methods seems to have been widely applied before modern contraceptive means and family planning services became available. Although some parents with relatively weak motivation for control may first have begun to restrict fertility when better methods came within their reach, experience shows that the operation of family planning services has mainly led to replacement of one method by another and better one (UN, 1983). Therefore, a focal point in fertility theory is to determine the factors which may induce parents and governments to restrict fertility.

Throughout history, the desire to seek security in numbers seems to have been the predominant motive for large family size. Rulers were preoccupied with defense and with the number of subjects who could be taxed, and parents wanted large families for physical protection and economic survival. At early stages of development, individual families or kin groups are left to provide their own physical security and economic support, and the parent generation depends upon the strength of the new generation for support in old age. The techniques of production and organization of work allow children to make a significant contribution from a young age. Such conditions do still exist in peripheral regions of some developing countries. In such regions, rural families are largely subsistence producers with small sales of agricultural products or labor and with little or no protection and support from government services. Child mortality is high and average family size smaller

---

"Shifts in the Determinants of Fertility in the Developing World: Environmental, Technical, Economic, and Cultural Factors." Reprinted with permission from *The State of Population Theory: Forward from Malthus*, edited by David Coleman and Roger Schofield. Basil Blackwell 1986: 239–55.

than desired, except for rich men in polygamous marriages. However, in most parts of the developing world subsistence production and labor investments in kind have been replaced by production for sale and monetized private and public investment, either as an indigenous process or as a result of colonization and neocolonization.

This process of specialization of agricultural and nonagricultural production is accompanied by the appearance and growth of occupations such as transport, trade, urban construction, and educational services designed to train the specialized labor force. As specialization proceeds, the share of subsistence producers in the population declines, and some family members or whole families take up new informal sector activities or become members of the modern sector labor force (E. Boserup, 1970a). These changes have important effects on family organization and desired family size, especially in cases when women as well as men replace or supplement subsistence production with money-earning activities.

The process of specialization does not only move production of consumption and investment goods from the family to specialized enterprises: many services previously performed by family members for each other also become specialized, and are taken over by private enterprises or public institutions and services. Among these are educational, health, and other social services, which gradually replace family training and family care, and police, courts, army, and other areas of government administration, which replace family discipline and tribal defense. Also, these changes strip the family of functions and create and expand specialized occupations, of which many employ a highly trained labor force of men and women, who have motivations for keeping their families smaller than those of other occupational groups. By these changes, the family loses not only functions but also power. When the government provides protection against physical and economic risks, family members become less dependent upon help from each other, and the government acquires more and more power over the family. By means of economic regulations, criminal law, compulsory education, marriage regulations, and in many other ways, the government becomes able either to reinforce the power of the family head over other family members, or to limit this power, giving women and youth more liberty or more security. Such changes have important effects on duration of marriage, age at marriage, and fertility in marriage.

Occupational Distribution and Fertility

Motivation for family restriction is much stronger for people working in the modern sector than for those in the informal sector. The labor force in the modern sector consists of government staff, members of the professions, and salary and wage earners in large industries and large construction, trade, transport, and service enterprises, while the labor force in the informal sector mainly consists of self-employed workers and workers in small family enterprises which produce goods and services for the market. Usually some of the personnel in the modern sector benefit from some limited social security, even in those developing countries at low stages of economic development. This means that they are less dependent upon family help than are people in the informal sector, who rarely have access to any sort of social security, except perhaps some health services. Moreover, enterprises in the modern sector do not use child labor, while children perform many jobs in the informal sector, working with their parents, or for wages, or on their own. Thus, in the modern sector, lack of dependence upon adult children for security in emergencies and old age and upon smaller children for household help provides little motivation for large family size. In the informal sector, there is more motivation for having a large family, but, even when children are active in the urban informal sector, there is often more motivation for limitation of family size in this sector than among people in rural areas, because in towns at least a part of the children's food must be purchased. Families who live in metropolitan areas or other large cities must buy all food for their children, while many inhabitants of smaller towns produce most of their own food, often with help from the children.

In some developing countries, wives and children of men who work in the modern sector may add to the family income through self-employment or by operating small family enterprises in the informal sector, so the inducement to reduction in family size is smaller. But often men in the modern sector prefer to have nonworking wives and children who qualify for modern sector employment by school attendance. Families in which the male head works in the modern sector are also likely to live in rented flats, which with a large family would be either very crowded or extremely expensive, while families in which the family head works in the informal sector often live in self-built slum housing and pay little or no rent (Loza, 1981).

The World Fertility Survey produced some information about differences in total marital fertility by husband's occupation, which is reproduced in table 1 (Alam and Casterline, 1984). The fertility differences by occupation are large. In twenty-three of twenty-eight countries there is a difference of 1.0–4.5 children between the group with lowest and the group with highest fertility. The exceptions with small fertility differentials are African or Moslem countries. The families with lowest fertility (occupational group 1) belong to the modern sector, are educated and largely urban, usually have their children educated and nonworking, often have some social security or property income, and rarely live in subsistence housing. These living conditions explain why their fertility is lower than that of the other groups.

Some of the families in occupational groups 2 and 3 share some of these conditions with group 1, but they usually have somewhat higher marital fertility than group 1, because of different age composition, lower marriage age, or less fertility restriction. The highest fertility levels are usually in the agricultural group (occupational group 4); in which the statistics unfortunately fail to distinguish between landless workers and members of cultivator families.

Decline of fertility may occur either because the families within a partic-

TABLE 1. Married women's fertility in developing countries, by husband's occupation

Country and technology group[a]	Marital fertility rates by husband's occupation[b]			
	Professional, managerial, technical, clerical (1)	Sales, service (2)	Manual (3)	Agricultural (4)
Nepal (1)	5.6	6.7	7.3	7.3
Bangladesh (1)	7.0	7.1	6.7	7.0
Haiti (1)	5.4	6.9	7.1	8.5
Senegal (1)	8.6	7.9	8.5	8.2
Pakistan (2)	7.6	7.9	8.2	7.8
Indonesia (2)	6.9	6.9	7.0	5.9
Sudan (2)	7.0	8.1	8.4	8.7
Kenya (2)	10.1	10.1	9.9	9.8
Ghana (2)	7.2	8.0	8.5	8.2
Lesotho (2)	8.8	8.0	7.4	7.5
Malaysia (3)	7.3	7.7	8.3	8.6
Thailand (3)	5.8	6.7	7.1	8.0
Sri Lanka (3)	6.7	7.4	7.1	7.2
Philippines (3)	7.7	7.9	8.9	9.5
Paraguay (3)	5.5	6.2	6.8	9.5
Peru (3)	7.8	8.3	9.1	10.2
Dominican Rep. (3)	5.4	7.2	7.2	9.8
Jordan (3)	9.4	10.7	11.0	11.8
Syria (3)	10.0	9.6	10.7	11.6
South Korea (4)	7.5	6.4	6.9	8.3
Guyana (4)	5.5	6.6	7.1	8.2
Venezuela (4)	6.2	10.4	7.6	7.5
Jamaica (4)	4.9	5.6	6.7	7.8
Trinidad (4)	3.8	4.4	5.2	6.5
Columbia (4)	5.7	6.5	7.0	9.8
Mexico (4)	7.6	8.7	9.4	10.1
Panama (4)	4.1	4.5	4.4	6.1
Costa Rica (4)	3.7	4.4	4.1	5.1

Source: Alam and Casterline (1984).

[a]A country's development stage (technology group) was determined by energy consumption, number of telephones, life expectancy at birth, and adult literacy (see E. Boserup, 1981a).

[b]Women aged fifteen through forty-nine were considered.

ular occupational group get more extrafamilial security or reduce their dependence upon child labor, or because development is accompanied by shifts of population from occupational groups with little motivation to groups with more motivation for fertility control. In many developing countries, a large share of the population is on the move from higher to lower fertility occupations, with more motivation for family restriction than their parents' occupations provided. A dynamic process of fertility decline is set in motion when economic development both increases family size by reducing child mortality and promotes major changes in the occupational distribution of the population. Some groups with motivation for relatively small family size will begin to use folk or modern methods of contraception when their family size becomes larger than expected, or when they move to an occupation with more motivation for restriction, or from rural to urban areas without change of occupation.

Table 2 gives an impression of the differences in occupational distribution of the adult male population in countries at different stages of development. Stage of development is measured by indicators and not by per capita gross national product, in order to avoid distortions due to changes in terms of trade and exchange rate problems. The indicators are energy consumption, representing technological levels in production, construction, and transport; number of telephones, representing levels of communication; life expectancy at birth, representing health technology and quality of food supply; and adult literacy, representing levels of skills and know-how. These indicators are given equal weights. For details of classification, and the countries belonging to each group, see E. Boserup (1981a). The first two occupational groups in the table include mainly male modern sector personnel, the next two mainly the male labor force in the informal sector. In the countries at the lowest level of economic development (technology groups 1 and 2), white collar workers accounted only for 4 percent and the whole of the modern sector for only 13 percent of adult men, while in the developing countries at the most advanced level (technology group 4), white collar workers accounted for 11 percent and the modern sector for more than one-third of adult men. Quite obviously, many more people were motivated to restrict family size in the more advanced developing countries. But these still fall far short of the industrialized countries (in group 5), which had 16 percent of adult men in the white collar group and 54 percent in the modern sector, to which should be added a much larger group of adult students than in developing countries. Moreover, even in the most advanced developing countries, families benefited less from social security systems than families in the same occupational group in industrialized countries, and so were more dependent upon family support or property.

Most occupational shifts are from occupations with lower income to occupations with higher income, but it is important to note that it is the occupational shift and not the increase of income which motivates a reduction of fertility. Income increases unaccompanied by occupational changes are unlikely to lead to reduced fertility, and occupational shifts to a lower

TABLE 2. Occupational distribution of adult males in thirty-nine countries, by national technological development, around 1960

Occupational group	Percentage of men by technology group of their countries			
	2	3	4	5
Professional, administrative, clerical	4	6	11	16
Employees in production, trade, transport	9	13	24	38
Total modern sector	13	19	35	54
Owners and family labor in production, trade, transport	10	8	9	6
Services and casual labor	6	8	9	6
Total nonagricultural labor force	29	35	53	65
Agricultural workers	8	17	14	4
Owners, tenants, family labor in agriculture	54	40	24	10
Outside the labor force (including students, army personnel, old people)	9	8	9	21
Total adult men	100	100	100	100
Number of countries	5	15	10	9

Sources: E. Boserup (1970a), appendix; national statistics.
Note: Adult males are all men fifteen years and over. There is no information for countries in technology group 1.

income group are unlikely to lead to higher fertility even if the new occupation is one which normally motivates larger family size than the previous occupation does.

Information about marital fertility differences by occupation are available for a limited number of countries, but intercountry and regional differences in total fertility rates are published annually by the World Bank. Since fertility levels and changes are dependent upon the stage of development reached by the country, comparisons are only meaningful for countries at similar stages of development. It can be seen from table 3 that fertility differences between industrialized countries are insignificant, but there are large regional fertility differences among the developing countries. The African and Arab regions have the highest fertility levels, with two to three more children per woman, than Asian and Latin American countries at similar levels of development. Fertility decline was also smaller between 1975 and 1981 in the Arab region, and fertility in Africa seems to be increasing (Tabutin, 1984; Lesthaeghe, 1980). Some of the changes reflected in table 3 are probably owing to revisions of earlier estimates for 1975, rather than estimated changes between 1975 and 1981 (World Bank, 1978, 1983). The higher fertility levels in the Arab world are related to the lack of security for women

TABLE 3. Fertility rates by national technological development and region, 1975 and 1981

Region	Fertility rates by technology group						Number of countries included in each technology group				
	1	2	3	4	5	Average[a]	1	2	3	4	5
Africa south of Sahara											
1975	6.3	6.3	6.6	5.6		6.3	18	14	1	1	0
1981	6.5	6.7	8.0	5.1		6.6					
South and East Asia and Oceania											
1975	6.5	6.0	5.7	3.3	2.7	5.1	4	5	5	3	3
1981	6.5	5.2	4.2	2.3	1.9	4.3					
Arab region											
1975	7.2	7.2	6.7	5.7		6.6	1	1	11	3	0
1981	6.6	70	6.5	4.4		6.1					
North and South America											
1975	4.9	6.2	6.5	4.6	2.3	5.1	1	1	8	12	2
1981	4.7	6.0	5.4	3.5	1.9	4.1					
Europe											
1975				3.0	2.3	2.4	0	0	0	5	20
1981				2.6	1.9	2.0					
World											
1975	6.3	6.3	6.4	4.3	2.3	5.1	24	21	25	24	25
1981	6.5	6.3	5.8	3.3	1.9	4.7					

Source: World Bank (1978).
[a]Unweighted.

in this region. In nearly all countries, married women have less security than men, because, in addition to the risks of life which they must share with their male provider, they are less economically self-reliant than men and are therefore in a more difficult position if their spouse dies or abandons them. Women in the Arab world are even more dependent upon the male members of their families—husbands, fathers, brothers and sons—than women elsewhere. Both legislation and custom discriminate against women, and prejudice against their participation in the labor market is stronger than elsewhere. Divorce is easily obtained by men, or repudiation and abandonment are legal (Allman, 1978). Dissolution of marriage and widowhood are far worse for women in societies in which there is no room for women in the labor market except as beggars and prostitutes than it is in societies where large numbers of women, illiterates as well as educated, are part of the labor force. The more secluded the labor market, the more women are limited to domestic work in their own home, and the larger the insecurity of married, and also of unmarried, women (Cain et al., 1979).

Risk of divorce, repudiation, and abandonment is largest for sterile women and women without sons. Therefore, in societies where they have no option in the labor market, women have a very strong motivation to have as many children as possible and to discriminate in favor of their sons with care and food (Chen et al., 1981; Miller, 1981). They are motivated to avoid spacing of children in order to increase the chance that their sons will survive to support them when they are old, widowed, or deserted. The extremely low level of labor force participation of Arab women around 1960 is shown in table 4. In the group with middle-level technology, in which comparison with other regions is possible, only 2 percent of adult Arab women were employed in the modern sector, against 4–5 percent of Asian and Latin American women. Most of these women were probably young unmarried girls, so the employment of married women was lower still. Even worse from the point of view of economic security for women, the share of Arab women in the informal sector was equally low, while three to six times more Asian and Latin American women worked in the informal sector, which is the one sector open to women with little or no education or professional qualifications. It is also the sector where women with responsibility for children have a chance to support their families or to earn incomes, which makes them less dependent upon male family members (E. Boserup, 1970a). In some Moslem countries outside the Arab region, for instance in Pakistan and Bangladesh, women's status is also low and their access to the labor market very low (Cain et al., 1979; Miller, 1981). Also in such countries, fertility is high, and in northern India, more influenced by Arab culture than southern India, fertility is higher than in the south (Dyson and Moore, 1983), although the level of development is higher.

Agricultural Systems and Fertility

Property owners are less dependent upon help from family members than people without property, and this is important in regions in which a large share of the population is small and middle-sized landowners. If child labor is little used in such regions, there is little economic motivation for landowners to have large families. In emergencies, they can obtain credit by giving security in land; in old age, they can cultivate their land with hired labor, or rent it out. A generation effect may also operate in favor of smaller families if sons who inherit a small share of the family land want to avoid further subdivision in the next generation (Poffenberger, 1983). Many dry regions of India, which afford little motivation for large family size (Vlassoff and Vlassoff, 1980; Cain, 1982), provide examples of landowning families with lower fertility than landless families in the same area, and studies of other countries have found the same (Stokes and Schutjer, 1984).

In order to understand the often complicated relations between landownership and fertility, it is necessary to distinguish between different agri-

TABLE 4. Women in the nonagricultural labor force around 1960, by region and national technological development

	Women in nonagricultural labor force								
	As percentage of adult women				As percentage of total labor force in sector				Number of countries
Region and sector	2	3	4	5	2	3	4	5	
Africa south of Sahara									3
Modern sector	1	—	—	—	9	—	—	—	
Informal sector	9	—	—	—	29	—	—	—	
South and East Asia and Oceania									11
Modern sector	1	4	12	21	6	20	23	28	
Informal sector	4	7	7	9	18	31	30	44	
Arab region									6
Modern sector	—	2	—	—	—	10	—	—	
Informal sector	—	2	—	—	—	11	—	—	
North and South America									14
Modern sector	—	5	8	22	—	23	28	30	
Informal sector	—	11	13	7	—	50	43	44	
Europe									5
Modern sector	—	—	—	18	—	—	—	28	
Informal sector	—	—	—	10	—	—	—	46	
Number of countries	5	15	10	9	5	15	10	9	39

Sources: E. Boserup, 1970a; national statistics.

cultural systems, which provide different motivations for family size. The agricultural system used in an area is related to its population density. Areas with high rural densities use systems which yield high outputs per unit of land, while areas with low rural densities use systems with low output per unit of land. Both the suitability of child labor and the system of land-ownership vary according to the agricultural system (E. Boserup, 1965).

Long-fallow systems, which are used in sparsely populated areas at low levels of development, for instance in Africa, encourage high fertility (E. Boserup, 1984). The land is tribally owned, and the user cannot mortgage or sell it. A large family can put into use more land than a small one, and child labor is widely used for herding, for gathering food, fuel, and water, for scaring birds and animals away from crops, for weeding crops, and for carrying them home. So parents are dependent upon children both for work when they are small and for support when they have grown up. Since child mortality is high in such regions, parents often have fewer surviving children than they would have liked to have.

In other sparsely populated areas with extensive land use—for instance, in many parts of Latin America—large-scale private landownership predominates, and most of the rural population are hired workers. These workers are either landless or have small plots for some subsistence production. Children help their parents both in the subsistence plot, by gathering, and by working for wages, either with their parents or on their own (Collins, 1983). Many plantations engage the whole family, and in tea plantations in Sri Lanka and Indonesia fertility is often higher than elsewhere in the region (Wijemanne and Wijeysekara, 1981; Saefulla, 1979).

In regions of Asia with high population densities and intensive agricultural systems, cultivator holdings are usually small or middle sized and are either owned by the cultivators or rented from landowners. Cultivators with large families and small holdings either cultivate the land very intensively or rent additional land from noncultivating owners or from families with small numbers in relation to the land they own. However, if holdings are small and the rural population is increasing, crop shares and other rents for additional land are extremely high, and this may provide motivation to restrict family size instead of renting additional land. Parents with many children often make distress sales of land in order to provide marriage payments, while landowners with small families become rich by renting out land. The difficulties which parents may have in finding suitable marriage partners and sufficient marriage payments for their children lead to delay of marriage and thus to reduced fertility. In other words, parents have more motivation for limitation of family size if they have land enough to support themselves in old age and emergencies, but not so much land that they can supply a large number of children with sufficient land or dowry. By contrast, landless laborers and people in areas with tribally owned land are more likely to be motivated to raise large families, because they are much more dependent upon help from children.

The Impact of Development Strategies on Fertility

Governments in developing countries influence fertility partly by actions designed to reduce or increase fertility, and partly by their choice of development strategy. The encouragement of industrialization provided by nearly all governments in developing countries tends to promote occupational changes, which reduce fertility, but in the least developed countries, especially in Africa, industrialization efforts are often unsuccessful. Moreover, there are large differences in agricultural policies between countries, which in some cases promote, but in others tend to delay, fertility decline.

In contrast to countries in Africa and Latin America, which often neglect agricultural development, it is characteristic for most countries in South Asia and East Asia to promote both industrialization and agricultural development. As a result, they have experienced large structural changes in both the urban and the rural labor markets. Most Asian countries promote not only import-replacing industrialization for the home market but also exports of manufactures. The increasing population provides an expanding labor supply at low wages, and increasing labor productivity in the modern sector keeps wage costs at levels which make Asian countries highly competitive in the markets of the industrialized countries, where the labor force has increased more slowly and there is strong upward pressure on wages (E. Boserup, 1981a).

Except for the most industrially advanced of the Asian countries, married women work mainly in the informal sector, if they take part in non-domestic work. This is partly because work in this sector is more compatible with child care, partly because employers in the modern sector prefer young single women, and, in some countries, because men do not want to have working wives but have less objection to working daughters (E. Boserup, 1970a). The rapidly increasing employment of young unmarried women in both national and multinational industries and services has had important effects on fertility and on the status of women, because it has helped to make young women more independent. The marriage age has increased either because parents have agreed to late marriage, because they can benefit from their daughter's wages as long as she stays under parental authority, or because the young woman herself has delayed marriage until she has saved enough money to finance a marriage of her own choice. In some Asian countries, including Malaysia and Thailand, economic change, increase of marriage age, other improvements in female status, and fertility declines have been large (G. Jones, 1981).

Agricultural policies in Asian countries have responded to their high population densities and high pressure of population on land. When population growth accelerated in the period after the Second World War, governments were concerned about how to achieve a sufficient increase in food supply. Therefore, nearly all of them promoted rural development and technological change in agriculture by means of credits, subsidies, and direct investment. The resulting Green Revolution led to increases in food production greater than the increase in population, and in nearly all Asian countries the dependency on food imports declined, with the notable exception of Bangladesh. Moreover, a number of Asian governments, including India, transformed tenants into owners, or organized settlement schemes in areas of relatively low population density. These types of land reform had different effects on fertility: tenants who became owners got a new motivation for fertility control, but the effect of settlement schemes was pronatalist, if land distribution gave priority to large families for social reasons, or if a family's new holding was substantially larger than its previous one.

Because the emphasis in Asian agricultural development is on irrigation, multicropping, and labor-intensive methods such as transplanting of paddy, output per hectare increased and so did the demand for labor. Therefore, it became possible for larger families to live better on smaller landholdings than before. There was some replacement of female and child labor by chemical and mechanical inputs, but there is still a demand for these types of labor in small-scale agriculture. In some cases, the first effect of the Green Revolution seems to have been an increase of family size, but this was temporary, and on

TABLE 5. Married women's fertility by her education, occupation of husband, and urban or rural location, twenty-one developing countries

Country and technology group	Low marital fertility rates			High marital fertility rates			Fertility differences		
	Wife has secondary education	Husband is professional, manager	Urban location	Wife is illiterate	Husband works in agriculture	Rural location	By education	By occupation	By location
Asia									
Nepal (1)	4.8	5.6	6.2	7.1	7.3	7.2	2.3	1.8	1.0
Bangladesh (1)	7.2	7.0	7.2	6.8	7.0	6.9	1.3	0.3	-0.2
Pakistan (2)	6.7	7.6	7.8	7.9	7.8	7.8	1.2	0.6	0.0
Indonesia (2)	7.3	6.9	7.4	6.0	5.9	6.2	-1.3	-1.1	-1.3
Malaysia (3)	7.3	7.3	7.4	8.1	8.6	8.0	0.7	1.0	0.6
Thailand (3)	6.0	5.8	6.5	7.5	8.0	7.7	1.5	2.2	1.3
Sri Lanka (3)	7.3	6.7	6.8	7.1	7.2	7.2	-0.2	0.7	0.4
Philippines (3)	8.1	7.7	7.5	8.8	9.5	9.4	0.7	1.8	1.9
South Korea (4)	6.4	7.5	6.6	7.8	8.3	8.1	1.4	0.8	1.5
Latin America									
Haiti (1)	5.6	5.4	6.3	8.3	8.5	8.3	2.7	3.1	2.0
Paraguay (3)	5.9	5.5	5.8	10.4	9.5	9.0	4.6	3.9	3.1
Peru (3)	7.7	7.8	7.8	10.3	10.2	10.4	2.6	2.4	2.6
Dominican Rep. (3)	6.2	5.4	6.7	8.9	9.8	9.5	2.7	4.4	1.8
Guyana (4)	6.9	5.5	5.6	8.2	8.2	7.5	1.4	2.7	1.9
Venezuela (4)	6.1	6.2	6.2	9.2	7.5	10.3	3.1	4.2	4.1
Jamaica (4)	6.3	4.9	5.2	7.4	7.8	7.3	1.1	2.9	2.1
Trinidad (4)	4.8	3.8	4.3	6.0	6.5	5.4	1.3	2.7	1.1
Columbia (4)	5.9	5.7	6.1	9.4	9.8	9.9	3.4	4.1	3.6
Mexico (4)	7.2	7.6	8.4	10.0	10.1	10.2	2.3	2.5	1.8
Panama (4)	3.9	4.1	4.0	6.6	6.1	5.9	2.7	2.1	1.9
Costa Rica (4)	4.0	3.7	3.7	5.8	5.1	5.1	1.9	1.4	1.4

Source: Alam and Casterline (1984).

the whole the development strategies of most Asian governments have helped both to reduce fertility and to ameliorate the effects of increasing population pressure on resources. The main exception is the Moslem countries of Pakistan and Bangladesh, which have had very little fertility decline in spite of official birth control policies. In some Asian countries, coercive government policies have played a major part in the reduction of fertility. This is true of China and Viet Nam, which have tried to improve the food-population ratio not only by efforts at intensifying agriculture, but also by introducing rationing of births (G. Jones, 1982). China, moreover, has tried to reduce family size by a marriage law which makes parents responsible for large numbers of relatives in addition to their own children ("China's new marriage law," 1981).

In Latin America, development strategies have been very different from those in most Asian countries. Some Latin American countries have had settlement schemes, but very few have transformed tenants into owners or redistributed land to agricultural workers. Thus a large share of the rural population continues to be landless or nearly landless labor, with no security except that provided by family members. Because of the abundant land resources in most of the continent, governments seem usually to have assumed that market forces would assure that food production expanded in step with demand, so they have done little to encourage expansion of food production. In many cases, they have directly discouraged food production by promoting imports of food from the industrialized countries in order to supply urban consumers with food at favorable prices, thus reducing urban wage costs and promoting industrialization. Because of the better opportunities for financing development with primary exports, the pattern of industrialization is more home-market and regionally oriented than in Asian countries, and less focused on exports to the industrialized countries. The result of the encouragement to industry and discouragement to agriculture has been an increasing gap between urban and rural employment opportunities and incomes. Rural-to-urban migration has become very large, with most migrants moving to metropolitan areas and other large cities. The abundant labor supply in these areas has encouraged the creation of industries and ancillary informal sector activities.

This Latin American pattern of development contains elements which have promoted fertility decline and elements which have delayed it. The occupational changes in the urban labor market and the rapid increase in the proportion of population living in large cities have helped reduce fertility, but the lack of rural development has kept rural fertility at high levels. It is true that migration from rural areas has tended to reduce fertility if spouses are separated, but if migrant youth of both sexes transfer part of their earnings to parents left behind, rural fertility decline will be delayed by good employment opportunities for migrants in urban areas and in the United States.

Table 5, which like table 1 is derived from the World Fertility Survey, shows differences in marital fertility in twelve Latin American and nine Asian countries. The differences between rural and agricultural families on the one hand, and urban population and white collar workers on the other, were much larger in Latin America than in Asia. There were usually differences of 2.0–4.0 children in Latin America, against 1.0–1.5, or less, in Asia. The large fertility differences in Latin America reflect a very high fertility in the groups of rural, agricultural, and illiterate women in Latin American countries, even some at high levels of economic development (technology group 4 in the table). These high agricultural and rural fertilities in Latin America, compared with Asia, seem to reflect the density-related differences in occupational structure. In Asia, population pressure on the predominant system of small-scale peasant farming induced governments to promote both rural development and fertility control, and many peasants were motivated to make use of family planning services, or they used folk methods of control, including late marriage. In Latin America, both rural development and rural fertility control have suffered from lack of government encouragement, and the landless rural population have had less motivation for control than the Asian peasants.

Although fertility has declined much in urban Latin America, even the most developed Latin American countries have considerably higher fertility than the highly industrialized countries. Not only are public social security systems less widespread and comprehensive, so the dependence of both sexes on their family is larger, but female access to employment in the modern sector is lower. Therefore married women have more fear of divorce and abandonment, and more are willing to accept the burden of many pregnancies and a life devoted to child care and domestic duties.

In most African countries, the burden on rural women is heavy. The nutritional strain of many pregnancies, long periods of breast-feeding, and heavy agricultural and domestic work often undermine their health (Harrington, 1983). In many areas, women still produce the subsistence food for the family with little or no male help, and the assignment of food production to women is a major reason for the lack of interest in conditions of food production by African male farmers and African governments. In many African countries, the growing towns are supplied mainly by food imported from industrialized countries, which is supplied at low prices owing to the support policies in industrialized countries and transportation by sea, which is cheaper than local African transport, because of the poor infrastructure in the sparsely populated continent (E. Boserup, 1981a).

The long-fallow system, which encourages high fertility, is still predominant in many regions of Africa; also, child mortality is high compared with most other developing areas, and widespread use of child labor continues to encourage high fertility (Dow and Werner, 1983). In African regions in which the long-fallow system with tribal tenure has been replaced by private property in land, either by legal reforms or by direct takeover, women have usually lost their cultivation rights in land without getting ownership rights, which have been granted or usurped by the men as family heads but preserved by the men even if they abandon or divorce their wives (Pala Okeyo, 1984). Thus in many cases women have become more dependent upon male members of their family, because they are less able to support themselves and children by agricultural work. Also, increasing monetization and the declining importance of subsistence production make it less feasible for women to be self-supporting, since the cash crops are usually produced by the men, who keep the income even when the women have helped produce the crops.

In many areas of Africa, there has been considerable expansion of export crops, which has benefited from increasing labor inputs. However, expansion of production of traditional export crops through traditional methods has not provided motivation to reduce fertility, and in many parts of Africa fertility has increased, owing to improvements in health, and to abandonment of traditional fertility-reducing measures, without replacement by contraceptive means (Lesthaeghe, 1980). Owing to the low level of development in most of Africa, African men have little inducement to change their pronatalist attitude: subfecundity of the wife is usually a cause of polygamy or divorce, and even the small elite of educated women often have large families under pressure from husbands and older family members (Oppong and Abu, 1984).

African governments, like those elsewhere, are in favor of industrialization, but because of the small and scattered population in most of the continent and the extremely poor infrastructure, efforts at industrial development are often frustrated. Therefore, the growing towns are usually service towns, with little, if any, modern industry. The population consists of administrators, educational and health personnel, persons handling foreign and internal trade and transport, and large numbers of informal sector workers, serving the above-mentioned occupational groups. As already noted, the informal sector provides little motivation for fertility reduction, and even the small elite groups often have high fertility, because their high incomes allow them to satisfy their desire for large families.

Prices for most African exports have fluctuated wildly. When export prices have collapsed, there has been large-scale emigration from the country with unfavorable prices to one with more favorable conditions, or to Europe. When export prices have fluctuated upward, a large share of the income increase has been used to raise consumption of imported manufactures and imported food. It is often assumed that increase of per capita income has a negative impact on fertility, at least when the families are not among the very poorest. But the factor which reduces fertility is structural change in the labor market, which may be the cause also of the income increase. If income increase occurs not because of structural change but because of windfall profits in terms of trade, and is used for imports of ready-made goods, the effects on fertility are more likely to be positive than negative. Improvements in prices of primary exports are likely to reduce fertility only if and when they induce national economic development, which causes structural changes in the labor market and in family organization. The large declines in fertility in recent years have occurred not in Arab and African countries, which have had improved terms of trade, but in Asian and Latin American countries, in which the governments have pursued policies leading to changes in the occupational structure.

When declining child mortality results in increasing family size, a family can either adapt income to family size or adapt family size to income. The husband, or the wife, or some of the children can take a job, or an extra job, in the modern sector, or they can engage in informal sector activity, or some family members can migrate for seasonal or more permanent employment elsewhere. All these options are alternatives to fertility control. Because of the economic expansion in both developed and developing countries in most of the period of rapid population growth, many families have had the opportunity to increase income by one or more of these options, and so avoid reducing family size. However, because of increasing protectionism and an unwillingness to receive migrants in both developing and industrialized countries, and because the debt crisis forces economic contraction in many countries, migrants return. It becomes difficult to find employment and extra jobs, and markets for products and services in the informal sector become less expansive.

In those developing countries which have become heavily dependent upon exports of manufactures or remittances by migrants or capital imports, the choice is narrowing. This situation is likely to force many families to choose fertility control as the means of restraining their expenditure. Some African countries, including Ghana, have for a long time suffered from a severe economic crisis, while others, including Kenya, have experienced strong economic growth. This may help to explain why use of family planning services is more widespread in Ghana than in Kenya, although in Kenya the services are available in a larger part of the country than in Ghana, and more people are aware of their existence (Lesthaeghe, 1984).

In an economic crisis, parents have more need for help from their children, but at times of crisis this is likely to be more than outbalanced by the reduced possibility of getting any help from children, either young ones or adults. In other words, while fertility will decline further, or begin to decline, in countries with continued economic development and occupational change, there are countries in Latin America in which the economic crisis may accelerate the existing downward trend in fertility, and the economic crises in large parts of Africa will probably make family planning acceptable to many more African families, especially in urban areas.

PART IV

Africa

Linkages between Industry and Agriculture

A SHORT ESSAY DEALING with the relations between industrial and agricultural development on the African continent must neglect many differences between individual countries and focus attention on some major features which seem to be characteristic of the countries in the region. There is a danger, however, in overstressing the similarity of basic conditions within Africa. The danger is that an autarchic attitude is taken in each country, if it is not realized that there are important differences between individual countries and that it is these which give scope for economic cooperation among them. Therefore, the present essay focuses attention not only on common features, but also on some important differences between African countries.

Since sparse population settlement is a common feature in Africa, it is natural to begin a discussion of the interplay between industrial and agricultural development with an analysis of the African labor market. The labor force needed for industrialization is not limited to the workers and employees of the new industrial establishments. It also includes the much larger numbers needed for the construction of industrial enterprises and for the creation of necessary infrastructure, such as transport facilities, power production, and urban expansion. In countries with little urbanization, most of the labor force needed for industrialization must be attracted from the countryside. This need to draw labor from a common pool creates a linkage between industrial and agricultural development.

While average population density in Africa is low, there are striking differences in density of settlement among individual countries. These contrasts, together with climatic differences, provide a basis for international specialization in industrial and agricultural production. Therefore, relative density of settlement is the chief criterion for the grouping of African countries adopted here. It must not be assumed that grouping by density of settlement is identical to grouping by access to waterways. The disadvantages of sparse settlement are not identical with the disadvantages of being landlocked: many coastal countries in Africa are sparsely settled, and some landlocked countries in East Africa are relatively densely settled.

"Linkages between Industry and Agriculture." UN Symposium on Industrial Development in Africa, Cairo; 27 January–10 February 1966.

Labor Supply for Industry and Agriculture

In the colonial period, most Africans preferred subsistence agriculture to wage labor. Europeans had great difficulties in recruiting labor for plantations, mines, and other nonagricultural activities, and they often had recourse to recruiters or even to forced labor. Wage employment was usually temporary: the young men returned to the villages as soon as they had earned the amount of money they needed for the payment of taxes, bride prices, and other purposes. In recent decades, the attitude of the rural African to wage labor outside his village has changed radically. Very large numbers of African youths have left the villages in order to establish themselves permanently in urban areas. Employment in construction and services, and sometimes also in industry, has been rapidly increasing in numerous African towns, but mostly the inflow of labor from the villages has been running ahead of demand for labor, and a certain amount of unemployment has become a characteristic feature of the urban scene in Africa.

The flow of villagers into African towns is sometimes explained as a result of population pressure in the villages. Closer inspection suggests, however, that this explanation is valid only in rare cases, at least in Africa south of the Sahara. In most of Africa, the agricultural system continues to be that of shifting cultivation on tribal land. This implies that all members of the new generation can find land to cultivate, even if population is growing at a fairly high rate. If all villagers, despite population growth, were to stay in the villages and take up the cultivation of land, it may sometimes be necessary to shorten the periods of fallow, which could lead to deterioration of the land in the longer run. This risk of land deterioration, however, does not deter the villagers from taking land under cultivation to obtain employment and income. As a result, agricultural experts are worried about the risk of land deterioration resulting from population increase in villages subsisting by engaging in shifting cultivation of tribal land.

It is true that there are rural districts in various parts of Africa where land is privately owned and where a part of the population is thus unable to start cultivation on their own account. However, these districts are mainly the centers of production of export crops, and the increasing volume for export has provided increasing employment; indeed, it has sometimes been difficult to recruit sufficient labor for export production. The producers of some traditional African export crops have suffered from declining export prices, but as a rule the decline of prices has not prevented output and employment from expanding.

Recent trends in production of food in Africa have been in marked contrast to the high rate of increase of export production. Statistical data on trends in food production are poor and few, but it is generally agreed that there has been little change in traditional methods of production. As a broad generalization, production of food may have increased roughly in proportion to increase in the *rural* population. This means that, in the typical case, there has been insufficient increase in the marketable surplus of food to feed the villagers who have emigrated to the towns. Thus the increased demand for food in the rapidly growing towns has had to be filled largely by imports. Some of this food has been imported from African countries which have had little urban growth or which have had some increase of productivity in food production, but a substantial part has come from non-African countries. Food imports into West Africa, for example, have been growing by more than 10 percent per annum in recent years.

The inflow of rural population to the urban areas has not only run ahead of the demand for labor and created unemployment, it has also created bad housing conditions, with the migrants living in congested shantytowns. It is important to note, however, that neither the risk of unemployment nor the lack of decent housing has been an effective deterrent to further migration. The attractions of the towns are obvious, and the gap between the range of private and public services which are offered in urban areas and in the villages is steadily widening. Under these circumstances, rural youth is willing to undertake a long waiting period, with unemployment and poor housing, in order to obtain the desired status of urban wage laborer or employee. They are able to withstand the waiting period because of solidarity among family members and covillagers, who support them during this period. They can, therefore, refuse to accept employment for less than the normal wages.

In the savannah regions, migration to urban areas usually begins as a seasonal migration by young villagers leaving their home village for the dry season. However, when the dry season is over, many of them have little desire to return to village life. They try to stay in the towns if they can obtain employment or support from other town dwellers or from their home village. The age and sex of the rural-to-urban migrants also suggest that the attractions of the town, rather than the lack of possibility for finding subsistence in the village, are the motivating force behind migration. It is much discussed, and much regretted, that the young people who leave the villages in search of urban employment are the more vigorous and promising members of rural life, including a large share of the literate in regions where literacy has begun to spread to the villages. This tendency is so pronounced that it has even been discussed whether it would be desirable, in the interest of rural development, to hold back the spread of primary education in rural areas. The suggestion seems self-defeating from the point of view of rural development, and it would not necessarily slow down rural-to-urban migration. The desire for education may be so strong that migration would increase if that were the only way to obtain literacy.

It has been a matter for debate among economists whether discussions about the possibilities and conditions of industrialization in underdeveloped countries should be based upon the assumption of an unlimited supply of labor. In the case of Africa, a realistic approach to this question requires that a distinction be made between the urban and the rural sectors. In the urban sector, it is pertinent to assume an unlimited supply of labor, because increase in employment will raise the inflow of labor from rural districts. With increasing employment, more former villagers will be able to support still larger numbers waiting for urban employment. Thus the inflow becomes larger and continues to run ahead of demand, so that the reserve of the unemployed waiting for employment tends to be maintained. This theory of an unlimited supply of labor in urban areas implies that there is little hope that industrialization can eradicate urban unemployment in the near future. Many developing countries have experienced this steady inflow from the countryside, which has prevented a decline of unemployment in spite of rapid expansion of urban employment. Italy continued to have mass unemployment during its period of rapid industrial growth in the fifties, because rural migrants continued to move in from the south, thus preventing a decline of urban unemployment in the northern regions, where industrial and other urban employment was growing at a remarkably high and steady rate. It is more than likely that this process will also take place in Africa. If the above reasoning is accepted, it serves to stress an important point for industrialization policy in Africa: the need for industrialization in Africa does not arise from the need to reduce or eliminate unemployment, but from the need to raise incomes.

Unemployment in *urban* regions must not be allowed to conceal the true picture of the *rural* labor market in most of Africa. Here, too, there is much unemployment in the dry seasons, and working hours are often short. But nevertheless, agricultural production is likely to decline proportionately when a share of the villagers leave the village for the town. There is no reason to assume that the remaining villagers would work harder because some are leaving, except in some regions of high population density, mainly in North Africa. Thus, in contradistinction to the urban scene, plans for rural development in Africa must be based upon the assumption of a limited supply of labor.

Food Supplies for the Urban Sector

Demand for food in Africa is increasing, partly because population is increasing and partly because of the growth of urbanization and the rise of per capita incomes in urban areas. Furthermore, growth in urban population causes a shift in the type of food demanded. Demand for processed food is rapidly increasing in urban areas, and imports of meat, vegetables, and fruits are rising to supplement local supplies in the seasons when this supply is insufficient.

The rising demand for food in urban areas is a challenge to African agriculture, but in meeting it there are several hurdles. The difficulty is not that the African soil cannot produce more than it does at present. There was a time when agronomists were in doubt about the ability of the African soil to bear more frequent harvests than it does under the traditional system of long fallow. This stage has been passed; virtually all experts now agree that the physical conditions for very large increases in agricultural production are excellent, given a radical change from long-fallow methods to more intensive methods, which use other types of fertilization, and taking account of the need to avoid erosion and other deterioration of the land. The experts agree up to this point, but no further. The long-fallow system can be replaced by several other systems. One possibility is to change to a relatively extensive system of short fallow or annual cropping, with plowing of the land and application of manure or chemical fertilizer. Another possibility is to change to an intensive system of mixed farming, where fodder for domestic animals is introduced into the crop rotation. A third possibility is to create facilities for irrigation, thus allowing more than one crop a year in regions where the agricultural population is without work in the long dry season. For short reference, the three types of agriculture just mentioned may be labelled as the North American, the West European, and the Far Eastern type of agriculture.

In the colonial period, most agricultural research and agricultural extension in Africa was concentrated on export crops. Some of the few and relatively small districts with dense population had an extension service, which devoted attention to improving the methods used in food production. What was needed in these districts was to raise the total amount of food crops and other crops which a family could produce on a given, and small, area of land. It was felt to be of less importance what effects the suggested changes had on average and marginal output per work hour. Therefore, agricultural research and extension work were focused largely on methods to raise output per unit of land by increasing annual labor input per family. There is little doubt that many of the new methods thus recommended added proportionately more to the input of labor than to the net output of agriculture, thus lowering net output per work hour.

The agricultural change needed in Africa today is of a different type. Since so much land is only rarely utilized for cultivation or grazing—or never utilized for any purpose—the aim should not be to raise the output of any particular piece of land. The aim must be to raise the output per unit of labor so rapidly that the marketable surplus can become sufficient to feed an increasing urban population with African-grown food, despite the fact that a share of the agricultural population will continue to leave agriculture and migrate to urban areas. In each rural district of Africa, the choice between the three agrarian systems mentioned above must be made with this goal in mind.

At this stage, our reasoning may be contradicted. It may be objected that, since most African long-fallow cultivators are working for a short part of the year only, or are working very short daily hours, the aim should be to raise the input of labor per cultivator family, thereby raising total output and total family income, while underemployment in agriculture is reduced. The answer to this possible objection is that it is based upon an unrealistic assumption regarding attitudes toward work. It must be remembered that in Africa—as in long-fallow communities in other parts of the world—agriculturalists value leisure highly in comparison with the utility of additions to output. (In technical parlance, income elasticity of demand for leisure is high). Therefore, agricultural changes that offer additional employment opportunities without raising output per unit of labor significantly are not likely to be widely acceptable. All Africans want higher incomes per work hour, but most of them have little desire for additional agricultural work which does not raise and might even lower average output per work hour.

If, on the other hand, agricultural changes make it possible to earn a significantly higher income from a workday of given length and strenuousness, cultivators may be tempted to put in more workdays per year or more work hours per day than they are doing now, thus raising their total income and output through the double effect of higher output per work hour and more work hours per year. In other words, if agricultural policy is designed to raise the output per work hour, it may have the secondary effect of raising labor input in agriculture, while on the other hand methods designed to raise labor input in agriculture without significantly raising output per work hour are unlikely to have the desired effect.

Our conclusion seems to be confirmed by actual experience in extension work in Africa. There are a few successful examples of improvement of food production by labor-intensive methods with low output per work hour, but these refer to untypical districts where land is very scarce and few employment opportunities are offered outside agriculture. In such cases, the cultivator had no alternative to working harder in agriculture and giving up his accustomed periods of seasonal leisure. By contrast, where cultivators have land enough to continue with the easy methods of long fallow or can avoid intensification by changing to nonagricultural employment, it is difficult or impossible to persuade them to take to labor-intensive farming with low output per work hour.

Intensive systems of farming are difficult to learn for a cultivator accustomed to long-fallow methods only, and desperately few people are available to teach him how to do it. Agricultural technicians and extension personnel specialized in food production were always few in Africa. Their ranks are now being depleted by the departure of expatriates, and few Africans are prepared to fill the gaps. This is not just a matter of too few years having elapsed since independence to train Africans to take over the jobs previously filled by Europeans. The problem is far worse, because there are so few Africans undergoing training for agricultural jobs requiring higher education. And this is not due to a lack of training facilities, since African candidates can easily get scholarships for training abroad. The fact is that educated Africans, like ordinary Africans, prefer any other activity to agriculture. Thus, few Africans seek scholarships for training as agricultural specialists, and the agricultural schools in Africa, although they are few and far between, often find it difficult to fill their capacity except by accepting the less qualified of the educated youth.

The immediate effect of African independence on economic policy was to focus attention on the expansion of the urban sector, while the modernization of African agriculture was considered to be less important. When African countries began to draw up development plans, agricultural expansion came into the picture as a means to reduce or avoid food imports, thus making foreign exchange available for the purchase of equipment for industrialization. It was generally agreed that expanding food production would require capital investment in agriculture. The purchase of agricultural equipment was foreseen in the import plans, and the cost of creating agricultural extension services and other rural development services were taken into account in plans for the agricultural sector. This concern for agricultural development was not exclusively due to pressure from the planners; it also reflected the desire of political leaders to make rural people feel that they had benefited from independence.

However, it is of limited avail that planners and politicians begin to take an interest in the modernization of African agriculture and make financial means available for equipment and personnel, if the general lack of interest in agriculture persists. Unfortunately, there is little reason to expect any change in this respect, and it is likely, therefore, that far too few and qualified top specialists will be available to work out the strategy of agricultural change and adapt it to conditions in various localities. It is likely, moreover, that it will take a long time to train a sufficient number of qualified extension personnel and technicians on lower levels, partly because there are too few to undertake the training and partly because too few qualified Africans are prepared to undergo this type of training—and to use it for the purpose it was meant to serve, once the diploma is obtained. The problem of a lack of qualified extension personnel is compounded by the likelihood that they will have to teach a rural population deprived of its more active citizens, who have migrated to urban work. It seems relatively safe to predict, in these conditions, that there will be much underfulfillment of agricultural development plans and considerable difficulties in supplying the towns with the quantities and qualities of needed food, if development plans for the urban sector are to be fulfilled.

Population Density and Type of Industrialization

It is a matter of much concern to governments of African countries that they are highly dependent on agricultural exports to industrialized countries as a source of foreign exchange. Nearly all exports of African countries are primary products, mainly agricultural, and nearly all of these exports are sold to industrialized countries on other continents. There are three ways to reduce the dependence of the economies of African countries on this type of export. One is to promote exports to developing countries on other continents, another is to promote exports of processed goods to non-African countries, and the third is to promote intra-African trade in all types of goods, thus replacing some of the imports from other continents. There is little doubt that in the longer run, Africa will reduce its dependence on primary exports to the highly industrialized countries in all three ways. However, in the short run, there seems to be scope primarily for progress along the third line of action, that is by increased specialization in the production for export to African countries accompanied by an increase in the volume of intra-African trade.

Individual African countries cannot carry out any systematic policy of import substitution without abandoning the hope of raising per capita incomes. Only three African countries—Nigeria, Egypt, and Ethiopia—have more than twenty million inhabitants, and nearly half of all Africans live in countries with less than ten million inhabitants, usually a few million only. Countries with a few million inhabitants—and even those with ten to twenty million—must export a large share of their domestic production in order to be able to pay for the very wide range of goods which cannot be produced economically for domestic use in countries with such small domestic markets. In all highly industrialized countries with populations in this range, exports are large in relation to national income.

Thus, there is no other route to high standards of living in individual African countries than to focus development efforts on the creation of an efficient export sector. It is important to note, however, that this in no way implies that the African continent, taken as a whole, does not have considerable scope for import replacement. A continent with 300 million inhabitants needs to import only a small share of the goods it is consuming or investing, if only the pattern of production within the continent is sufficiently diversified, with a high level of trade between countries. As the range of goods produced in Africa for exports to other African countries becomes larger, the range of goods imported from other parts of the world can be narrowed, thus leaving more room for imports of the type of goods which cannot with advantage be produced inside Africa at the present stage of development.

There are many obstacles to a rapid expansion of intra-African trade, but only two of them fall within the scope of this essay. One is the desire for self-sufficiency in food, shared by many African governments. The other is the widespread resentment felt by countries who take the risk of becoming exporters of agricultural products in exchange for imported manufactures, not only in trade with non-African countries but also in intra-African trade. There are large differences among African countries with respect to climate, mineral resources, population density, and degree of economic development. Therefore, there is considerable scope for intra-African trade in agricultural and mineral products. Some such trade is already taking place. For instance, the savannah countries south of the Sahara deliver considerable quantities of livestock to the coastal countries of West Africa. However, the coastal countries are planning to replace these imports by introducing intensive systems of livestock and fodder production in northern regions within their own frontiers.

The coastal countries have usually better possibilities for exports to other continents than savannah countries in the interior of the continent and better possibilities for setting up many types of industries. It was mentioned above that the limiting factor for the expansion of food production in Africa is more likely to be human resources than physical capital or financial allowances for agricultural extension in development plans. This is important to note in any discussion of the possibilities for intra-African trade: if financial and physical limitations mattered, these would be likely to be the least severe

TABLE 1. Intraregional trade in East Africa, 1961 (millions of US$)

Exporting country	Importing country		
	Kenya	Uganda	Tanzania[a]
Kenya		19.7	24.9
Uganda	14.4		4.8
Tanzania[a]	5.1	1.1	

Source: UN (1963).
[a]Excluding the trade of Zanzibar.

in the richest countries with the best conditions for economic development. These countries might then be able to overcome these limitations and become self-sufficient in food, with the result that there would be little scope for intra-African trade in food. On the other hand, if human resources are the limiting factor, then the difficulties are likely to be most pronounced in the countries with the best possibilities for development of the urban sector. This is so because countries with rapid growth of the urban sector give both the highly skilled technicians and the ordinary villager the best chance to satisfy their wish of avoiding agricultural work. If these countries encounter a food deficit for their urban sectors and thus have to allow food imports, other African countries could fill the gap, and intra-African trade in food may thus expand.

Thus, one obstacle to the expansion of intra-African trade is the widespread desire to be self-sufficient in food and other agricultural products. Another and probably more formidable obstacle lies in the fact that the less industrially successful African countries are likely to resent being allocated the role of importers of manufactures from the African countries which have more success with their industrialization policy. Recent developments in East Africa provide a good example of this obstacle to the expansion of intra-African trade in industrial products. It is unavoidable that those African countries which have proceeded more rapidly with industrialization should take the lead in exports of industrial manufactures, while the countries which are less advanced in industrialization must begin by replacing imports of European manufactures by African ones, without themselves being able to export manufactures. Kenya is more advanced in industrialization than Tanzania, and under the free-trade arrangement between these two countries and Uganda, exports from Kenya to Tanzania have increased much more rapidly than trade in the opposite direction. The resulting pattern of intraregional trade is shown in table 1. It appears from the table that Kenya has a considerable export surplus in its trade with Tanzania. The latter country resents having to pay for African-produced industrial manufactures (textiles, footwear, beer, etc.) with part of the earnings derived from exports of agricultural products to Europe, and insists that Kenya must take industrial manufactures of Tanzanian origin in exchange. In these conditions, the prospects for the free-trade arrangement and for Kenya's exports are not too bright.

Tanzania is far from being the only African country to take a pessimistic view of its chances of industrialization under a system of free trade among African countries. Therefore, discussions about industrial coordination held under the auspices of the United Nations Economic Commission for Africa have been focused on attempts to arrive at a mutually agreed planned distribution of industries among African countries. The idea is that industries should be allocated among the countries in such a way that all countries obtain an appropriate share. It is hoped that in this way not only countries with a late start, but also countries with more permanent handicaps due to small markets, lack of mineral resources, or awkward geographic position, could avoid falling behind the others in their rates of industrialization and development of per capita incomes.

In discussions of the industrialization of Africa, it is necessary to distinguish between the obstacle to industrialization caused by the smallness of population and the obstacle caused by low density of settlement. In densely peopled Europe, small countries need only make free-trade arrangements or common markets in order to overcome the handicap to industrial growth from which they are suffering. But in Africa, most countries have small home markets not because they have small territories but because their often huge territories are very thinly populated. Countries with very low population densities are unsuitable as locations for medium- and large-size market-oriented industry. This handicap cannot be overcome by free-trade and common market arrangements, and if market-oriented industries are set up in sparsely settled regions, they cannot compete with similar industries in more suitable locations without being permanently subsidized.

Although population density is exceedingly low in most of Africa, there are regions (north of the coast of Benin and districts near Lake Victoria, for example), where populations of twenty-five to fifty million live within a relatively small area. Such regions must unavoidably exert a strong attraction to market-oriented industries. Small centers in sparsely populated regions with smaller markets will find it difficult to compete with them. The attraction of the big population in the Victoria region is already being felt in East Africa. A foreign firm which had agreed to set up its East African processing plant in Tanzania instead of in Kenya chose to place it in northern Tanzania rather than in Dar-es-Salaam, which is less favorably situated for serving the Lake Victoria region. In addition to big, densely settled regions, there are a number of much smaller, densely settled districts which are usually separated from each other and from the larger agglomerations by vast areas of very sparsely peopled forest, savannah, or desert. These smaller districts will no doubt become centers for market-oriented industries of the kind which lend themselves to economic production even at a medium size, while they will be unable to compete for the location of large-size market-oriented industries. Sparsely populated countries with still smaller markets are best suited for specialization in raw-material-oriented industries producing mainly for export. According to local circumstances, these may process either ores and other minerals or products from agriculture, pastures, forestry, and fishing.

In advanced industrial countries it is usual, in grouping industries according to their preferred location, to distinguish several groups in addition to the broad and basic groups of market-oriented and raw-material-oriented industries. For instance, it is usual to distinguish between labor-oriented industries and "footloose" industries, the latter group consisting of industries which can be located almost anywhere in the territory without making much difference to the costs of production. The special conditions of Africa are such that all the industries which elsewhere in the world might be classified as labor-oriented or as footloose would seem to be market oriented, since they are likely to have much lower costs of production if they are set up in major urban centers in regions of large and dense population, rather than in other parts of Africa.

Take first labor-oriented industries. Even in densely populated and highly industrialized countries, labor-oriented industries are attracted to the big centers of market-oriented industries, which are by definition the largest agglomerations of potential industrial workers. They may, however, be attracted to other locations if these have significantly lower labor costs. In Africa, it seems most unlikely that labor costs would be lower in sparsely populated regions than in the centers of regions with a large and dense population. Wage rates may be lower far from these centers, but in view of the high incidence of labor migrations in Africa (including labor movements from one country to another), it is unlikely that the difference would be large enough to outweigh the higher efficiency of labor and other advantages of the centers. The population in the densely populated regions is more familiar with modern techniques and types of work. Literacy rates are higher and schools usually of better quality.

It is true that a large share of the population in the big towns is composed of recent immigrants from rural areas, including some from sparsely populated regions, but it has been noted already that it is often the best elements that migrate to the centers and the less qualified who are available for employment in their home districts. The high labor costs in the less urbanized regions are partly due to the fact that workers in such regions are more likely to spoil materials and equipment by misuse and carelessness than are workers with some urban experience and education. This factor is reinforced by the difficulty of providing spare parts and qualified repair work outside the industrial agglomerations. These factors together with the fact that transport costs are high all over Africa, except in the most densely settled regions, lead to the conclusion that there cannot be footloose industries under African conditions. There must necessarily be a very strong tendency for the concentration of manufacturing industry in the densely settled regions which can afford better infrastructure and can attract the best qualified workers, technicians, and managers.

Outside these locations, the only medium- and large-size industries which can be competitive are raw-material-oriented industries either of the heavy type, processing ores and other minerals, or of the light type, processing raw materials from agriculture. Even raw-material-oriented industries of both types will prefer locations near markets, unless the raw materials (or power) they use can be produced more cheaply in sparsely settled regions away from the location of market-oriented industries.

It is of course possible for a country to choose a type of industrialization which runs counter to these considerations, but the result is likely to be unsatisfactory. Such a country will lose the advantage of profitable trade with neighboring countries with different types of industrialization, and when other African countries will have outgrown the need for infant industry protection and take steps to liberalize their trade, the country with unsuitable industrialization may not find it possible—without painful adjustments—to take part in this movement, because it has set up industries in need of permanent protection.

The Integration of Agriculture and Raw-Material-Oriented Industry

For sparsely populated regions without possibilities for the establishment of low-cost market-oriented industries, the advantage of raw-material-oriented industries is not in the processing costs but in the costs of the raw materials (counting fuel and power as raw materials). Processing costs are likely to be higher than elsewhere, because labor costs are likely to be higher. Thus industries are raw material oriented only if it is more convenient or cheaper to transport the industrial product than the raw materials used in its production. Otherwise, it is likely to be cheaper to undertake the processing in the market region.

Take cotton for instance. Raw cotton loses weight in the process of ginning. Therefore, cotton ginning takes place in the region where the cotton is grown. Ginned cotton, on the other hand, is as easy and cheap to transport as cotton yarns and cotton textiles, and there is thus no particular advantage in setting up textile industries in the region where the cotton is produced. If this region happens to be densely populated and thus provides a sufficiently large local market for textiles, a textile industry may be set up to serve this market, but otherwise the crude cotton is likely to be transported away from the region. It is only at a later stage, when the country has become highly industrialized, that the cotton industry can become footloose, because there are no longer significant regional differences in the efficiency of labor or in the quantity and quality of infrastructure.

It has been suggested during discussions among African governments about the possibility of an agreed geographical distribution of industries in West Africa that cotton industries producing for exports to other West African countries might be located in some landlocked countries which now export raw cotton and in which the domestic market is too small to support a cotton textile industry. There seems to be a considerable risk, however, that such industries would long remain high-cost producers, unable to pay the producers of cotton as much as they could obtain by exporting unprocessed cotton.

In contrast with cotton, many other agricultural products are inconvenient to transport in crude form. This is true of perishable products like fruit and vegetables, livestock products, and fish. Such products are expensive to transport over long distances under tropical conditions while suitable processing can solve the transport problem. Forest products, too, are inconvenient to transport in crude form, because there is considerable loss of weight in the processing. Owing to the gradual exhaustion of forest resources near seaports, there is demand for timber from more remote regions where the timber may more conveniently be processed locally. Thus food processing, wood, and paper industries would seem more suitable for location in distant and sparsely populated regions than textile industries, provided, of course, that the crude products can be produced at costs low enough to enable the processed goods to bear the cost of transportation to the large urban centers of Africa without becoming noncompetitive in relation to local products or to imported non-African products.

It is often recommended that small-scale food processing industries should be set up in rural areas as a means of reducing seasonal and other underemployment in agriculture and to improve the incomes of the rural population. The further suggestion is often made that such industries should be organized as cooperatives run by the farming communities, and that agricultural extension and other types of rural development services might assist cultivators in producing the type and quality of products needed in these industries. It is not possible to base the processing of agricultural products for export on this type of enterprise. Those African countries which will most need to base their industrialization on a specialization in agricultural processing industries are among those which have hitherto been least affected by modern influences. Their agriculture is overwhelmingly a nonmonetized production for consumption by the cultivator's family, with the sale of only a small share of the output of food or of a small quantity of other products, which are usually of poor quality. The social system is highly traditional in such rural areas; elders and traditional chiefs dominate, and the younger members of the communities are subservient to them. Cooperative industries set up in such regions must necessarily be dominated by the least enterprising and most traditional elements of the local population, and there is thus a risk that these industries, instead of being a means for modernization and increased efficiency in traditional agriculture, will themselves be contaminated by the traditional inefficiency of primitive agricultural economies.

Industries producing for export markets must have managers and technicians of high quality. The flow of production must be uninterrupted (apart from seasonal interruptions) and consist of products of uniform and reasonably high quality. Food processing industries catering to export markets must maintain high hygienic standards. In order to meet these requirements, enterprises producing for export must be large enough to be able to pay high salaries to managers and technicians. (An enterprise can consist of a number of relatively small industrial plants under the same management). Moreover, the enterprises must not be dependent for their supply of raw materials on the whims of the leaders or members of traditional rural communities, unaccustomed to meeting firm timetables and with little regard for quality and hygienic standards. Thus, the industrial enterprises must be autonomous and should organize and supervise the agricultural production on which they depend for their supply of raw materials.

In sparsely populated African countries which have possibilities for setting up this type of industry, the rural population consists either of tribes of herdsmen or of agriculturalists cultivating tribal land by very extensive labor systems of shifting cultivation. These types of activities may produce low yields per unit of land, but food can be produced for subsistence with a small input of labor per family, usually less than one-thousand hours per year. In other words, in activities of these types, labor productivity, as measured by output of food per hour of labor, is not particularly low. In fact, it is much higher than in regions where agriculture is more intensive but where the use of modern equipment or chemical fertilizers has not yet been adopted. Annual output per family is low not because output per hour of work is low but because the number of hours worked per family is low. This traditional pattern of work in sparsely populated regions is an important factor to keep in mind in discussions about industrialization in Africa. A labor force accustomed to very short daily hours or to long periods of idleness between short seasons of agricultural work cannot easily be adapted to modern types of regular work in industries or in modern agriculture. All parts of Africa are suffering from this obstacle to economic development, but the handicap is more serious, the more sparsely populated the region and the more labor extensive the traditional agricultural system. It is generally agreed that the problem is most formidable where the local population is composed of nomadic herdsmen accustomed to no other work than pasturing their flocks.

The youths belonging to tribes of herdsmen or to cultivating tribes applying extensive systems of long fallow on tribal land usually have no desire to become independent, landowning farmers. The more enterprising among the young people desire, first of all, to leave the village dominated by the elders and obtain well-paid employment in a distant area, where they are able to freely dispose of the earnings of their labor. In order to obtain employment of this type, they are willing to accept longer working hours than the ones to which they were accustomed in their home village (although it may require intensive training and considerable time before they agree to work with consistent effort throughout the working day). Thus it would seem advisable for several reasons, in the case of agricultural or pastoral production related to the food processing industry, to recruit wage labor from among the young people who are eager to leave their home village, instead of having production organized by the villagers themselves in their traditional surroundings. It should not be difficult to find suitable land on which to organize production of this kind in the very sparsely populated countries.

Many European plantations organized agricultural production around a processing plant, relying on wage labor, but their labor policy was usually to recruit a large, rapidly shifting and poorly paid labor force, which continued to be uncommitted and inefficient and needed steady and intensive supervision by a European staff. If industrialization is to have a chance in the least developed regions of Africa, labor policy must be the exact opposite of the above. Workers must be carefully selected from among the best elements of the rural population. All of them, industrial as well as agricultural workers, must be systematically trained in the classroom and on the job, and the wage system must be one which gives strong incentive to individual effort and to careful work and careful handling of equipment and materials.

The organization of local agricultural production under the auspices of a large processing industry has the further advantage of helping to mitigate the scarcity of agricultural technicians. It has already been mentioned that educated people willing to specialize in agriculture are a desperately scarce resource in Africa, and it is therefore important that such people should be utilized in the most efficient way and offered the best possible conditions of work and other facilities. Agricultural technicians are more efficient when they can give orders to a staff of wage laborers than when they are engaged in persuading traditional cultivators to change their methods and types of crops. They can obtain more attractive living conditions and have a better chance of promotion if they work on the staff of a modern integrated processing industry than if they are dispersed in traditional villages.

Africans do not seem to be firmly tied to their home districts. They are inclined to leave regions where they cannot obtain as high a remuneration for their qualifications as elsewhere in Africa. If agriculture-based industries in sparsely populated countries can become efficient and able to pay high salaries and wages to qualified persons, they may become poles of attraction for people who would otherwise have emigrated from the country. Ordinary villagers, as well as the best educated youth, may then choose employment in such industries and in ancillary activities, such as offices, workshops, and technical schools attached to the industries.

Industrial processing of agricultural products is often regarded as a less desirable type of industrialization, because it is thought to have little or no local spread effects. It is certainly true that such processing industries, established in regions of sparse settlement, are unlikely to attract market-oriented industries, but this is because of the small population in the region. A heavy mineral processing plant of similar size would not have much spread effect either. Even the exceptionally large and rich mines in the African copper belt have little spread effect, because the region where they happen to be located is very thinly populated. In such regions, it is difficult if not impossible to achieve the agglomeration effect where new market-oriented industries attract other market-oriented industries and immigrants. However, agriculture-based industries can have important spread effects if they contribute to raising labor productivity in agriculture in the region where they are located.

A thinly populated country specializing in industries which process agricultural or mineral products for export becomes dependent on markets in more densely populated countries which buy the former's products for consumption or for use in their own market-oriented industries. However, the dependence works both ways, since the thinly populated countries can offer the densely populated countries an outlet for their industrial products. In other words, the sparsely settled country which chooses the type of industry to which it is best suited enjoys the advantage of having an economy which is complementary to and not competitive with those of its more densely populated neighbors, with resulting better possibilities for economic production in market-oriented industries.

Trade agreements and coordination of development plans are likely to be more easily arranged between local groups of neighboring countries which are developing complementary patterns of industrialization than between the wider groups of African countries which are competing to attract foreign investment in the same types of market-oriented industries. By promoting the right type of industrialization, sparsely populated countries can link their economies to those of African countries which have better possibilities for setting up a wide range of industries. Thus, instead of making vain attempts to compete with other African countries in the fields where they are at a disadvantage, they may gain from the growth of market-oriented industry in other African countries by improving the markets for their own industrial and primary exports.

Use of Industrial Input

The preceding sections of this essay deal with the contribution of the rural sector to industrial development in Africa: the transfer of labor and food from the rural to the urban sector and the input of agricultural raw materials to industry. It must now be asked to what extent African industry can help solve the problems of the rural sector. In other words, what is the scope for use of industrial input in African agriculture?

It is generally agreed that there will be a widening market in Africa for chemical fertilizers and insecticides, and some African countries are setting up or planning to set up industries to produce such chemical inputs to agriculture. The future demand for equipment for agriculture is less easy to foresee, because the type of equipment needed depends upon the system of cultivation which African countries will choose to replace the long-fallow system. In a previous section, the possible alternatives were briefly referred to as the Far Eastern system, the West European system, and the North American system. The first would require widespread use of irrigation equipment if it were to be applied in the dry regions of Africa; the second system requires plows and other equipment suited for animal draft power; and the third one requires the use of mechanical traction and ancillary equipment. Thus the amount and kind of equipment needed vary widely according to the system of agriculture, and it is therefore necessary to discuss the scope for the introduction of each of these types of agriculture in various parts of Africa.

There are in Africa large areas of land in humid regions which are used very extensively in long-fallow systems or not utilized at all. These underutilized or unutilized areas could be opened up for farming by the building of access roads and by land clearing. Therefore, production for export on artificially irrigated land is unlikely to be profitable, unless the costs of irrigation are low and the distance to markets relatively short compared with the distance which separates the same markets from humid land suitable for growing the same type of crops. Irrigation projects which are being set up or are being planned in dry regions of Africa are mostly large-scale schemes for the damming of rivers. Usually, such schemes are very costly: investment per hectare of irrigated land seems to range from US$1,000 to US$2,500. Crops grown on such land must be sold in the home market at prices which are likely to be far above those at which the products could be imported, or the full capital costs of the project cannot be covered.

Large irrigation projects are not the only possibility of bringing water to dry regions of Africa. In many parts of these regions, this can be done much more cheaply by small-scale irrigation. In addition to having lower capital costs per hectare of land irrigated compared to large-scale projects, small-scale irrigation has the further advantages that the equipment can be produced more easily by African industry than can the equipment for large-scale schemes, and that small-scale irrigation allows a more flexible adaptation to the available supply of labor than does large-scale irrigation. In large-scale irrigation schemes, full utilization of the capacity can be obtained only if the input of labor in agriculture in the district where the project is located can be increased rapidly either by the immigration of labor or by a sufficiently radical change in the work habits of the local population. Some large irrigation projects in Africa, created with a view to providing additional employment for the local population, have in fact been unable to recruit sufficient labor to produce more than one crop annually and have been forced to use highly mechanized methods of production. This would appear to be a striking example of misconceptions about the true supply elasticity of agricultural labor in Africa.

Small-scale irrigation projects are not dependent on whether a large or small share of the local population desires to obtain additional employment. Enterprising villagers who desire to grow some irrigated crops in the dry season, for local use or for exports, can do so, while less enterprising villagers may continue with their traditional system of work until the improved living standards of the former become a sufficiently strong motivation for emulation. In this way, small-scale irrigation may spread slowly in step with the change of attitude of the villagers.

The choice between animal and mechanical power to replace the traditional hoeing of land is a much discussed dilemma. A priori, there seem to be several arguments in favor of the introduction of mechanical power in African agriculture: the increasing need of the urban sector for agricultural products combined with the steady migration of part of the rural population to the urban sector makes it desirable that output per agricultural family should increase rapidly. The attitudes of the rural population make it unlikely that this can happen through a rapid and radical increase in labor input per family, but the introduction of mechanized equipment might help to provide a break with old attitudes. The low man-land ratio in most of the continent makes it physically possible to expand very rapidly the area that is tilled and harvested in any given year, since the long-fallow periods can be shortened or eliminated when chemical fertilizer is applied to the land.

The chief advantage in using animal draft power and animal manure instead of power-driven equipment and chemical fertilizer is that less money expenditure is required. But although money expenditure per unit of output may be lower if the first alternative is chosen, the cultivator family must provide a much larger input of labor per unit of output. This is the chief reason for using this type of labor-intensive agriculture in preference to agriculture with more industrial input in those parts of the world where the agricultural population is dense in relation to available land, and it may also be suitable, for the same reason, in districts of Africa where the man-land ratio is higher than usual, where land is privately owned, and where there is fragmentation of land. By contrast, it seems less suitable in those parts of Africa where a more rapid expansion of cultivated area could be obtained with the use of mechanized equipment than with the use of animal draft power.

Actual experience with the use of mechanized equipment in African agriculture is rather mixed. In some regions of white settlement, mechanized traction has been spreading very rapidly, but in areas farmed by Africans it has usually proved uneconomic. There seem to be several reasons for this difference. Africans usually had no experience in handling mechanical equipment; it was misused and deteriorated rapidly. Sometimes the land was also damaged by incorrect use of the equipment or by the use of unsuitable equipment. In most cases, insufficient or no preparation was made before the introduction of the equipment. Finally, in some cases the cultivators seem to have used the equipment not to increase output but to add to their hours of leisure. Many agricultural experts have concluded from these experiences that the introduction of mechanized equipment in African agriculture should be deferred until cultivators have learned from experience with simple animal-drawn equipment how to handle equipment without spoiling it, and have learned from experience with more intensive systems of irrigated and mixed farming to value additional income more than additional leisure.

The transformation of African agriculture will necessarily be slow if it is to take place in step with a change of attitude in favor of additional manual work. There is considerable risk that the less enterprising villagers will avoid the adoption of labor-intensive farming or will adopt them so half-heartedly that the results may fall short of expectations. The more enterprising villagers are more likely to seek an outlet for their energy in the more attractive, and more mechanized, nonagricultural occupations. It has also been proposed that mixed farming with animal draft power and produced fodder be introduced as an intermediate stage preceding the introduction of mechanized power. This seems seriously to underestimate the difficulty of teaching African cultivators to operate such a complicated and wholly new system. Cultivators must learn not only to operate the equipment and to use and feed the animals but also to use more complicated systems of rotation which require that the different crops are sown at the right time and that all operations throughout the year are timed in such a way that crops benefit from the growing season most suitable for them. As mentioned before, there are very few technicians available who can teach cultivators and supervise their activities to ensure that they follow instructions.

It would seem less difficult to teach some of the more alert young villagers how to handle mechanized equipment and to introduce simple systems of specialized cropping with the use of chemical fertilizers and insecticides instead of having to teach all the villagers how to operate systems of mixed farming. In fact, rural youth are operating lorries and busses in all regions of Africa where a modern road system is available. It is true that the motor vehicles deteriorate rapidly and thus are very costly to operate and that the same would be the case with tractors. But this may have to be accepted as an inevitable weakness of an infant industry, which could be overcome only by systematic training and long experience.

It was suggested above that in sparsely populated regions where very extensive systems of long-fallow cultivation are practiced and where there is a traditional social structure, it might be preferable for processing industries to undertake the production of their own agricultural raw materials. Such an agricultural organization would be well suited to the mechanization of agricultural operations, if that were desired, since the industrial enterprise could train the necessary mechanics and drivers and control the use of the equipment. A hire service with mechanized equipment for use in neighboring villages might be attached to such an enterprise, and this could be the first experimental step toward partial mechanization of more traditional systems of farming. If the villagers had to pay for the hire service without any subsidization, there is little risk that they would use the services to lower their input of labor instead of using it to raise total output. This risk arises only when cultivators obtain the equipment too cheaply.

In many regions of Africa, the changeover from long-fallow systems to other types of cultivation requires heavy investment in the leveling of land, removal of roots, and so on. If heavy tractors were used for this type of work, it would increase the willingness of cultivators to change their system of agriculture. Subsequent use of tractors for cultivation raises some intricate problems of land tenure in communities used to applying shifting cultivation on tribal land. This is because cultivators who can afford to pay for tractor services can occupy a disproportionate share of tribal land. The need for tenure reform would also emerge, however, in such communities where the change is to plowing with animals instead of hoeing the land, since this change also enables wealthier cultivators to encroach upon the land rights of other villagers. The need for tenure reform does in fact arise as soon as the system of long fallow is replaced by any other type of agriculture.

The remarks made above make no claim to have solved the dilemma of the type of agriculture to be applied in sparsely populated regions of Africa; they only attempt to show that it is a dilemma. It is difficult to accept the idea that Africa could completely reverse the traditional sequence of development, with mechanization of agriculture occurring after the urban sector has reached a high stage of mechanization. The idea of introducing mechanized or partly mechanized farming in villages still dominated by traditional leaders belonging to the old, nonliterate generation seems farfetched and unrealistic. But it may seem equally unrealistic to advocate a change to farming used in densely populated regions with a shortage of land, since the chief advantage of the sparsely populated regions lies in the abundance of land which can be taken under cultivation or can be used for improved grazing if modern mechanical equipment is introduced. Therefore, the inevitable conclusion is that much more thought and research must be applied to the problem of future farming systems in Africa before the question of the role of African industry in solving the problems of African agriculture can be conclusively answered.

[1980]

Population Growth and Prospects of Development in Savannah Nations

WHEN THE DISTRIBUTION of nations that come within the intermediate tropical zone (ITZ) is examined (see figure 1), it is obvious that some include large areas of savannah environment, which nevertheless account for a small proportion only of national territory (e.g., Australia, with 20 percent ITZ), whereas others lie entirely within the ITZ (e.g., Viet Nam, Zambia). Only a very small proportion of the population of Australia lives in the continent's savannah region, which contributes relatively little to the Australian economy (principally minerals, cf. Calaby, 1980), but in many African and Asian countries the population is wholly or largely confined to savannah environments.

In this essay, a savannah nation is defined as a country that has at least half its territory within the ITZ. By this definition, there are forty-four savannah nations, twenty-six of which are in Africa south of the Sahara, ten in Latin America, and eight in Asia; however, if the distribution of countries with 75–100 percent of their national territory within the ITZ is examined, it is found that there are none in Latin America, five in South and Southeast Asia, and fifteen in Africa (table 1).

Nearly all the countries with such high proportions of their national territories in the ITZ are at very low levels of technological development and have very low average incomes. Of the twenty countries with 75 percent or more of their territory in the ITZ, only two were at medium, and all others were at low, technological levels. Technological levels were higher in the category of 50–74 percent ITZ, largely because Latin America has attained higher levels than either Africa south of the Sahara or South and Southeast Asia and because nearly half of the countries in that category are in Latin America. However, even this category of savannah nations lagged far behind nonsavannah countries, 77 percent of which were at medium or high technological levels by 1970.

There are large differences in population density among the savannah nations. The world distribution of these differences in 1975 is generalized in figure 2. Most savannah nations have low or medium density, but seven

"Population Growth and Prospects of Development in Savannah Nations." Reprinted with permission from *Human Ecology in Savannah Environments*, edited by David Harris. Academic Press, 1980: 407–14.

TABLE 1. Technological level and population density in savannah nations, around 1970

	Number of savannah nations		Number other nations	Percentage of savannah nations		Percentage other nations
	75–100% in ITZ	50–74% in ITZ		75–100% in ITZ	50–74% in ITZ	
Region						
Africa south of the Sahara	15[a]	11[b]	17	35	26	39
South and Southeast Asia	5[c]	2[d]	14	24	10	66
Latin America	0	10[e]	17	0	37	63
Other	0	1[f]	60	0	2	98
Technological level						
Low	18	13	21	90	54	24
Medium	2	11	41	10	46	47
High	0	0	26	0	0	30
Population density						
Low (<16/km²)	9	13	39	15	21	64
Medium (16–64/km²)	8	7	29	18	16	66
High (>64/km²)	3	4	40	6	9	85

Note: All nations and dependent territories, except for ministates (which are defined as areas of less than 10,000 km² and with less than 1 million inhabitants), are included in regions. Technological level is determined by energy consumption, number of telephones, life expectancy at birth, and adult literacy (E. Boserup, 1981a). Twenty countries and dependent territories have been omitted from countries under technological level for lack of these indicators. ITZ = intermediate tropical zone.

[a] Angola, Benin, Gambia, Ghana, Guinea, Guinea Bissau, Ivory Coast, Mozambique, Sierra Leone, Tanzania, Togo, Uganda, Upper Volta, Zambia, Zimbabwe
[b] Botswana, Cameroon, Central African Republic, Congo, Gabon, Kenya, Madagascar, Mali, Nigeria, Senegal, Zaire
[c] Bangladesh, Kampuchea, Laos, Thailand, Viet Nam
[d] India, Sri Lanka
[e] Bolivia, Brazil, Colombia, El Salvador, Guatemala, Guyana, Honduras, Mexico, Nicaragua, Venezuela
[f] Taiwan

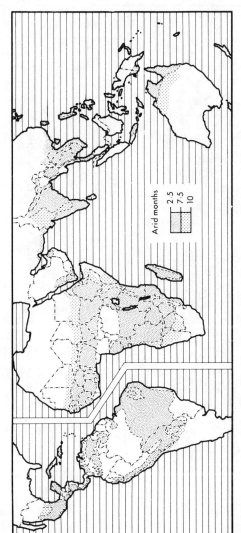

FIGURE 1. World distribution of savannah nations

Source: Harris (1980).
Note: Savannah nations are those with over 50 percent of their territory falling within
the intermediate tropical zone.

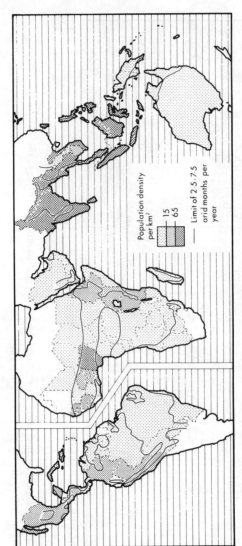

FIGURE 2. Variations in population density among savannah nations, 1975

Source: Harris (1980).
Note: Savannah nations are those with over 50 percent of their territory falling within the intermediate tropical zone.

countries, including such large ones as India and Bangladesh, have very high population densities. By contrast, typical savannah-nation densities in Africa and Latin America are below ten persons per square kilometer, and the density in the savannah region of northern Australia is far lower. Agricultural land use in the savannah areas has adapted to population densities. In the near-empty savannah of northern Australia, the indigenous population were hunter gatherers until recently, and to some extent still are (R. Jones, 1980); in the sparsely populated savannahs of Africa and Latin America, the land is used mainly for pasture and for shifting cultivation (Dyson-Hudson, 1980; Walker, 1980; Medina, 1980; and Parsons, 1980); but the people living in the densely populated savannah region of the Indian subcontinent and in parts of West Africa, particularly Nigeria, have long ago learned to use their savannah environments more intensively (Sopher, 1980; and Burnham, 1980). In these latter areas, permanent agriculture with annual cropping is maintained by the application of manure or other fertilizers and sometimes by irrigation.

The rapid increase of population in recent decades has led to further intensification of agricultural land use in the savannah nations, both the sparsely and the already densely populated ones. The acceleration of rates of population growth is due mainly to the improvement of health services, the rates of growth being lower in areas where such services are least developed than in areas with better services and therefore lower mortality. However, there are very few savannah nations in which rates of population growth are less than 1.5 percent per year, and in some they exceed 3 percent. On average, population in the savannah nations grew at 2.7 percent per year between 1970 and 1976, as table 2 shows. An annual rate of population growth of 2.7 percent means that the population doubles in twenty-six years, that is, within a single generation. The implication is that, unless a large part of the increased population in savannah areas emigrates either to towns or to nonsavannah areas, agricultural land use in the savannah areas will need to change rapidly if the larger population is to be fed and employed.

However, the increase of population is only one of the radical changes that is occurring in the savannah countries. It can be seen from table 2 that both in savannah and nonsavannah nations the nonagricultural sectors of the economy are growing more rapidly than the agricultural sector. Moreover, the table shows that in middle-income nations (including most of those with 50–74 percent ITZ) gross domestic product (GDP) is growing much more rapidly than population. In such countries, the expanding nonagricultural sectors of the economy offer attractive employment opportunities for rural youth, which reduces (or eliminates) the tendency for pressure of population on land to intensify as a result of population growth.

In many Latin American and in some African savannah countries, only a small proportion of the total population of the country lives in the savannah areas, and economic development is rapid outside those areas (Parsons, 1980). Urban expansion, the development of mining, and the growing of export crops in wetter tropical areas all offer attractive employment opportunities to the youth that grow up in the savannah areas. Population pressure on the land

TABLE 2. Percentage growth in population, gross domestic product, and agricultural output, savannah nations, 1970–1976

Country group	Population	Gross domestic product	Agricultural output
Savannah nations 75–100% in the ITZ	2.7	2.7	2.3
Savannah nations 50–74% in the ITZ	2.7	4.9	1.7
Low-income nations	2.4	2.9	1.6
Middle-income nations	2.7	6.0	3.2

Source: World Bank (1978).
Note: The division between low- and middle-income nations in 1976 was US$250 per capita annual income. ITZ = intermediate tropical zone.

thus is reduced not only immediately but also in the longer run, because the large-scale migration of young people from savannah to nonsavannah areas creates differences in age distribution, which result in higher birth rates in the nonsavannah and lower ones in the savannah areas than would have occurred without migration. The most urgent need is therefore to improve agricultural and other production in those nations in which most of the population lives in savannah environments and in which nonsavannah (including urban) areas have low rates of economic growth. Unfortunately, such countries are precisely the ones that have the least means to invest in development.

In many African countries that have 75–100 percent of their territory in the ITZ, a large proportion of the total population lives as cultivators and pastoralists in savannah areas, while other sectors of the economy are small and expand relatively slowly. It can be seen from table 2 that, on average, GDP increased from 1970 to 1976 at the same rate as population in the group of countries with 75–100 percent of ITZ. In these countries, unless there is considerable emigration abroad, the savannah areas must accommodate the rapidly increasing numbers of people. Even in the absence of any direct or indirect governmental development of agriculture, the local population in such countries is forced to use their savannah environments with increasing intensity, and both cultivation and livestock spread into more and more marginal land.

The methods by which savannah populations intensify their subsistence production vary between savannah areas with low and with high population densities. In the sparsely populated savannahs, changes are mainly from shifting cultivation to permanent agriculture, or from pastoralism to crop cultivation or more intensive animal husbandry. In the densely peopled parts of the ITZ, for example in India, crop production is intensified and dry cultivation is replaced by irrigation. In most savannah areas, intensification of land use is carried out by the local population using traditional methods.

This means that the change consists mainly of an increase in labor input, for example better care of more animals, the cultivation of more land with heavier applications of fertilizer, and more frequent watering of crops. Even when local producers are able to make such improvements without causing overgrazing, overcultivation, and erosion, they are likely to have to increase labor input as much or more than output. Therefore, their living standards tend not to increase but to fall further behind those of the national urban population.

In order to increase not only total agricultural production but also living standards in savannah regions, some modernization is necessary, such as the introduction of better breeds and seeds, increased use of chemical inputs, or improved equipment. However, local populations in savannah regions—and in other rural areas—are often prevented from carrying out such modernization because of a lack of rural infrastructure or the poor quality of the existing infrastructure. A precondition for the modernization of agriculture is, for example, that there are adequate roads to the villages, local warehouses, and repair shops; irrigation facilities and extension services may also be required. Moreover, the price ratio at the village level between modern inputs and marketable agricultural products must be low enough for the use of modern inputs to be profitable. This second condition for the modernization of agriculture is related to the first because poor transport and lack of other services raise the costs of modern inputs in the village and reduce the price that the producers can obtain, so that production becomes locally unprofitable, although it may be profitable in the neighborhood of the towns or in other areas with better infrastructure.

By devoting a large share of public revenue and public investment to the development of rural infrastructure, governments can reduce the difference between the prices received by the rural producer and the prices paid by the urban consumer for agricultural products, and thus induce modernization and the higher output that is necessary to improve rural living standards. Unfortunately, few governments in developing countries have chosen to do this. Most have devoted their resources mainly to urban development, a policy that they could follow without risking food shortages in the towns because imports of surplus food, produced in industrialized countries, provided an attractive alternative to the development of local agriculture, at least until the reduction of the surplus stocks in the early 1970s made reliance upon food imports less attractive.

If some savannah areas have suffered from lack of attention from their national governments, others have suffered from ill-conceived schemes of modernization designed either by national governments or by international organizations. In the planning and implementation of such schemes, insufficient attention has been given to local environmental conditions and to locally adapted methods of resource utilization (Scudder, 1980). Methods of development that have succeeded in temperate environments or in densely populated tropical Asian countries may fail in sparsely populated savannah nations. More careful studies of local conditions, including the traditional methods used by the local people to adjust to the seasonal and interannual variations that are so characteristic of savannah environments, would have made it possible to avoid some of the failures, and should be incorporated into future development plans in savannah nations.

[1980]

Food Production and the Household as Related to Rural Development

THE PROBLEM OF WOMEN'S work in production and in the household is a crucial one in African development, because the role of women in rural areas is different in Africa from that of most other parts of the world, as we shall see below. However, Africa is a large continent, and women's roles are not everywhere the same. The discussion below will focus on women in Africa south of the Sahara and leave out the very different conditions in North Africa. Moreover, the focus will be on women belonging to agricultural families, excluding those of families of pastoral tribes.

The best way to understand the peculiar role of women in African agricultural families is to compare them to the roles of women in peasant families in Europe in the days before the beginning of agricultural modernization. The characteristic feature of European peasant societies was that they consisted of family enterprises. These family enterprises produced a number of crops, and the head of the family enterprise, that is, the oldest man in the family, organized and was responsible for the production of all these crops and for the animals belonging to the farms. This responsible male would have his wife, children, daughters-in-law, and grandchildren as unpaid family aid, performing different agricultural operations according to his orders and under his control as the head of the family.

The female members of the family would besides their agricultural work perform the household tasks, which would to a large extent be their responsibility, but the agricultural part of their work, which was considerable, would be performed as assistants to the man. The men were decision makers in all agricultural matters; it was their responsibility that the crops were selected and produced. Women might at the most take independent charge of a vegetable garden and of the poultry.

Another characteristic feature of the European peasant farming system was that the same crops were produced partly for family consumption and partly for sale. Production for sale was in reality a sale of a surplus, which was unneeded for family consumption, and one has to go far back in European

"Food Production and the Household as Related to Rural Development." Reprinted with permission from *The Household, Women, and Agricultural Development*, edited by Clio Presvelou and Saskia Spijkers-Zwart. H. Veenman & Zonen, B. V., Wageningen, 1980: 11–16 and 35–40.

history to find peasants who produced crops exclusively for family consumption without selling any surplus. Families who did not sell a surplus were not peasant families, but families of agricultural laborers, who had at their disposal only a vegetable garden.

In Africa, the situation is fundamentally different. Agricultural production in Africa is not a family enterprise with men and women producing the same crops, the women as assistants responsible to the men. In Africa men and women are both independent producers, both producing different crops. In most cases, women produce the basic food crops consumed by the family, while men produce other crops. Usually, men specialize in producing crops not used by the family, but sold. These may be crops such as coffee, cocoa, tea, and cotton, which are not used by peasant families except after processing elsewhere, or they may be crops such as rice, groundnuts, and palm oil, which are little used by peasant families.

Women give some help to the men with the production of their sales crops, and the men often help the women to clear the ground before they sow or plant the food crops, but each sex is an independent producer responsible for their own crops. The women must use their food crops to feed the family, including the men, but they carry out their production independently and dispose of the surplus when the needs of the family are fulfilled. In other words, while peasant women in Europe were unpaid family aid in enterprises belonging to the male members of their families, African women are independent producers and decision makers, disposing of their own labor and of the money they can earn by producing a surplus over and above the food needs of the family.

In order to understand this African system, it is necessary to look at its origin, that is, to look briefly at the development of African agriculture before and during the colonial period. In most of Africa, population density is very low compared to that of Europe, and we need not go far back in time to find that gathering of food and hunting were more widespread than food production. Men hunted and women and children gathered vegetable foods in forests and bushland. When population density became too high to permit the continuation of these methods of food supply, women, instead of gathering crops, planted or sowed these crops in small plots which they—or the men—cleared in the forests or the bush. This system of food production is still predominant in most of Africa except North Africa.

In the colonial period, the Europeans took advantage of the African system of food production. They discovered that the women took care of the food production with little, if any, aid from the men, and that the men devoted their time to hunting and warfare. The Europeans either incited the underemployed men to work in plantations, mines, or other activities, which were part of the colonial economy, or they forced the men to undertake these tasks as obligatory labor. Moreover, many African men discovered that they could earn money by planting and selling the same types of crops which the Europeans were cultivating in European-owned plantations and farms, so they started small-scale production of these export crops. In other words, men became engaged in new activities, either nonagricultural activities or production of new cash crops for export to the markets in Europe. Women, on the other hand, continued to produce food crops for the family in the usual way. Men could leave the villages and transfer to employment on plantations or in nonagricultural enterprises, because the women were accustomed to producing all the food needed for themselves, their small children, the aged, and other nonworking members of the family. The men's role in food production had always been limited to giving some help with land clearing; that role could still be performed by the minority of men and young boys left in the villages. Thus large parts of Africa became areas of labor migration. In such areas there were few adult, able-bodied men left. Women were heads of households; it was they who went to the fields, sowing, planting, weeding, watering if necessary, harvesting and carrying the crops back to the villages.

The regions which became areas of labor migration were those where transport systems were nonexistent or so primitive that it did not pay to produce cash crops. In these districts, the only way to earn money income was to send some members of the family off to other regions and they would send money back. Women became the sole providers for nonworking members of the family. They became independent, because men were away for years or even forever. During the colonial period, however, the role of women changed, especially in more advanced regions where it was possible to produce cash crops and transport them to markets elsewhere, because men who produced cash crops often demanded that the women help them with some of the work on these crops. In these regions, women acquired a double, or even a triple role, if domestic duties are also taken into account. Women became unpaid family workers in the men's cash crop production, but at the same time, they continued to be independent producers of food crops for family use and sellers of food surpluses. Nevertheless, the change in women's work was less radical than that in men's work. The main role of women continued to be food producers for the family and performers of domestic services, and, in many cases, they did not take any part in production of the men's crops.

The colonial system meant that both men and women had to do more work. Men worked with cash crops and with nonagricultural activities, and women either had to support the family alone, if the men went away, or they often had to help men with the cash crops. Many conflicting and incorrect statements are made about the work input of men and women in African agriculture. The crucial role of the women often is overlooked by people who focus only on the production of crops for sale and overlook or underestimate the production of food for family consumption. In other cases, women are said to do all or nearly all the work in agriculture, because this statement is made with the focus on food supply, and export crops, which provide the main agricultural work burden for men, are overlooked.

Some quantitative studies have been made in regions in which both cash crops and food crops are produced. These studies sometimes only cover a few families, but a compilation of eighteen larger studies from different parts of Africa reveals that men spent an average of fourteen hours on agricultural work per week, while women spent fifteen hours (E. Boserup, 1970a). The difference is not very large, but it must be taken into account that, over and above their agricultural work, women had a very large burden of domestic work to perform; this not only includes cooking, cleaning, and child care, but also the crude processing of food, water carrying, and the gathering of fuel. All these tasks are considered women's work. So African women in rural areas have a heavy work burden compared to men.

The end of the colonial period did not reduce the work burden of African rural women, but enhanced it further. The reason for this was that the end of the colonial period coincided with two other changes: an acceleration in the rate of population growth and a further acceleration of labor migration.

Rates of population growth accelerated because of a decline in mortality, especially child mortality. This means that families are larger than previously, and therefore women need to produce food for more people. Increasing food production means that more land has to be cultivated, either by using land that is less fertile or further from the village, or by using more intensive methods of cultivation, for instance hoeing the land better or weeding it more often. Regardless of the method used, it means a larger labor input than before, so women have to work more in order to supply their families with food. And women have even less help from men than previously, because migration of men from the villages has become even more frequent than in the colonial period.

In other words, the task of producing enough food for the whole family has become much more difficult for women than previously, and this means that they cannot produce as large food surpluses for sale as they could earlier. The lack of surpluses implies that when towns grow in size they cannot get sufficient supplies of food from the countryside but must be supplied by increasing imports from other countries.

It is not a new feature that African towns are supplied by means of food imports from other continents; this also happened in the colonial period. The relatively few and small towns that existed at that period were mainly inhabited by non-Africans, that is Europeans and Asians, who preferred to eat food of the types they were accustomed to from their countries of origin—thus food was imported from non-African countries. In contrast to peasant farming regions of Europe, the African rural population supplied little food to the towns, and few of the products of the urban areas reached the surrounding countryside. African peasants earned money by selling export crops to foreign countries, and they used this money to purchase imported manufactured products. African towns did little more than handle this import and export trade, and the traders were nearly all non-Africans.

This system has changed fundamentally since African countries have become independent. Foreigners have left either voluntarily or have been expelled, and there has been a very large migration of Africans to the towns. The town population has increased much more rapidly than the food surplus in the countryside, and with the increasing town population food imports have been rising very rapidly in most African countries.

Let us now see, what role food producing African women have played in this development, and return to the comparison between European peasant production and agricultural production in Africa. Family production in Europe consisted of crops, of which a part was consumed by the family and a part sold to neighboring towns. When the population in Europe increased and agricultural production became more intensive, total crop production increased, and more food became available to the increasing families and the enlarging towns. Subsistence production and production for sale both expanded, without any change in the organization of family production. Men continued to be responsible, and women remained unpaid helpers.

In Africa, by contrast, expansion in production by men meant only an expansion of export crops, but no additional food to feed the enlarging towns. Food produced for sale increased little, because it was done by women, and women were overburdened due to the increasing size of family and male migration. Women could do little more than supply the food needed for subsistence in their own family. Moreover, because they produced for subsistence, they did not earn money which could be used to purchase fertilizer and other agricultural inputs. Men used the money they earned on their own export crops, not on women's crops. They also used the better land and left the poorer land to the women, who could therefore obtain only low yields, especially when they were unable to buy fertilizer.

It is more and more obvious to many African governments that a change in the system of food production is necessary. It is true that many Arab and Latin American countries import food, but many of these are rich countries, which can pay for food imports because of large incomes from the exports of oil or minerals. African countries which import food are by contrast poor countries. They need their export incomes for the purchase of equipment and other goods which they cannot produce themselves, rather than for the purchase of food. Nearly all African countries have large areas of unutilized land, suitable for food production. It is not lack of land but lack of proper organization of food production, food trade, and food transport which explain the increasing food deficit of Africa.

Moreover, African governments want to become more self-sufficient in food in order to become less dependent upon the agricultural policy of the big food exporting countries. These countries produce food surpluses as a part of their farm support policy, and their supplies to the world market are irregular and dependent upon changes not only in harvests, but also in internal agricultural policies, which create fluctuations in prices and supplies to the world market. Therefore, African countries want to become more self-reliant, and this means that a better organization of food supplies from African villages to African towns in an urgent problem.

Mechanization and the Position of Women

The way in which this problem is solved will become crucial for African women in rural areas. Will subsistence production continue to be important, or will it quickly give way to commercial production of food? Will there be a rapid change to modern technology, a change to intermediate technology, or a continuation of primitive agricultural systems and methods? Will small-scale or large-scale production gain ground, and how will production be organized? And what are the implications for women in each case? We shall look at these problems one by one.

Let us begin with the choice between commercial agriculture and improvement of subsistence production. It is a just criticism that, both in the colonial period and after independence, virtually all efforts in the agricultural sector have gone into expansion and improvement of the commercial production of export crops, and virtually nothing has been done to help women improve the production of subsistence crops. Therefore it is argued by many that a reversal of policy is needed and that both donor and African countries should focus on improvement of subsistence production and social development in the villages.

However, it is an illusion to believe that social development and improvement of the subsistence level can ever be a realistic alternative to further expansion of and improvement in commercial agriculture. Donor aid is very limited and is likely to remain so. Sooner or later, the donor will move out and another way will have to be found to pay for the clinics and other services which have been set up with outside aid. It could be argued that this could be done, if the governments would devote less of their total resources to industrialization and urban development and more to social development and improvement of subsistence production in the villages. It is true that rural development has been neglected by many African governments, and that some are willing to engage in a somewhat less urban-biased policy. The taxation of rural areas, accomplished mainly by large levies on export crops, may be somewhat reduced, but it is quite unrealistic to assume that the change could go so far that the small urban sector could finance improved social services and other aid in the rural areas. Lasting social improvements in rural areas will be possible only if these areas are able to pay for these services themselves, and that can happen only if their commercial production is expanded and becomes more efficient. So, there is no real choice between social or economic policy or between subsistence production and commercial production. Social improvements and improvement of subsistence level are only possible in the long run by means of expansion of and improvement in commercial agriculture, with markets either in the export or urban areas. Only by means of a rapidly increasing surplus of village products for sale elsewhere can the villages get the means to finance social improvements and better living standards.

Like the choice between social and economic development, the choice between modern and intermediate technology is no real choice. This is so because the lack of, or poverty of, infrastructure makes the use of modern technology impossible in most of Africa.

Let us just take the example of chemical fertilizer. It is impossible to use large amounts of chemical fertilizer unless there is a railway network or a very good road network to transport the fertilizer. In Europe, agricultural modernization did not start before the second half of the nineteenth century. At that time, railway density in Europe was already ten times larger than it is in Africa today. Of course, today road motor transport has become possible if there are good roads, but while there are thousands of meters of roads per square kilometer in Europe, there are only some twenty or thirty meters per square kilometer in most African countries, and very few of these small networks are hard-surface roads (E. Boserup, 1981a). Under such conditions, utilization of fertilizer becomes risky, if not impossible, as was proved by the recent difficulties in Zambia, when its small railway network broke down because of military transports, leaving the peasants without supplies of fertilizer.

In the middle of Africa there are hundreds and hundreds of square kilometers devoid of any transport networks or other economic infrastructure. In such regions there is no possibility of using modern technology, and the types of intermediate technology that can be applied are very limited. Costs of infrastructure investments are closely linked to population density. In a densely populated region, there are many who may use the facilities and services and help to pay off the cost of the investment, but Africa generally is sparsely populated, and the small, scattered, and poor population is unable to secure sufficient usage to make infrastructure investment feasible. Therefore, agricultural modernization is severely handicapped in Africa, compared, for instance, to densely populated Asia.

The lack of infrastructure limits the number of crops which can be grown in Africa, except for a few areas which are better provided with infrastructure. Most African export crops are durable and easy to transport even under difficult conditions, but many food crops can be grown only in the immediate neighborhood of the areas of consumption, because they would perish in transport under the given conditions.

The lack of infrastructure also influences the choice between large-scale and small-scale farming. Small-scale farming with sale of a surplus is possible only if there is some public infrastructure in the region, but large plantations, set up by multinational corporations or national companies, are able to finance and build their own infrastructure, including roads and railways. African export products that are difficult to transport, such as fruits and flowers, therefore, are often produced in large-scale farming. Small-scale farmers, either male or female, are unable to compete in these fields, because of the poverty of the infrastructure in their areas.

The examples above indicate that there are many conditions to take into account if a policy for improvement of agriculture in general and of female farming in particular is to be achieved. Because men in a given area can sell the cash crops they produce, it does not necessarily mean that it is also possible for women to sell their food crop surplus. Large plantations can produce fruits and other nondurable goods, but this does not mean that it is by any means certain that women can make a living by producing these products. Programs for helping women to change from subsistence producers to commercial farmers, or just helping them to earn some money, requires a careful study of the region in which the women live, the natural conditions, the existing infrastructure, and the likelihood that this infrastructure may be improved in the near future.

The tenure system in the region also plays a role as to whether it is possible for the women to produce crops both for subsistence and for sale. According to the traditional tenure system, which still exists in most of Africa, land belongs not to individuals but to the tribe. If the population is sparse, a woman may start cultivation of crops on vacant land without asking permission from anybody. If land is less abundant, she may need to have land assigned to her by her husband, or by the tribal chief. If population density has become relatively high and men have occupied much land for their cash crops, most or all the land may have become considered the private property of the occupier, and women may therefore be unable to get hold of land on which they can start cash crop production, and may even have difficulties getting hold of land for cultivation of subsistence crops. Due to the rapid increase of population in Africa in recent decades, more and more land is passing into private possession, and in this process women tend to lose their rights to cultivate land and become more and more dependent upon their husbands and other male villagers, who have secured themselves permanent rights to the land to which previously access had been free. A result may be that women may now have to pay rent or deliver a share of the crop to a male landowner, while men will more frequently be able to cultivate land without such levies.

In many cases, the change from tribal tenure with free access to land to private property occurs when large-scale irrigation systems are introduced in a region. In such cases, individual ownership rights are often granted to men as heads of families, but no cultivation rights are given to women, who become wholly dependent upon their men. If women are divorced, they are cut off from land for subsistence production.

Large irrigation projects create many difficulties besides the problem of the loss of women's rights in land. One of the most serious problems is the effect on health. A number of waterborne diseases appear in the wake of irrigation projects. Many technicians have been ignorant of the risks of flowing or stagnant water as breeding grounds for disease, and some regions which were meant to be improved habitats for people have become instead so heavily infected by disease that the population has left the areas, when river blindness, malaria, or other diseases became widespread.

Women have not only greater difficulties in getting access to land for cultivation, but also greater difficulties in getting access to other inputs, because they have almost no cash income and usually no access to credit, and because they are legally dependent upon their husbands, who may be unwilling to honor their obligations. Therefore, the shift from subsistence producer to commercial producer is very difficult for women, and in a situation in which it is urgent that commercial food production replace food imports, it seems likely that we will see female subsistence production of food replaced, not by female commercial food production, but by male commercial food production. There are parts of Africa where this is happening. Men have engaged in food production for the market, sometimes with use of modern inputs, and women have changed from independent producers either to unpaid family labor for their husbands or to wage labor for other men. The results of such a change are serious in a period when the traditional family system is breaking down and leaving women unprotected, because they no longer can count on the solidarity of a large family group. We have already mentioned that increasing family size and increasing male migration from the rural areas make women so overburdened with work that they have great difficulties in producing surpluses of food for sale. Also, this invites a shift of food production from female to male family members, when food production becomes commercialized. It could be avoided if women were helped to modernize their production, to get credit, and to become trained in better, more labor-saving methods in both their agricultural and domestic activities. Deliberate efforts in these fields are necessary—otherwise there is likely to be a gradual shift to male-organized food production.

In some parts of Africa, women are trying to start commercial food production or the production of other commercial crops by establishing women's cooperatives, in which they pool their resources of labor and money for purchase of inputs. Women may more easily be able to get credit when more than one can help to pay back the loan, and their husbands cannot demand that women hand their earnings over to them when these earnings belong to the cooperative and are reserved for purchase of inputs.

In regions with large-scale farming, women have the possibility of earning money by wage labor on large-scale farms, and thus retain some economic independence and means of support in case of divorce and desertion. Women can also obtain money by participation in cooperatives, but unfortunately, many cooperatives are family cooperatives, which hand the rewards for the work of the whole family to the men as the head of the family. Many women both in Africa and elsewhere have obtained their first independent money income by joining a cooperative of the nonfamily type. Because they provide the possibility for earning independent incomes, such cooperatives are often much more popular with women than with men. Wage labor on private plantations and farms, which men regard as socially inferior to family farming, may also be considered a mark of prestige for women, because they can earn their own money in this way. Men may, however, for the same reason, resent the existence of income-earning opportunities, which make women able to support themselves.

A pattern of mixed tenure, in which large-scale and small-scale farming coexist in the same region may sometimes provide women with better opportunities for some economic independence than well-meaning attempts to teach them production and sale of their own crops, if the prospects for remunerative production and sale of such crops are bleak in that region, either for lack of markets or economic infrastructure, or for other reasons. Modernization of male farming can also sometimes bring so many economic and social improvements to a region that women get possibilities for employment or self-employment in processing industries or rural services. The jobs created in this way may be available only to a minority of rural women, but they may provide a possibility for economic independence for deserted women, and for women who need an alternative to an unhappy marriage.

Future Outlook

It was mentioned above that two factors are very important for African women in rural areas: large male emigration and large family size. It is pertinent to ask if these are likely to be permanent features. Let us begin with migration.

African men, especially young ones, migrate from rural areas either to developing districts in the same country or to other countries in order to earn money incomes. Income differences between rural and urban areas are large and they have become larger since independence. Although industrialization in Africa has been limited, many employment opportunities were opened up in the towns in construction, administration, and other urban services, while it was difficult to earn money in the backward rural areas, in which cash crop production was handicapped by poor infrastructure. Emigration from areas with widespread cash cropping was also large. Cash crop prices were sometimes low, and when they were high, the government took a large share of the profit by levies on exports. Villagers were looking for security by having some members of the family in urban employment. Modern services in towns, including movies and sports facilities, also attracted young villagers. Rural services have sometimes been improved, especially by the establishment of rural schools, but this has enhanced rather than deterred migration, because school was considered the means of qualifying for urban employment. Rising unemployment in many African towns and restrictions on access to the European labor market for foreign workers may help slow down the emigration of young men from African villages. Emigration of women will possibly become less infrequent than before, but it is nevertheless certain that a surplus of women will continue to exist in African villages, so the problem of women who must support themselves is a permanent feature.

Large family size will also be characteristic of Africa for many more decades. There are signs of declining family size, due to fertility control, in a large number of developing countries, but these do not include African countries. In this as in other respects, African development is retarded compared to other continents. Child mortality is still so high that parents are disinclined to restrict fertility when they do not know how many or how few of their children will survive. Moreover, child labor is widespread in rural areas, so children, even small ones, may contribute more to family production than to consumption. African agriculture still relies on human muscle power, and many operations in rural production and services can be performed by children. The large number of children in African families are an added work burden for women, but they try to alleviate this work burden by making use of the labor power of the children. Children therefore become increasingly useful as they grow up, and they are the parents' hope for survival and a decent life in old age.

Since most African countries are underpopulated, and both agricultural and industrial development is handicapped by low population density, most African governments have few motives to promote fertility control, and they are under little pressure from the population to engage in such activities. The new generation of African women will therefore also probably have many children and be forced to lead more traditional lives than young women on other continents.

[1985]

The Primary Sector in African Development

IN SUBSISTENCE ECONOMIES, individual families consume within the family all that they have produced. A primary sector emerges when a large number of families begin to sell food or other commodities which they have produced. Raw products may be exported for use by consumers or industries in other countries, or a secondary sector may develop to process the materials and food sold by the primary sector.

In large parts of Africa south of the Sahara nearly all of the production of the primary sector is exported, because secondary-sector development remains far behind that of the rest of the world. No less than thirty-seven out of forty African countries derived less than 15 percent of their domestic product from manufacturing in 1970; worldwide, three-fifths of all countries with such low degrees of industrialization were African countries (E. Boserup, 1981a). Moreover, Africa is also behind in primary-sector development. In many African countries, the rate of urbanization is low, and nearly all food consumed in rural areas is produced for subsistence only. In African countries with some urbanization there is also little commercial food production, so that a large share of the food produced in urban areas is imported from other countries, usually from countries on other continents. Thus primary production of nonfood crops, forest products, and minerals are of crucial importance for African economies. These exports are virtually the only source of foreign exchange; further, in many African countries, taxation of these primary exports supplies the bulk of government revenue.

Africa is not the only part of the world that developed primary production for exports before the development of a secondary sector. Exchange between producers or gatherers of primary products and producers of secondary products has taken place during several millennia, not only through trade within the same village or country, but also by long distance trade. Often densely populated, urbanized areas ran short of building materials, certain types of food, metals, and other materials and acquired them by long-distance trading, by plunder, or both (E. Boserup, 1981a) Some peoples specialized in long-distance transport and trade, and many urbanized societies extended

"The Primary Sector in African Development." Reprinted with permission from *The Primary Sector in Economic Development*, edited by Mats Lundahl. Croom Helm 1985: 43–55.

their military domination in order to protect trading routes and sources of supply. Thus, over time, a development took place with primary sectors producing a surplus for trade appearing in regions of previous subsistence production. Sometimes the primary producers were independent producers selling to foreign merchants; in other cases the primary-producing areas became colonies of foreign powers, which acquired the products by trade or as tribute.

The ancient societies of Mediterranean Europe got supplies of materials and food both from other shores of the Mediterranean and the Black Sea and from western and central Europe. Later when the latter areas became urbanized societies, they got supplies of raw materials and food from the less developed areas in northern and eastern Europe, causing the emergence of large primary sectors in these areas. With improvement of transport technology before and after the Industrial Revolution, areas on other continents also developed primary sectors to supply Europe with raw materials, food, and tropical products. Further, the primary-producing regions in northern and eastern Europe developed secondary sectors and became importers of overseas raw materials.

It is implied in what is said above that nearly all European countries were exporters of food and other primary products before they developed their own secondary sectors. This is true even of England, which relied on exports of wool and cereals to Continental Europe before becoming an exporter of manufactures and an importer of food. Also, the non-European countries which are industrialized or semi-industrialized today began as exporters of primary products, before they developed industrialized sectors. But there was an important difference between primary exporters in Europe and those on other continents. The primary sector in European countries belonged wholly or mainly to indigenous producers, and the profits earned by export production financed the development of secondary and tertiary sectors in these countries. By contrast, on other continents, a large part of the primary sector was foreign owned, and part of its profits was transferred to the homelands of the foreign owners and so did not finance investments in development of secondary and tertiary sectors in the exporting countries and colonies.

Both in most European colonies and in countries that remained independent, small indigenous family enterprises or settlers gathered or produced primary products and sold them to foreign or indigenous merchants in competition with large-scale companies running mines or plantations. Some of the large companies were integrated enterprises, which not only produced primary products but also processed them, either on the spot or in Europe, and transported and traded them. Competition between multinational companies, operating in several countries and colonies, and small indigenous primary producers is by no means a recent feature.

It is interesting to note that for many mining products the primary sector has nearly disappeared on a world scale, because large national and international companies handle not only the extraction of one or more minerals and ores, but also the secondary activities (processing) and the tertiary activities (transport, trading, and research) related to these products. A similar development can be observed for some types of food, especially horticultural products. For these products, the primary sector seems to be gradually disappearing; if such development spreads to more and more products, it is conceivable, although it seems improbable, that we may end up with vertically integrated economies without an independent primary sector.

Obstacles to Development

In the nineteenth century, when non-European areas developed into important exporters of primary products to the industrializing regions, many parts of Africa developed large primary sectors producing for exports. However, both in the nineteenth and in this century, the development of secondary sectors proceeded much more slowly in Africa than elsewhere. Several features characteristic of Africa contributed to make development of secondary sectors particularly difficult. Overall population density was low, population was widely scattered, and infrastructure was extremely poor.

The colonial powers built a few railway lines, linking rich mineral deposits to export harbors or strategic lines, but except for the Union of South Africa, no African country has more than six meters of railway line per square kilometer, and many have no railways. European countries have 75 to 100 meters per square kilometer (International Railway Statistics, 1972). Most African railway lines run through sparsely populated or empty areas. They have little traffic, so little that it is uneconomic to build feeder roads serving the lines. Road density in Africa is also extremely low. While western European countries have over a thousand meters of road per square kilometer, mostly hard-surface roads, only a few African countries have as much as a hundred meters and some have less than ten, nearly all of much poorer quality than European roads (UN, 1974b; International Road Federation, 1973). Building good roads in sparsely populated areas is uneconomic; therefore transport becomes prohibitively expensive for most types of products.

In an area with the overall population density of Africa there will live 100,000 persons in a circular area with a radius of sixty kilometers, but in the same area with the overall density of Europe there will live one to two million people. In a densely populated area with reasonably good transport facilities, the home market may be sufficiently large for the establishment of local industries, even when the majority of the population is poor and has low per capita purchasing power for industrial goods. This helps to explain how manufacturing industries could be installed in densely populated areas of Asia in spite of colonial resistance to industrialization and how, after independence, industrialization has been more rapid in Asia than in Africa.

Overall population density in Latin America is not much different from that of Africa, but because Latin America was populated to a large extent by immigration, most of the population lives in coastal areas with high population densities and much better infrastructure than that of African countries. It is mainly these coastal areas and the densely populated plateau of Mexico that are becoming rapidly industrialized. In Africa, some mining towns grew up in the colonial period, but because they were located in sparsely populated areas they did not, as usually happened elsewhere, attract other industries. They remained small enclaves of extracting and crude-processing industry in a largely unindustrialized continent which failed to develop secondary sectors in spite of its rich, unutilized resources of land, minerals, and water for hydropower.

The low population density, the scattered population, and the poor infrastructure in Africa were serious obstacles not only to the development of manufacturing industries, but also to the development of a commercial food producing sector. As is usual in areas of low population density, the predominant African subsistence systems are forest fallow, bush fallow, and pastoralism (E. Boserup, 1981a; 1965). In a region where forest and bush fallow systems are used, the land is cultivated for a few years, usually with hand tools, and left in fallow for many years. Adult men and young boys fell the trees and bushes when land is retaken into cultivation after several years, but most or all of the other field operations are done by women and children with very primitive tools or without any tools (E. Boserup, 1970a). Only in small parts of Africa with relatively high population densities has this system of subsistence food production become supplemented or replaced by development of a primary sector of commercial food production.

Several factors have combined to produce this result. One is the lack of rural infrastructure, which makes long-distance transport uneconomic, if not impossible, except for high-value and durable crops. Another factor that causes delay in development of commercial food production is the organization of work, and especially the sex distribution of work, in traditional African agriculture. The large increase of rural population in recent decades and expansion of the areas under export crops have forced the women, who produce food crops for family consumption, to cultivate poorer land with shorter fallow periods, or to cultivate land far from the villages. Thus women have had to put more time into food production and transport of crops from the fields. Since African women must combine food production with domestic work, gathering fuel, and fetching water, and must often help the men with the production, transport, and processing of cash crops, they are of course unable to produce any significant surpluses of food above the quantities needed to feed their own families. So even the small minority of African villages which are linked to urban areas with good transport facilities have little to sell (Presvelou and Spijkers: Zwart, 1980).

In regions where efforts were made to modernize and expand agricultural production, both male farmers and male government officials focused on the export crops for which the men are responsible, while the women's food crops were neglected. Women received no information about improved agricultural methods and, if they had, they lacked both time and money to change and expand their production of food. Add to this the fact that African food production is exposed to severe competition from imports of subsidized food from the industrialized countries. Owing to heavy income or price support to farmers in industrialized countries, their exportable surpluses of many agricultural products have been rapidly increasing, resulting in the need to get rid of this surplus. This availability of surpluses has kept food prices low in the world market; costs of sea transport from the industrialized countries to Africa are also quite low. Further, imported food has also benefited from overvalued exchange rates and from direct government subsidies to keep food prices low in the towns (World Bank, 1982). Because rural infrastructure in Africa is so poor, producers in rural areas generally obtain only a small fraction of the prices paid in urban areas. As a result, prices in most of Africa at the village level are too low to encourage commercial food production. Food continues to be subsistence production with traditional methods and low productivity, and food imports are growing rapidly. Moreover, the subsidized food exports from the industrialized countries prevent African countries with good natural conditions for commercial food exports from engaging in export production of food (IFPRI, 1980).

Under these circumstances, producers can usually earn more by producing traditional nonfood export crops than by producing food crops in spite of the high taxes levied on many export crops (World Bank, 1981). Moreover, some large government projects designed to establish commercial food production had to close down or be kept alive with heavy subsidies because they could not compete with imports. Examples are projects for sugar and rice production linked to large-scale irrigation projects (Dumont and Mottin, 1983). In spite of the mounting imports and shortages of foreign exchange, government policies in most countries continue to encourage food imports. The politically powerful urban middle class, including civil servants and military personnel, benefit from low prices for the type of food which they prefer to consume. Moreover, by importing food, the towns can obtain sufficient supplies without the government having to use part of the revenue to finance rural infrastructure investment and other expenses which would have been necessary if the country were to remain self-sufficient in food in spite of the rapid increase of urban populations.

The surplus production of food in the industrialized countries has not only depressed world market prices, it has also induced the industrialized countries to grant large amounts of these surpluses as food aid in order to prevent an even greater pressure on world market prices. When African governments received food imports as food aid, not only did they save foreign exchange, they could also sell the food supplies and use the counterpart funds from these sales as budget aid. Except for countries with large mineral exports which can be taxed, African government budgets are fed mainly by taxes on export crops and from counterpart funds related to food aid. In both cases, African agriculture bears the burden. Although some governments are becoming worried about the increasing dependence on foreign supplies of basic foodstuffs, there is little sign of a radical change of government policy. Food imports into Africa continue to increase by leaps and bounds, while African food production stagnates. In a number of countries, food production is declining due to competition from imports.

There were small food imports into Africa already in the colonial period, because the European and Asian populations in African towns imported and consumed non-African types of food. But for the rural population and most Africans in the towns, the basic foods were sorghum, millet, yams, or bananas. Because imports are multiplying and the prices of imported food are favorable, more and more African families add foreign types of food, like wheat, rice, maize, sugar, and dairy products, to their diet, often abandoning the use of traditional foods. The foreign types of food have become so popular that change in taste is a frequently used argument against suggestions to promote the production of African types of food. However, the experience both in Africa and elsewhere is that food habits adapt to changes in relative prices of various foodstuffs. Therefore, it seems likely that import duties on imported food would be an effective means to encourage African food production and reduce imports, especially if simultaneous efforts were made to reduce costs of internal transport and to improve methods of food production.

Prospects for Development of the Primary Sector

Except for wheat, the types of food imported into Africa can be grown on most of the continent. Moreover, growing sufficient food for the rapidly increasing African population need not reduce the rate of growth of production of export crops. More food can be grown around the existing villages by changing the traditional system of bush fallow into a more intensive system of permanent land use with much more use of fertilizer and other inputs. Moreover, nearly all African countries have unused or underutilized cultivable land, which can be taken into use either for food production, or for export crops, or both. What is needed is making this land accessible by investment in transport networks and other infrastructure and, sometimes, radical changes in the traditional use of forests and pastures (E. Boserup, 1965).

A considerable share of the African rural population lives so far away from centers of export production or towns that it is uneconomic for them to produce either food or other crops for sale. They produce most of what they need themselves and earn money income by labor migration. This migration may be either seasonal migration to mines, plantations, towns, or farms in other regions, or it may be more permanent migration by the head of the household or one or more adult children, who transfer part of their earnings to the family members who have remained in the home village.

Labor migration from peripheral areas to regions of primary production for exports had already become large in the colonial period, and it has continued to be of major importance. But emigration of a substantial share of the able-bodied, adult population makes development of a peripheral area by infrastructure investment less urgent and even less economic than it would have been without emigration. Both public and private investments tend to be attracted to the areas of labor immigration, and so bypass those of labor emigration. Thus, the contrast between areas overcrowded by immigrants and other empty or nearly empty areas becomes more and more pronounced. The low population density, which makes transport and other infrastructure uneconomic, is the main cause of these labor exports. Therefore, the continued rapid natural population growth in the labor exporting areas is a potential advantage. With a larger local population establishment of commercial production and improvement of infrastructure might become feasible in many such regions, assuming that the emigration could be contained. It would require considerable investment in long-distance transport, local transport, and other infrastructure, but it would increase primary production and raise employment also in construction, food processing industries, and services. By such a policy of rural development, increasing congestion in the traditional centers of immigration, especially the metropolitan areas, could be avoided.

The rapid increase of population in Africa, which will continue far into the next century (Tabah, 1982), will also improve the possibilities for industrialization. Many more parts of Africa will have a sufficiently large and dense population for economic operation of home-market industries, as well as industrial processing of food and minerals for exports and domestic use. But to finance this industrialization, African countries must still, during a long period, rely mainly on income from exports of primary products, crops as well as minerals and forest products, to more industrialized countries on other continents.

It has been suggested that Africa should avoid depleting its mineral resources for the benefit of industries in other parts of the world and preserve them for use in future African industries. Delay of exploitation has also been recommended in the hope that increasing scarcity of raw materials will result in a more favorable development of export prices. However, in our world of rapid advancement of science and technology, it is more than likely that threatened scarcities of a particular raw material will be averted by technological improvements and new substitutes. Appearance of new substitutes and other technological changes may also reduce the future value of some natural resources.

In any case, African countries have little choice. Today, the secondary sector in African countries is too small to make any significant contribution to exports from the continent. Only gradually, as this sector expands, can the primary sector become less predominant as supplier of foreign exchange, but this is not necessarily a serious handicap. It must be taken into account when evaluating the future prospects for Africa, that Latin America, Asia, and the Arab world are industrializing rapidly. These areas have not only much lower wage costs than the highly industrialized countries, they also possess recently established industries in many branches, while many industrial enterprises in the older industrialized countries are of earlier date. For these reasons, the highly industrialized countries restrict the access to their home markets of imports of manufactures from developing countries, but they have no means to avoid competition in their export markets in the developing world from low-cost producers in these areas.

It is likely, therefore, that export markets for most industrial manufactures will become so competitive that the old industrialized countries cannot continue to adapt their export prices to increasing wage costs in their own countries, without losing market share. Thus there is some reason to believe that exports of manufactures will become less attractive than they were when the old industrialized countries had a near monopoly on this type of exports. If for that reason the price gap between manufacture prices and prices of raw materials becomes reduced in the future, countries which, like the African ones, rely mainly on raw material exports will gain, and they may be able to finance their industrialization by means of the foreign exchange earned by primary exports. But this requires that they do not use their foreign exchange earnings on imports of food, which could better be supplied by African agriculture.

Economic and Demographic Interrelationships in Sub-Saharan Africa

As THE EXPERIENCE OF many developing countries has demonstrated, high rates of population growth are compatible with rapid economic growth over long periods (Chesnais, 1985). But the fertility declines now under way in nearly all countries outside of Africa confirm the expectation that economic development eventually induces reductions in fertility. Sub-Saharan Africa is now the only major region not experiencing fertility decline.

The main causes of the lack of fertility decline in the region are obvious. Mortality decline—usually the first stage in the demographic transition—began later in Africa than elsewhere, and economic development has been less successful in Africa than in most other parts of the world. Whereas there was considerable natural increase of population in both Asia and Latin America in the colonial period, there seems to have been very little growth of the indigenous population in Africa, and net outmigration by slave transport to the Americas was substantial. So Africa remained sparsely populated, accounting for a declining share of world population. This trend has only very recently reversed.

Fertility decline in Asia, Europe, and the Americas has been the result of structural changes in economies, accompanying increasing industrialization (E. Boserup, 1984). In this process, larger and larger shares of the populations become engaged in occupations that are conducive to lower fertility—for instance, because they are located in urban areas or require higher education. Moreover, the supports for large family size are eroded as the use of child labor declines, as land reforms provide security through landownership, and as sources of nonfamilial support in old age and emergencies develop. In most of Africa, this process has barely begun. The level of industrialization and urbanization is still low, and agricultural technology is primitive. Furthermore, special features of African land tenure and family organization encourage high fertility. These factors are also related to the delayed economic development that explains the preservation of cultural features that have disappeared in most other parts of the world.

"Economic and Demographic Interrelationships in Sub-Saharan Africa." Reprinted with the permission of the Population Council from Ester Boserup, "Economic and Demographic Interrelationships in sub-Saharan Africa," *Population and Development Review* 11, no. 3 (September 1985): 383–97.

The Effect of Population Distribution on Economic Development

The highly uneven spatial distribution of the population is a major factor in the low level of industrialization in Africa (E. Boserup, 1981a). With its hot climate and rich mineral resources, Africa is complementary to Europe with its moderate climate, dense population, and relatively poor natural resources. In the colonial era, to utilize African resources, the Europeans opened mines and plantations and created a basic infrastructure, mainly transport facilities, linking mines and major plantation districts to coastal harbors. In most cases, local populations were too small and scattered to provide sufficient labor for production for export to Europe, and for the construction and upkeep of the infrastructure. Therefore, labor was brought in by voluntary or forced migration from more remote parts of the continent and, in some cases, from Asia.

In many of the scattered enclaves around mines and plantations, which had been supplied with some infrastructure, the local African population began to produce crops for export. The money income they earned from sale of these crops was used mainly for taxes, for local services, and for purchase of European manufactured goods, while they continued to produce food and other goods and services for family use. Migrants from the interior of Africa were attracted to these enclaves of small-scale indigenous production of export crops. Thus, the enclaves, most of which were located in coastal areas, became areas of higher population density and more intensive agricultural production than the vast, thinly populated areas in the interior of the continent, which continued to produce mainly for subsistence.

In most of Africa, the lack of transport facilities prevented production of export crops, except for high-value products that were worth transporting long distances carried on the head or on the backs of animals. Therefore, for a large share of the African population, the best, if not the only, means to acquire money incomes was short- or long-term labor migration to the areas with export production. Large-scale labor migration contributed to the highly uneven spatial distribution of the African population. Today, there are some large and many small areas in which the population is dense in relation to natural resources; but in between these, and particularly in the interior of the continent, are vast areas within all climatic zones with very sparse population and large unutilized resources of land, water, and minerals.

While many parts of Asia, the Arab region, and Latin America had preindustrial urbanization many centuries ago, Africa had very little indigenous urbanization. The towns that grew up in the colonial period were service towns, centers of colonial administration and foreign trade. They produced little for either urban or rural African consumption and consumed few African products. In most of Africa the small urban populations were largely Europeans and Asians, who imported food and manufactured goods from their home countries.

Thus, in the colonial period, most African economies consisted of three sectors: a vast sector of subsistence production with labor migration; a partly monetized sector in the enclaves, with indigenous export production supplemented by subsistence production; and a monetized sector of towns, European-owned mines, farms, and plantations. The population in each town and enclave was too small to make industrial production economical, and the large underdeveloped regions that separated them prevented creation of larger markets. The mining towns did not, as they do in more developed and densely populated regions, attract processing industries, except for some crude processing of ore by the mining companies.

Although both towns and enclaves have been growing rapidly since independence, the structural pattern inherited from the colonial period continues to predominate in most countries and acts as a powerful obstacle to industrialization. The level of urbanization is lower than in other parts of the world; most towns are still mainly service towns, separated by large rural areas with poor, if any, transport facilities. The few industries suffer from lack of sufficient markets, and only a very small part of the African population is occupied in modern production and working under conditions that provide incentives to smaller family size.

The Slow Pace of Agricultural Modernization

Because past rates of population growth were much lower in Africa than in other parts of the world, extensive land-using subsistence systems—that is, long-fallow agriculture and pastoralism—continue to be much more prevalent than elsewhere. In large parts of Africa, there is more land than the sparse population needs for growing crops. Most of the land is either forested or is used as pasture for herds and flocks. Only small plots are cleared for cultivation. When a plot becomes infested with weeds, or when crop yields decline for other reasons, the plot is abandoned and another one is cleared and brought under cultivation. The result is an agricultural system characterized by a low frequency of cropping on each piece of land, while large areas are left to grow natural vegetation and are available for hunting, grazing, and gathering of food, fuel, and other materials (E. Boserup, 1965).

It is often assumed that an area with sparse population and long-fallow systems from which labor migrates in search of employment has submarginal land or is overpopulated. In fact, labor usually leaves because there are no opportunities to earn money income in the region. Not poverty of the uncultivated land, but lack of markets for surplus production is to blame. When transport facilities are very poor, local producer prices become unprofitable, even if prices are high in export harbors or internal centers of consumption. Under these conditions, labor migration becomes more economical than production for sale.

Subsistence agriculture is conducive to large family size. The primitive long-fallow system practiced in most of Africa provides greater motivation for large family size than other systems of subsistence agriculture (E. Boserup, 1984). Under the long-fallow system, men and adolescent boys fell trees and bushes to clear the land for cultivation, but all other work in the fields is usually performed by women and children. Because women are responsible for the production of vegetable food for the family, they make extensive use of child labor. Moreover, in regions with pastoralism and long-fallow agriculture, members of the local tribe or village community are entitled to clear as much land for cultivation as they need for family consumption, and they have the right to pasture animals in the common grazing land that is not cropped in a given year. A chief in such a community assigns land for cultivation in direct proportion to the size of the family. Thus, a man with several wives and a large number of children has access to many times more land than a man with a single wife and few children.

Where women and children perform nearly all the agricultural work, the father of a large family is likely to become a rich man, while the father of a small family will remain poor. Therefore, this system provides motivation for a much larger family size than do more intensive agricultural systems in more densely populated areas such as obtained in Europe prior to its demographic transition.

Except for countries that impose a system of collective agriculture for ideological reasons, regions with intensive land use have private property in land. Where nonagricultural employment opportunities are scarce or unattractive, neither private landowners nor persons who must rent land at high cost have an economic interest in rearing a larger family than can be supported by the land area at their disposal. Their status in the village depends upon the amount of land they own, and their status is reduced rather than enhanced if they have a larger family than their land can support. Moreover, substantial landowners do not depend upon support from their children in old age and emergencies: they can lease or sell land or have it cultivated by hired labor.

By contrast, an African cultivator in an area with tribal tenure cannot sell or mortgage land, and he cannot obtain status as landowner. His status and wealth depend not upon land, but upon family size. By having several wives and many children, he is provided for in old age and other periods of disability. Similarly, pastoralists in areas with common grazing land obtain status, wealth, and security by having large herds, cared for by large numbers of offspring. So, in regions of traditional African production and land tenure, polygyny is frequent, family size is large, and bride prices are high (E. Boserup, 1970a). Formerly, many African chiefs in cultivating tribes obtained high status and great wealth by having numerous wives and very large numbers of children. Even today, when much land has passed into private property and many Africans live in urban areas, a large family continues to be a male status symbol.

The situation is changing because of the rapid growth of population. Fallow is shortened and land passes into private property, whether through land reform, by illegal action, or by gradual change of custom. In many areas, emerging land shortages are inducing the young to emigrate to sparsely populated areas to find more land for cultivation. There is scattered evidence that differences in population density and in agricultural methods influence age at marriage. In Rwanda and Burundi, the most densely populated countries in Africa, age at marriage has been increasing gradually and is now relatively high by African standards (Lesthaeghe, 1984). There is evidence also from a region in Nigeria that shortage of land prevents young people from setting up independent households, causing them to marry later (Johnson-Stone et al., 1984).

The marriage pattern in Africa differs from that in Asia. In most Asian countries, the recent fertility decline is partly attributable to an increase in the age at first marriage among females, but in Africa age at marriage has apparently changed little, except in some large cities and a few densely populated rural areas. Because of the traditional male preference for polygyny and for a large number of children, marriage is virtually universal for women, and girls are married off at a young age. Divorce and abandonment are frequent events, but both after these and after widowhood, remarriage follows quickly if the woman is of childbearing age. With this marriage pattern, the period in which women do not live in a sexual union is short. By contrast to Asia, the reduction in fertility caused by women living without a sexual partner is much smaller than the reduction due to birth spacing. An increase in the female age at marriage could be an important means to reduce fertility (Lesthaeghe, 1984).

While girls marry early in most of Africa, age at marriage for men is much higher. This is related to the sex distribution of agricultural work and its effects on male migration. When most or all food is produced by women and children, adult men can leave the village in large numbers, not only for seasonal work but for several years. Moreover, a man does not forfeit his right to land assignment by emigration. He can reassert this right when he returns to the village. These features have contributed to the high mobility of Africa's rural male population and the excessively heavy workloads of many African women.

Where export crops are produced, they are usually cultivated by men. But their wives often help in production and sometimes also in processing and selling these crops, in addition to producing food crops for family consumption and engaging in domestic work and child care. Therefore, women in such regions also use child labor extensively, and men have economic motivation for polygyny and for having many children. Both in areas with export crops and in areas with subsistence production, bride prices are high, and the need to earn enough money to pay the bride price motivates young men to migrate to obtain employment.

In some regions, especially in southern Africa, many married men migrate and leave their wives as heads of household, sometimes under the supervision of the older generation. As a result, marital fertility seems to be somewhat lower in these areas than in other parts of Africa (Lesthaeghe, 1984). However, this migration pattern is not typical for Africa. In most regions, it is the young, unmarried men who migrate, often upon finishing school. In order to obtain the bride price and because early female marriage is customary in most of Africa, parents obtain husbands for some of their young

girls by marrying them off as second wives to much older men, not infre-
quently to men who are twenty or thirty years older (E. Boserup, 1970a).
Young men who return to their villages marry women who belong to a cohort
that is younger and larger than their own. Again, there is a large age difference
between spouses. In four of the five countries for which information about
age differences in women's first nonpolygynous marriages is available (Cameroon, Ghana, Kenya, and Senegal), the difference was eight to nine years.
This compares with differentials of no more than two to five years in the rest
of the world, except for Bangladesh and Egypt (World Bank, 1984). The age
differentials would of course be even larger if polygynous marriages were
included.

The Status of Women

The young age at marriage for women, the large age difference between
spouses, the frequency of polygyny, the unequal work burden between the
sexes, the high bride price, and the low educational level of women all combine to perpetuate the low status of women. Traditionally, the status of African women has been that of nonadults. Even in countries in which there is
now legislation to protect women's rights, they suffer from de facto discrimination. Most often they have no say in their own marriage and divorce. Their
husbands or other male family members have legal or de facto control over
them and their children. Usually women cannot accept employment, engage
in money transactions, or dispose of own income without permission from
male family members. Even though African women often provide the primary or sole economic support of children, their husbands or older members
of their husband's or their own family usually have the right to decide on the
living arrangements, education, future occupation, and marriage partners of
their children ("Symposium on Law and the Status of Women," 1977).

As a rule, in countries in which the status of women is low, men and older
family members strongly favor large families, and girls are told from a young
age that their role is to be obedient and to bear many children. Moreover,
where women are unable to support themselves economically and risk divorce if they fail to bear many children, it is easy to explain why their families
are large and demand for contraception is low or nonexistent. The regions of
the world in which women's status seems to be lowest—Africa, the Arab
countries, and Muslim countries in South Asia—have higher fertility levels
than other areas.

There are indications that the economic position of African women is
deteriorating. By contrast to women in Muslim societies outside Africa,
women in traditional African societies were less economically dependent
upon male relatives because they had access to land and could support themselves and their children by subsistence agriculture. The organization of food
production in Africa differs from the system of family production prevalent in
Asia today and earlier in Europe, in which women assisted their husbands in
the production of crops. African women traditionally had the right to culti-

vate one or more plots of land on which to produce food for family consumption and, if possible, a surplus for sale in the local market. In many parts of Africa, this is no longer the case. Both under formal land reforms and when land has been privatized through change of custom, women's cultivation rights have been overlooked or eliminated. Men have become owners of the land, either as individuals or as heads of families, and women no longer have any claim to the land if the men want to dispose of it or if they become widowed, divorced, or abandoned (Pala Okeyo, 1984).

Even when women have access to land to cultivate, their economic position has often deteriorated. Producing a surplus of food for sale has become more difficult as family size has increased. When the village population increases or when men want to expand production of export crops, women must shorten the fallow periods and use more labor-intensive methods, and they must cultivate poorer or more distant land. This means additional work for the women—weeding and fertilizing, or long transports between the fields and the village, or both. If they cannot produce a surplus for sale, women have no money of their own to buy fertilizer and other inputs. Husbands often use the money earned by sale of export crops on their own fields. Women are also handicapped in obtaining credit, because they have neither land to offer as security nor independent legal status (E. Boserup, 1980).

These changes reinforce women's interest in having many children, because they make women increasingly dependent upon both child labor and support from adult children later in life. In many rural areas of Africa, even small children may contribute more to family provision of goods and services than they consume—partly because of their direct contribution and partly because they allow the mother to use more of her time on higher productivity work. Older children, especially girls, are an important labor force at the disposal of the mother, who may withdraw them from school, thus making it less likely that they will later be motivated to restrict family size.

If modernization of agriculture reduces reliance on the labor of women and children, or if women are deprived of cultivation rights, mothers will need less help from their children while they are young. But, with fewer employment opportunities in agriculture, women will become more dependent upon their husbands and, subsequently, on their adult children. Their increasing need for children as economic security may outbalance their reduced need for children as sources of labor.

Women's changed position has important effects not only on fertility, but also on African food production. Because food production is considered a part of women's domestic duties, neither male farmers nor most African governments have taken much interest in its development. Agricultural research and extension, credits, and sales promotions have focused on export crops, and as extension services and training facilities are established for food crops, men alone have been approached by and have benefited from these services (E. Boserup, 1970a; ISNAR, 1985a). With larger family size, women need to produce more food for subsistence, and in most areas they have less help from children because of the rapid increase in school attendance. So, decline of women's food surplus for sale occurs alongside a rapidly increasing urban demand for food.

Income Change versus Economic Structural Change

There have been many economic changes in Africa that could be expected to influence fertility. In the early years after independence, many Africans experienced large increases in income. Many moved into well-paid administrative jobs; others obtained higher income from urban employment, especially in the construction and service industries. Some secured well-paid industrial employment, and many rural Africans' incomes grew as a result of increasing prices for export crops. Many families with migrant members benefited from remittances. But the prosperity did not last. Prices declined for many African export crops and minerals. In some countries, employment and wages in the modern sector declined, and it became more difficult to earn a living by self-employment or in a small family business. The opportunities for migration also declined, and migrants often had to return home because they could not obtain or retain jobs in their new locations. The shortage of educated persons was reduced, and unemployment among those with some education rose.

In order to evaluate the likely effects of these economic changes on fertility, it is necessary to distinguish between income changes and the structural changes in the economy that often cause the income changes (E. Boserup, 1984). Changes in income have a positive effect on fertility; structural changes in the economy, a negative effect. People may enter an occupation or move to an area that is conducive to lower fertility. They may in such cases begin to restrict fertility, despite the fact that the new situation provides them with a larger income. On the other hand, if they obtain a higher income because of an increased wage, or a windfall profit in their usual occupation and residence, the only change in their situation is that they can now afford to have a larger family than before. This is more likely to retard than to accelerate fertility decline. Moreover, the increase in income accompanying occupational, spatial, and educational change can be so large that the fertility-reducing effect of these structural changes is delayed. In other words, the income effect on fertility may outweigh the structural effect.

It is often assumed that the spread of education, especially for girls, makes parents more inclined to limit family size, because school attendance reduces the productivity of children in the home. However, while educated children are less valuable as child labor, they are more valuable as support for the parents later in life. Given the high value placed on education in Africa, the great expectations of support from educated offspring probably more than counterbalance the reductions in benefits from child labor in the parental calculus. Due to the severe scarcity of trained people in Africa in the period after independence, skill differentials in Africa are much larger than elsewhere, and until recently employment opportunities for educated persons were favorable in large parts of the continent. Because of the large skill differentials, educated parents, especially those living in metropolitan areas, had very large incomes by African standards, and they were willing to make sacrifices in order to raise a large educated family that would give them both prestige and economic security in the future. There is little doubt that the unusually large skill differentials in wages and salaries and the exceptionally large rural-urban income differentials in Africa help explain the very high fertility and the low contraceptive use in urban areas in the period after independence.

Many members of the African elite probably descend from the large and wealthy rural families, who could afford to give their children, or some of them, high levels of education. The high incomes of the small elite allow them both to satisfy the desire for the luxuries of modern life and to continue the tradition of large families. Members of the elite who come from relatively small families may want to prove that they have advanced in status by having large families. In contrast to the pattern of occupational fertility differentials in other parts of the world, the wives of men in administrative, managerial, and professional occupations have higher fertility than wives of men in lower occupational groups in three of the five African countries for which such information is available in the World Fertility Survey (Alam and Casterline, 1984).

The majority of Africans experienced little, if any, increase in income after independence. But most anticipated a brighter economic future and better conditions for rearing a large family. In subsequent years, however, both income trends and expectations changed for the worse. In most African countries, the optimism has been replaced by disappointment and pessimism over future prospects. It is feared that educated children may be unable to find jobs. With diminishing employment opportunities for educated children, salary differentials by educational level are diminishing or likely to diminish in the future. Moreover, governments are concerned about the pressure on the labor market posed by increasing numbers of educated youth. In the face of such concerns, some governments are beginning to alter their hostile attitude toward family size restriction.

These changes are likely to make many more Africans, especially in urban areas, inclined to delay the next birth or terminate childbearing. This is especially likely in countries in which a change in government attitudes facilitates the spread of knowledge of, and access to, contraception. The effect of economic crisis on attitudes may help to explain the differences in contraceptive use between Ghana and Kenya. Ghana was hit by economic crisis much earlier and much harder than Kenya, and contraceptive use seems to be higher in Ghana than in Kenya, although educational levels are lower and family planning services are less widely available. Kenya has one of the oldest family planning programs in Africa, with much better coverage in rural areas than the Ghanaian program. A much larger share of the women are aware of the existence of the Kenyan program, but it is less widely used than that in Ghana (Lesthaeghe, 1984).

The Motivation for Fertility Limitation

Men are usually quicker than women to give up traditional attitudes and customs that no longer coincide with their economic interests. Moreover, in Africa, husbands and fathers are much more likely to be decision makers in family matters than women of childbearing age. Many of the recent changes in African societies—in availability of land and urban housing, in employment opportunities, and in possibilities for migration—have either increased the economic burden of children from the father's point of view or reduced the actual or expected contribution from children. Yet there has been little effort to investigate men's attitudes toward family size. Those studies of family size ideals that have been carried out in Africa have usually involved summary interviews with women, asking them about desired family size and desire or lack of desire for additional children.

The women's responses are difficult to interpret. The instructions for the World Fertility Survey did not clarify whether it was "expected, intended, desired, or ideal family size" that was to be studied, and women were often "guided into giving more meaningful numerical answers" by the interviewers (Lightbourne and MacDonald, 1982). It may be questioned whether "meaningful numerical answers" can be given by women who from a very young age have been socialized to put their own desires and interests behind those of their husbands and other family members. Their answers may well reflect what the women—rightly or wrongly—assume would be the answers of these others.

Some studies are more revealing (Oppong, 1983; Oppong and Abu, 1984). Both men and women were interviewed, and instead of questionnaires based upon large samples but yielding ambivalent answers, a limited number of open-ended interviews were conducted by highly qualified interviewers. The responses reveal stress due to the conflict between traditional pronatalist attitudes and the economic constraints to rearing a large family. They also reveal differences in attitudes between spouses to continued childbearing, and the particular difficulties women face when spouses differ.

In many countries outside of Africa, providing economic support for the family is mainly the obligation of the father, whereas the mother is primarily or exclusively occupied with domestic chores. Most African fathers contribute less to family support than fathers elsewhere. This is in part because African family legislation and custom give the fathers all rights over wives and children but little responsibility for economic support of either. By the same token, African women are accustomed to and, at least in the past, were able to support their children without male help.

Where fathers are allowed to pass the burden of family support onto the mother, men's motivation for fertility limitation is weak, even if the economic motivation for large families has disappeared. In these circumstances, the effect of economic and structural change on family size is delayed. This is very important in Africa because of the strong sex hierarchy, in which men are the decision makers in family matters and women are socialized to the role of hard-working mothers of large families, seeking economic security in this role. Changes in family legislation giving men more responsibility for their children and wives would no doubt promote their interest in family limitation. Women might also be more motivated to restrict family size if their marital insecurity were reduced by changes in family legislation.

It has been suggested that both parents may be more motivated to have a large family when they can rely on a wider kin group to support them and their children, whether in the extended household, through child fosterage, or through other forms of support (Caldwell, 1976; Oppong, 1985). But the effects of kin solidarity on fertility are far from obvious. If the system of kin support were to disappear, parents would not necessarily be more motivated to restrict family size, because they would be even more dependent upon their own adult children for support in old age and emergencies. In fact, while access to wide kin support has been adduced to explain delay in fertility decline in Ghana and Nigeria, the lack of wider kin support is said to contribute to delayed fertility decline in Bangladesh (M. Cain, 1982). In the absence of extrafamilial insurance systems, even if both the kin support system and the system of support to parents by adult children began to break down, these trends might make at least the mother even more inclined to seek security in a larger number of children.

The Practice of Fertility Limitation

It is generally believed that contraceptive use, whether by modern or traditional means, is very low in Africa. Evidence comes from tallies of numbers of visits to family planning clinics and answers to questionnaires—the latter unlikely to cover fully the use of abstinence, abortion, and other traditional means of reducing fertility. Where the age distribution of pregnant women is used to decide whether fertility is controlled or "natural," deliberate delay of births in periods of economic distress will escape discovery, because it is likely to affect all age groups proportionately. For the same reason, reduction of fertility by precautionary spacing will escape attention or be underestimated. Such behavior is likely to be prevalent among populations that have access only to unreliable contraceptive methods—namely, industrialized countries in the early period of fertility decline (David, 1984) and most of contemporary Africa. Moreover, lack of data on induced abortion in Africa may be a serious gap, because abortions tend to be frequent when reliable means of contraception are scarce or unavailable.

Lesthaeghe (1984) has made an interesting attempt to measure the combined effects of contraception and other intermediate variables in different parts of Africa by means of a method developed by Bongaarts. In most cases, the levels of the variables (period outside sexual union, infertility and subfecundity, spacing by abstinence after childbirth and lactation, and contraception) produce fertility far below the fifteen children usually considered to constitute natural fertility.

Long periods of female sexual abstinence after childbirth are traditional in Africa, probably as a means to protect the health of child and mother. Today, these periods of deliberate birth spacing show large national and local variations, from two months to two years. The custom of sexual abstinence for married women promotes resort to prostitution and the spread of venereal disease, with the result that infertility and subfecundity have reached high levels in many parts of Africa. Men usually divorce a wife if she is thought to be infertile or subfecund, but both husband and wife remarry, thus spreading venereal disease if that was the cause of the reduced fertility. Before modern health services began to reduce the incidence of venereal disease, total fertility rates in some parts of Africa were as low as four children or less, as the result of infertility, subfecundity, and spacing of births. In addition, high infant and child mortality further reduced family size.

Declines in traditional postpartum abstinence and improvements in health conditions that limit family size both tend to occur with economic development. This seems to be the main explanation for the observed increases in fertility and family size in regions that earlier had a high incidence of disease. Further increases of family size in such regions are to be expected. Besides the traditional period of abstinence after childbirth, the custom of prolonged lactation contributes to reduced fertility. In some cases, African children are weaned after six to nine months; in others, breast-feeding continues until the child is aged eighteen months or older. Nearly everywhere in Africa, infant mortality is high, as is child mortality in the period immediately after weaning. The apparent trend toward shortening or abandoning breast-feeding causes concern because of the negative effects on child health and on spacing of births.

The problem is a difficult one. Repeated pregnancies and long periods of lactation after each birth place a nutritional and health strain on mothers, especially rural women, who must also work hard in agriculture (Harrington, 1983). From the point of view of women's health, birth spacing ought to be measured by the interval between the end of lactation and the beginning of a new pregnancy, not by the interval between one birth and the next pregnancy. If spacing by female sexual abstinence is replaced by spacing through prolonged lactation, the father and the children benefit, but at the cost of a threat to the mother's health. Where the traditional period of abstinence is discontinued, it is important that it be replaced by contraception rather than by reliance on prolonged lactational amenorrhea, as is sometimes recommended.

Wide spacing of births and long periods of lactation between pregnancies are serious impediments to wage and salary employment for married women. This employment itself is another means to reduce fertility. The shift to small family size in the industrialized countries was accompanied by reduction in the total length of the reproductive period, by rapid succession of a few births, and by relatively short periods of lactation. The change to this pattern of reproduction was accompanied by increasing female employment in types of jobs that are difficult to reconcile with prolonged breast-feeding. The reduction in the period of lactation observed in some African countries may be a first step in such a development, with early termination of reproduction being the second step. Such a transformation of the reproductive pattern is a means to facilitate women's participation in modern sector employment. Promotion of wide spacing of births and prolonged breast-feeding may, therefore, be a step in the wrong direction.

African men are in a better position to avoid their sexual partner's pregnancy than the women themselves are, as long as women's status is low and family planning services rare. If significant numbers of African men in urban areas, and perhaps some in rural areas too, become interested in prevention of births, it is unlikely that objections from their partners will prevent increasing use of contraception. Husbands are more likely to use contraception without asking their wives' permission than the reverse. Many wives would probably follow the advice of their husband, if he wished to delay the next pregnancy or terminate childbearing. Others may be eager to use contraception as soon as the husband is willing. They may welcome the chance to reduce the heavy burden of pregnancies, breast-feeding, and child care, if they can do so without risking a marital conflict.

Implications for Research

Population increase will be rapid in Africa for many decades, so a very large expansion in agricultural production is needed. Agricultural production in many sparsely populated areas can be multiplied if long-fallow agriculture and pastoralism are replaced by more labor-intensive systems. Increased output requires improved transportation networks and other public infrastructure investment. Opening up new areas between existing urban enclaves would relieve population pressure in the most densely populated areas and provide industries located in these areas with larger markets. There would be wider scope for the development of secondary towns to lodge the public and private infrastructure that is needed for modernization of the surrounding agricultural base (Commission of the European Communities, 1984).

Studies are being made of the agricultural possibilities in different climatic zones of Africa. These studies should be coordinated with studies of other natural resources in the same area, to identify priority areas for investment in transportation and other public infrastructure that could help to create larger markets for both agricultural and industrial products. Research of this type is urgently needed, because the large investments in transportation networks planned for the coming decades seem more focused on long-distance transport than on opening new regions for productive activities.

Some African governments are now taking steps to speed up commercial food production in order to reduce imports. Since women are the main food producers in most of Africa, government support to agriculture should include measures to improve women's access to credit, training, extension services, more advanced technologies, and land. Studies of the best means to promote women's food production should be given high priority (ISNAR, 1985a).

There is a need for more information on the conflict between traditional attitudes and the economic strains resulting from recent development of the African economies. What are parents' economic expectations for the future? To what extent are their family size decisions influenced by increasing difficulties in finding good employment for children, educated or not? If parents risk rearing a large family, how do they expect to obtain sufficient income to support themselves and their children? It would be useful to have more systematic studies of how land shortages and privatization of land affect age at marriage and male and female attitudes toward family size. Finally, to complement such information, research is needed on prospects for the practice of fertility limitation, deliberate as well as unintended.

PART V

Policy

[1973]

Population Growth and Employment

The Need for Infrastructure Investment

INVESTMENT IN INFRASTRUCTURE is a major source of capital demand in developing countries, and countries that are short of capital try to economize on infrastructure investment by limiting such investment as much as possible. Often investment in infrastructure—both economic and social—is limited to one or a few major towns and harbors and to the transport network that links these centers to major cash-crop districts or mining districts.

The result is that all new investment and government activities are set up in these favored locations. Employment and incomes are growing rapidly in these places, which tend to attract both the elite of the youth from other regions and a larger number of ordinary workers than can be productively employed in these centers. The rapid concentration of population in these centers makes it necessary to devote still more infrastructure investment to these already favored locations, while the rest of the country continues to be starved of infrastructure and, therefore, of opportunities for modern type employment.

The concentration of infrastructure in a few locations may be a necessary first step toward development in a country with a limited supply of capital, but the sharply increasing labor force makes such a policy of concentration less feasible. Population and labor force in developing countries will double in the remaining decade of this century, and it is necessary to prevent a large share of these additional people from converging on and overcrowding existing large towns. The future rapid increase of the rural labor force will provide the labor for major investments in rural infrastructure and for the building of new towns, and such investments can provide young villagers with money incomes and thus help to contain the stream of migrants to the large towns.

There are two purposes for infrastructure investment: (a) to provide the rural areas with transport and marketing facilities and link them up with the centers, thus making new types of agricultural production feasible in such areas; and (b) to provide other economic and social infrastructure to make rural areas and small towns attractive as locations for modern sector activities and more attractive to live in for educated youth.

"Population Growth and Employment," reprinted from *Ceres* 10, 1973.

In some developing countries there is large scope for agricultural development by expansion of arable land and settlement in undeveloped regions, but it is often suggested that such investments should be avoided because this type of development is more expensive per additional unit of agricultural output than modernization of agriculture by means of modern inputs in densely populated regions of old settlements. This may be true, but in a period of sustained and rapid growth of population and labor force, the investment cost of opening up for development in undeveloped areas should not be seen in the narrow perspective of expansion of agricultural output. It should be seen as a means to spread not only agricultural but also nonagricultural and—in a longer perspective—urban activities more widely, thus avoiding overcentralization, which tends to become more and more disadvantageous the longer it is allowed to last.

Rapid population growth makes it necessary to step up the share of investment in national income, and in view of the shortage of capital in most developing countries, this implies that it is necessary to use less capital-intensive techniques within each branch of investment and current work than what would be feasible with less rapid rates of population growth. Moreover, it is necessary to make full use of the possibilities for promotion of savings. Infrastructure investment can contribute to these aims in two ways: (a) It is well known that there is a wide choice between labor-intensive and capital-intensive techniques in infrastructure investment and other construction activities. (b) In most developing countries, people in rural areas and sometimes in smaller towns provide by their own efforts the economic infrastructure they need for traditional activities. They make their own dwellings of local materials, fetch the water and fuel they need, and provide local transport by carrying headloads or using pack animals or carts on tracks and rudimentary roads. By contrast, the corresponding goods and services in large urban centers are provided by relatively capital-intensive activities financed through the organized capital market. By slowing down the rate of concentration of population in the large urban centers, it becomes possible to increase the amount of savings-cum-investment provided by the population, especially by self-constructed or self-financed rural housing.

The Choice of Agricultural Techniques

The discussion of the effects of rapid population growth on employment in developing countries has been focused rather too much on the industrial sector. There is a tendency to assume that most of the additions to the labor force ought to be employed in the industrial sector, while the need for additional employment in other sectors of the economy in periods of rapid population growth have been underestimated.

The increasing employment opportunities in infrastructure investment were discussed above. This section raises the problem of employment opportunities and of the choice between labor-intensive and capital-intensive techniques in agriculture. When the discussion of agricultural development became focused on the problems caused by the acceleration of population growth, it was in the first instance the increasing demand for food that caused concern. The role of agriculture was viewed primarily as that of producing sufficient food to the rapidly rising population, and it was suggested that this should be done by rapidly increasing use of capital-intensive inputs, both chemical and mechanical, combined with new types of seeds selected for use in capital-intensive farming and designed to give very high yields per hectare. The possible effects of such a policy on employment were considered of secondary importance, because of the urgent need to rapidly raise total agricultural output.

It is often said that Green Revolution techniques are labor-intensive. Whether this is so depends upon which system is seen as the alternative. Green Revolution techniques with double cropping of irrigated land require more agricultural labor per hectare—but less per unit of output—than the traditional Indian farming system with one crop per year without irrigation or fertilization. But Green Revolution techniques require less labor per hectare and per unit of output than the traditional East Asian farming system, in which double cropping of land was based upon fertilization by compost, hand weeding, and very labor-intensive systems of irrigation.

Experience has shown that, under certain natural conditions, population densities, and systems of land tenure, the techniques of the Green Revolution can rapidly raise both total agricultural output and employment in agriculture, but this is not a sufficient reason for recommending their transfer to other regions with different conditions. It is true that there are regions where a major expansion of total output can be achieved only by the use of capital-intensive inputs, but most of the agricultural population in developing countries live in regions where there is a wide choice between labor-intensive and capital-intensive methods to expand agricultural output. This is true not only of regions with unused land that can be brought into cultivation, but also of more densely cultivated regions, where fallow can be reduced or land use can be made more intensive by other means. Too little attention is paid to the possibilities for using the increasing labor force to shift over from traditional patterns of extensive pasture and forest to labor-intensive fodder production and to intensive forestry, thus releasing land which can be made arable after clearing and other land improvement.

There is a wide choice between labor-intensive and capital-intensive techniques, both in the production of crops and in animal husbandry. Moreover, investments needed both for clearing new land for cultivation and for other means to intensify land use can be in either labor intensive or capital intensive techniques: land clearing can be done by young men climbing trees and cutting them down with an ax, or it can be done with bulldozers; irrigation ditches can be dug with spades or with mechanized equipment, and so can terraces and leveled fields. A suitable choice of agricultural technique can help alleviate the capital shortage and avoid unemployment. The techniques of the Green Revolution are but one set of a large number of possible combinations of labor and capital inputs. There is need for agricultural research aimed at developing other combinations of inputs suited for regions with different degrees of shortage of capital, land, and labor.

The advantages of labor-intensive agricultural techniques are not only that they reduce the demand for capital-intensive inputs per unit of output. Labor-intensive techniques have the additional advantage that, if used for investments, they may induce savings, which would not have been forthcoming if capital-intensive techniques had been used. This is because peasant families can make labor-intensive investments as nonmonetized investment-cum-savings. Much of the agricultural investment needed in periods of increasing rural population can be done in this way—by the increasing number of adults in peasant families or, if necessary, by reducing the leisure time of family members.

Most developing countries do not include nonmonetized investment in agriculture in their national accounts, but the labor required for such investments is considerable in periods of rapidly rising population. It is not only subsistence production of food that benefits from this type of investment. Even today, nonmonetized investment provides much of the investment for land clearing, for planting crops and trees for export crops, and for irrigation of such crops. This helps to explain why agricultural production has tended to expand in step with rapid growth in population in many developing countries whose governments did nothing to facilitate and promote monetized investment in agriculture.

Foreign Trade and Agricultural Employment

The scope for employing increasing numbers of people in agriculture is of course largest when there is a rapidly expanding market for agricultural products. This is the case in many developing countries because of rapid population growth, increasing urbanization, rising urban living standards, and an attempt to replace food imports with home production. However, in the least developed countries, the home market for agricultural products is small, because most of the population produce their own food. In such countries, export markets must absorb most of the additional output if the increasing rural population will be able to obtain remunerative employment in agriculture. There are two possibilities: exports to industrialized countries and exports to other developing countries with larger urban sectors.

It is often emphasized in discussions about agricultural trade between developing and industrialized countries that, in the industrialized countries, rates of population growth and income elasticities for agricultural products are low. Therefore, it is said that industrialized countries cannot provide rapidly expanding markets for agricultural products from developing countries. However, there is a whole range of agricultural products with high income elasticities in the industrialized countries. These include many types of vegetables, all types of fruits, and nearly all types of animal produce. All these products can be produced by labor-intensive techniques in developing countries, and it is mainly the protection of high-cost domestic production in industrialized countries that limits the possibility for expanding agricultural employment in developing countries by means of such exports.

In the coming years of rapid growth of the labor force, the employment problem will be most difficult to solve in the least developed countries, which are dependent on agricultural exports and are unable to finance either urban or rural development, unless they can rapidly expand their earnings from exports of agricultural products. Usually such countries are neighbors of developing countries that are at a somewhat more advanced stage of economic development and that, therefore, have larger internal markets for agricultural products. Unfortunately, the protection of agriculture is as widespread in developing countries as in industrialized ones. This prevents the least developed countries from exporting to countries with a relatively large internal market for food and other agricultural produce.

If the more advanced countries within a developing region were more willing to open their markets for imports of agricultural products from their less-developed neighbors, these would become better customers for the growing industries in the more advanced developing countries, which often suffer because the size of their home market is too small for efficient operation.

Development Strategy and Demographic Transition

In the 1950s, when economists began to study the development problems in unindustrialized countries, very few took the unfolding demographic transition into account, and the focus was not on total income, but on per capita income. In conformance with Malthusian population theory, these countries were assumed to be overpopulated, and marginal labor productivity in agriculture was assumed to be zero. No distinction was made between seasonal unemployment in agriculture, short work hours in many areas of subsistence production, and a general labor surplus due to overpopulation. Therefore, it was assumed that, in order to increase per capita output in agriculture, the surplus labor had to be transferred to productive employment in other occupations.

At the time, no distinction was made between modern and informal production in industry and services, and the whole service sector was assumed to be a huge reservoir of surplus labor, because the low level of productivity in the informal service sector was defined as underemployment (ILO, 1969). Thus, the widely accepted strategy consisted of encouraging industrialization and rural-to-urban migration, not only for the sake of industrialization itself, but as a means to improve agriculture.

Not all economists believed in the theory of a chronic labor surplus in agriculture. W. Schultz (1964) based his theory of transformation of traditional agriculture on the assumption that labor was fully utilized with traditional techniques, so that per capita income could not be raised by reducing the labor force but only by promoting the use of industrial and scientific inputs. However, although Schultz's book first appeared in 1964, he took no account of the demographic transition. The term *population growth* is hardly mentioned, and the problem is considered that of raising output with a constant or declining labor force working in a constant area of arable land.

When development economists became more and more concerned with the demographic transition, the attitude to the agricultural problem changed, and the need to raise total output took precedence over that of improving per capita output. At that time, it was generally assumed that uncultivated land

---

"Development Strategy and Demographic Transition." Reprinted from *Economic Essays in Honour of Jorgen H. Gelting*. Tillagsnummer til *Nationalokonomisk Tidsskrift*, 1982: 43–50.

in all developing countries was too poor to be able to support additional populations (E. Boserup, 1965). Moreover, the possibilities for intensification of traditional agriculture by increasing frequency of cropping were ignored (E. Boserup, 1974). Therefore, pessimists prophesied worldwide famines before 1980 (Dumont and Rosier, 1969), while less pessimistic development strategists recommended the industrial input solution suggested by Schultz, or they recommended that the population increase be fed on food imported from the industrialized countries, especially North America, until the population problem could be solved by birth control.

At the early stage of the birth control discussion, it was generally assumed that a large share of the children born in unindustrialized countries were unwanted, and that birth rates would decline rapidly, if safe means of prevention could be developed and put at the disposal of the population. Thus, focus was on research and on convincing governments of the need to promote birth control services. However, the relation between the availability of modern preventive means and birth rates is much less close than had at first been assumed. Many of the efforts to propagate modern techniques of birth control in unindustrialized countries gave small results, while birth rates declined in many regions where modern techniques were unavailable. In other words, when parents were motivated for family limitation, many succeeded in reducing the number of births by traditional methods, although these might be both illegal and dangerous. By contrast, the availability of modern family planning services often failed to motivate parents to limit family size.

Induced by this experience, the experts began to study the different attitudes toward family limitation in industrialized and unindustrialized countries, with the result that the problem of the economic role of children came into focus. The lower the level of economic development in a region and the less monetized the local economy, the more scope there is for child labor, and the smaller the cost of rearing children. Moreover, lack of public support in old age makes most parents dependent upon the goodwill of adult children. So, children are economic assets for parents in the most underdeveloped regions, but an economic burden for parents in industrialized societies.

The first time a large number of governments engaged in a discussion of the interrelationship between population trends and economic development was at the United Nations World Population Conference in Bucharest in 1974. There was sharp disagreement at that conference in attitudes toward family limitation. In most cases, governments in densely populated countries urgently wanted to reduce family size, while those in sparsely populated countries wanted larger populations as a means to develop and defend their national territories (UN, 1975b). However, concerning the importance of economic development for rates of population growth, there was no disagreement. It was generally agreed that economic development is a precondition for the success of population programs. Only if certain economic and social levels are reached is fertility likely to decline.

Of course, this does not mean that the economic level, at which family size will begin to decline spontaneously, due to new attitudes of parents, is the same in all parts of the world. The status of women in the family and in society at large, as well as many other cultural, economic, and structural factors, seems to be important for the level of development at which parents attitudes change. And, of course, governments may cause a delay in fertility decline by hampering and making illegal methods of control, or they may hasten fertility decline by stern measures in favor of it—especially, of course, when a formal rationing of children is enforced by community pressure, as in China (Bergmann et al., 1981).

When population growth accelerated in the unindustrialized countries, nearly all development economists expected that the rapid growth of population would prevent economic development. Later development proved that this assumption was wrong. Many developing countries combined high rates of population growth in the 1960s and 1970s with very high growth rates of both total income and per capita income. Others had very slow growth of per capita income in the 1960s and 1970s and have fallen more and more behind other developing countries in income. These differences in income development were not related to differences in rates of population growth but to differences in the stage of development reached at the onset of the demographic transition. In the least developed countries, infrastructure, both economic and social, was—and is—much inferior to that of developing countries at somewhat later stages of development. In such countries, lack of transport facilities and other economic infrastructure prevented sales of local products to towns and foreign countries (E. Boserup, 1981a). Therefore they were prevented from taking part in that process of export-led growth, which helped countries with better infrastructure and already established export markets to have rapid economic growth.

As long as economic infrastructure is poor, it is not possible to modernize agriculture, to establish rural industries, or to develop decentralized patterns of industrialization. The rural population continues to produce mainly for subsistence, and its most enterprising members emigrate to distant urban centers or to foreign countries to earn better incomes. For the remaining population, life continues in the old way, parents have little motive to change their attitudes to family size, and fertility remains high. By contrast, fertility is declining in the countries at higher stages of development with rapid economic growth, due to the change in parents' attitudes that accompanies economic change.

Many developing countries have now passed the first stage of the demographic transition, in which the number of surviving children per family is increasing. But even in such countries, the youthful age distribution implies that they must look forward to a very long second stage, in which population continues to increase rapidly because of rapid growth in the number of families. The most recent UN forecasts of future population growth suggest a doubling of the population of South Asia in the next fifty years but more than a trebling of that of Africa, which is still at an early stage of demographic transition, with high child mortality and increasing family size (Tabah, 1982).

Since rapid population growth will continue for many more decades, one would expect that long-term development strategies would be focused on future changes in the size of the labor force and its geographical and occupational distribution. But this is not so, because the notion of surplus labor continues to find widespread support among development economists. The long-term models used for national and international development planning continue to be based on the concept of labor surplus. In his recent projections of world development until 2030, Leontief makes the assumption that in the developed countries population growth and the corresponding increase in total labor force will be one of the determinants of the rise in output until around the year 2000, but after that time the importance of human labor as a factor of production will diminish due to substitution by machines and natural resources (Leontief et al., 1977; Leontief and Sohn, 1982). In view of this, one might expect that his assumption for developing countries would be a much higher dependence of output on labor input than in industrialized countries, but instead of that, he simply assumes that the rise in population and labor force in developing countries has no effect whatever on the rate of growth of output.

The lack of long-term labor force planning, coordinated with regional and national population forecasts and plans for public infrastructure, has serious consequences, because it implies that the spontaneous concentration of private investment and population in the areas with the best infrastructure will continue. In a short-term perspective, it may seem to be a good policy to let development proceed by improvement of capacity utilization of existing infrastructure (rural and urban, economic and social) and avoid the cost of creating new facilities in new places. However, when rapid population growth is continuing, it soon becomes cheaper to create new growth poles for industry and agriculture instead of having mushrooming growth in a few centers and districts. Transformation of backward regions into new growth poles by means of more decentralized infrastructure investment will create employment opportunities in public works, new industries, formal and informal ancillary services, and the expansion and modernization of local agriculture, thus reducing migration from backward areas to the metropole, and relieving both rural and metropolitan poverty.

The tendency to concentration of population in one or a few mushrooming cities was most pronounced in countries which tried to solve their food supply problem by means of massive imports. The assumption of inelasticity of food production, which was mentioned earlier, made large-scale transfer of food from industrialized to developing countries look like a desirable solution to the agricultural problems of both developing and developed countries. Earlier, food exports had gone from unindustrialized to industrialized countries. North America and other non-European areas had built up a large capacity for exports to the industrialized countries in western Europe, but as demand for food in these exporting countries and in Europe decelerated, due to decelerating rates of population growth and decline of the income elasticity of food consumption, a choice had to be made between reducing export capacity and developing new markets. The last solution was chosen. Access to the expanding markets for food in developing countries was obtained by grants of food and other special advantages, including heavily subsidized prices for commercial exports. On the other hand, aid to development of food production in developing countries was only given on a small scale or was bluntly refused, if it concerned products that would offer competition to exports of surplus products from the industrialized countries. Moreover, the industrialized countries discriminated against or prohibited agricultural imports from developing countries that competed with their own production.

Governments in many developing countries were tempted by the favorable conditions for food imports to supply their urban populations, and sometimes also rural populations, with imported food. By this means they could avoid using scarce investment resources for rural infrastructure and development of agriculture. Such a policy may increase overall growth rates in countries with good possibilities for production and exports of nonagricultural products, but it will keep growth rates low in countries with the bulk of their population in agriculture. In many developing countries, the competition from imports of cereals led to steep decline of production (Valderrama and Moscardi, 1977; World Bank, 1981).

Because the low growth rates for agriculture in many developing countries are viewed not as the result of insufficient demand, due to food imports and lack of access to national and international markets, but as the result of low supply elasticity, most experts continue to recommend ever-increasing food imports into developing countries from industrialized ones. A recent FAO projection for the year 2030 suggests that imports of cereals into developing countries, which increased from 40 million tons in the early 1970s to 96 million tons in 1980/81, may increase further to 150 million in 2000 and 350 million in 2030. Only a small share of this trade is assumed to be exports from developing countries (Islam, 1982). The effect of such projections is to encourage continued government support of surplus production in the industrialized countries and to encourage governments in developing countries to continue to neglect development of their own food production.

Early warnings from economists against massive food imports have not been lacking (M. Boserup, 1966) but it is widely believed that, on balance, food imports into poor countries have positive effects, because malnutrition among the poorest would be worse without food imports and food-for-work programs. However, a large share of the poorest are rural people with little or no land, who would have more employment and better incomes if the towns were supplied by national food production instead of imports. Most of the remaining poor are slum dwellers in urban areas, who would have been better off if expansion of national food production had allowed them to remain in— or return to—their villages. Food-for-work programs would of course be of more benefit to the poor if donors did not insist on delivery of imported food but instead financed production of local food.

Increasing reliance on imports of basic food in a period of continuing rapid population growth is undesirable not only because of its effects on local agriculture but also because the world market in food is heavily dependent on a few large exporters. These countries have no interest in keeping large stocks, because exporters gain more from soaring prices in bad harvest years than they lose when prices fall in years of good harvest, since they can support the market by building up stocks and cutting production. Moreover, demand in the world market fluctuates strongly, not only in response to climatic changes but also because of the frequent breakdowns in food supplies in communist countries. Therefore, developing countries that are heavily dependent upon food imports risk going hungry if exporters, for political reasons, give preference to competing claims on their stocks.

At the second stage of the demographic transition, when the number of families is rapidly increasing, there is need for rapid growth of employment (including self-employment). However, many of the policies discussed in this essay contribute to keeping overall growth rates of employment low. This is true of massive food imports, which keep rates of growth of food production low, and of agricultural modernization policies, which rely more upon use of industrial inputs than upon expansion of cropped area and other types of more labor-intensive intensification of land use. Also, the lack of decentralized rural development keep rates of employment low.

Except for developing countries with exceptionally rapid industrial growth, which had overall labor shortages, the combined effect of the policies mentioned above were probably more important for growth of unemployment than the much-discussed pattern of capital-intensive industrial growth.

Bibliography

I. Selected Works by Ester Boserup

1965. *The Conditions of Agricultural Growth.* Chicago: Aldine.
1966.* "Linkages between Industry and Agriculture." Paper prepared for symposium on Industrial Development in Africa, Cairo. New York, UN Center for Industrial Development.
1968. "Surpluses in the Third World—who wants them?" *Ceres* 5.
1970. "Population Growth and Food Supplies." In A. Allison, *Population Control.* Harmondsworth: Penguin.
1970.* "Present and Potential Food Production in Developing Countries." In Zelinsky, Kosinski, and Prothero, 1970.
1970. "The Interrelation between Population Trends and Agricultural Methods." In P. Gray and S. Tangry, *Economic Development and Population Growth: A Conflict?* Lexington: D. C. Heath.
1970. *Woman's Role in Economic Development.* New York: St. Martin's. London: Earthscan 1989.
1971. Ester Boserup and Ignacy Sachs, eds. *Foreign Aid to Newly Independent Countries.* The Hague: Mouton.
1972. "Population Change and Economic Development in Africa." Paper prepared for seminar on Population and Economic Growth in Africa, Leiden. Africa Studies Centrum.
1973.* "Employment of Women in Developing Countries." In *International Population Conference, Liege 1973.* Liege: IUSSP.
1973. "Integration of Women in Development: Background Study." In *Report of the Interregional Meeting of Experts on the Integration of Women in Development.* New York: UN.
1973.* "Population Growth and Employment." *Ceres* 10.
1974.* "Food Supply and Population in Developing Countries." In Islam, 1974.
1975. "Employment of Women in Developing Countries." In Tabah, 1975.
1975. Ester Boserup and Christina Liljencrantz. *Integration of Women in Development: Why, When, How?* New York: UNDP.
1975.* "Population and Agricultural Productivity." In UN 1975b.
1975.* "The Impact of Population Growth on Agricultural Output." *Quarterly Journal of Economics* 89.
1975.* "Women in the Labour Market." In Jain, 1975.

1976.* "Environment, Population, and Technology in Primitive Societies." *Population and Development Review* 2.

1980.* "Food Production and the Household as Related to Rural Development." In Presvelou and Spijkers-Zwart, 1980.

1980.* "Population Growth and Prospects of Development in Savannah Nations." In Harris, 1980.

1981.* "Indian Agriculture from the Perspective of Western Europe." In Sarma, 1981.

1981. *Population and Technological Change: A Study of Long-Term Trends.* Chicago: University of Chicago Press.

1982.* "Development Strategy and Demographic Transition." In *Economic Essays in Honour of Jorgen E. Gelting. Nationalökonomisk Tidsskrift,* special issue, ed. S. Andersen et al.

1982. "Research for Population Policy Design." Paper prepared for seminar on Studies on Determinants of Fertility Behavior, Colombo. Liege: IUSSP.

1983.* "The Impact of Scarcity and Plenty on Development." In *Journal of Interdisciplinary History* 14.

1984.* "Demographic Pressure, Growth, and Productivity in a Historical Perspective." In IEA World Congress, *Human Resources, Employment, and Development,* vol. 5. London: Macmillan.

1984.* "Technical Change and Human Fertility in Rural Areas of Developing Countries." In Schutjer and Stokes, 1984.

1985.* "Economic and Demographic Interrelationships in Sub-Saharan Africa." *Population and Development Review* 11.

1985.* "The Primary Sector in African Development." In M. Lundahl, ed., *The Primary Sector in Economic Development.* London: Croom Helm.

1986. "Economic Growth with Below Replacement Fertility." In *Below Replacement Fertility in Industrial Societies. Population and Development Review* 12, supplement, ed. K. Davis et al.

1986.* "Shifts in the Determinants of Fertility in the Developing World: Environmental, Technical, Economic, and Cultural Factors." In Coleman and Schofield, 1986.

1987.* "Agricultural Growth and Population Change." In J. Eatwell et al., eds., *A Dictionary of Economics,* vol. 1. London: Macmillan.

1987.* "Agricultural Development and Demographic Growth." In Fauve-Chamoux, 1987.

1987.* "Inequality between the Sexes." In J. Eatwell, et al., eds., *A Dictionary of Economics,* vol. 2. London: Macmillan.

1987.* "Population and Technology in Preindustrial Europe." In *Population and Development Review* 13.

1988. "Population Growth as a Stimulant to Agricultural Development." In G. Steinmann, et al., eds., *Probleme und Chancen Demographische Entwicklung in der Dritten Welt.* New York: Springer Verlag.

1990.* "Economic Change and the Roles of Women." In I. Tinker, ed., *Persistent Inequalities: Women and World Development.* New York: Oxford University Press.

1990.* "Population, the Status of Women, and Rural Development." *Population and Development Review* 15, supplement.

II. Works Cited and Other Sources

Abdullah, T., and Zeidenstein, S. 1982. *Village Women of Bangladesh.* Oxford: Pergamon Press.

Adams, R. 1965a. *Land behind Bagdad.* Chicago: University of Chicago Press.

———. 1965b. *The Evolution of Urban Society: Early Mesopotamia and Prehispanic Mexico.* Chicago: Aldine.

———. 1968. "Early Civilization, Subsistence and Environment." In Y. Cohen, 1968.

Adams, R., and Nissen, H. 1976. *The Uruk Countryside.* Chicago: University of Chicago Press.

Ahmed, E., ed. 1985. *Technology and Rural Women.* London: Allen and Unwin.

Alam, I., and Casterline, J. 1984. *Socio-Economic Differentials in Recent Fertility.* World Fertility Survey Comparative Studies 33. Vorburg: International Statistical Office.

Allan, W. 1965. *The African Husbandman.* London: Oliver and Boyd.

Allman, J., ed. 1978. *Women's Status and Fertility in the Muslim World.* New York: Praeger.

Angel, L. 1975. "Paleoecology, Paleodemography, and Health." In Polger, 1975.

Arrow, K. 1973. "The Theory of Discrimination." In Ashenfelter and Rees, 1973.

Ashenfelter, O., and Rees, A., eds. 1973. *Discrimination in Labor Markets.* Princeton: Princeton University Press.

Bairoch, P. 1969. *Revolution Industrielle et Sous-Developpement* Paris: SEDES.

Becker, G. 1960. "An Economic Analysis of Fertility." In *Demographic and Economic Change in Developed Countries.* Princeton: Princeton University Press.

———. 1981. *A Treatise on the Family.* Cambridge: Harvard University Press.

Bergmann, T.; Hazard, B.; and Senghaas, D. 1981.*Wiedersehen mit China nach zwei jahren.* Saarbrucken: Breitenbach.

Berrill, K., ed. 1964. *Economic Development with Special Reference to East Asia.* London: Macmillan.

Binford, L. 1968. "Post Pleistocene Adaptations." In Binford and Binford, 1968.

Binford, L., and Binford, S., eds. 1968. *New Perspectives in Archaeology.* Chicago: Aldine.

Binswanger, H., and Ruttan, V. 1978.*Induced Innovation, Technology, Institutions, and Development.* Baltimore: Johns Hopkins University Press.

Bloch, M. 1931, 1956. *Les caracteres originaux de l'histoire rurale francais.* Vol. 1. Paris: Les Belles Lettres. Vol. 2. Paris: Armand Colin.

Boserup, E. 1965. *The Conditions of Agricultural Growth.* Chicago: Aldine.

———. 1970a. *Woman's Role in Economic Development.* New York: St. Martin's. London: Earthscan

———. 1970b. "Present and Potential Food Production in Developing Countries." In Zelinski, Kosinski, and Prothero, 1970.

———. 1974. "Food Supply and Population in Developing Countries." In N. Islam, 1974.

———. 1975a. "Population and Agricultural Productivity." In UN, 1975b.

———. 1975b. *Employment of Women in Developing Countries.* In Tabah, 1975.

———. 1975c. "Women in the Labour Market." In Jain, 1975.

———. 1980. "Food Production and the Household as Related to Rural Development." In Presvelou and Spijkers-Zwart, 1980.

———. 1981a. *Population and Technological Change: A Study of Long-Term Trends.* Chicago: University of Chicago Press.

———. 1981b. "Indian Agriculture from the Perspective of Western Europe." In Sarma, 1981.

———. 1984. "Technical Change and Human Fertility in Rural Areas of Developing Countries." In Schutjer and Stokes, 1984.

———. 1985. "Economic and Demographic Interrelationships in Sub-Saharan Africa." *Population and Development Review* 11.

———. 1986. "Shifts in the Determinants of Fertility in the Developing World." In Coleman and Schofield, 1986.

Boserup, M. 1963. "Structure and Take-off." In Rostow, 1963.

———. 1966. "Bistandsteori—kommentarer til den nyeste litteratur." *Nationalokonomisk Tidsskrift* 5–6.

Brown, L. 1963. *Man, Land and Food.* Washington, D.C.: U.S. Department of Agriculture.

Buck, J. 1979. *The Village Woman in Ghana.* Uppsala: Scandinavian Institute for African Studies.

Buck, J. L. 1937. *Land Utilization in China.* Nanking: Nanking University Press.

Bunster, X., et al., eds. 1977. *Women and National Development.* Chicago: University of Chicago Press.

Burnham, P. 1980. "Changing Agricultural and Pastoral Ecologies in the West African Savannah Region." In Harris, 1980.

Buvinic, M., Lycette, M., and McGreevey, W., eds. 1983. *Women and Poverty in the Third World.* Baltimore: Johns Hopkins University Press.

Cain, G. 1985. "Welfare Economies of Policies Towards Women." *Journal of Labour Economics* 3, special issue.

Cain, M. 1982. "Perspectives on Family and Fertility in Developing Countries." *Population Studies* 36.

Cain, M., et al. 1979. "Class, Patriarchy, and Women's Work in Bangladesh." *Population and Development Review* 5.

Calaby, J. 1980. "Ecology and Human Use of the Australian Savannah Environment." In Harris, 1980.

Caldwell, J. 1976. "Toward a Restatement of Demographic Transition Theory." *Population and Development Review* 2.

Caldwell, J., and Okonjo, C., eds. 1968. *The Population of Tropical Africa.* New York: Population Council.

Carneiro, R. 1956. "Slash-and-Burn Agriculture: A Closer Look at its Implications for Settlement Patterns." In *Men and Cultures: Papers of the Fifth International Congress of Anthropological and Ethnological Sciences.*

———. 1961. "Slash-and-Burn Cultivation among the Kuikuru and Its Implications for Cultural Development in the Amazon Basin." In Wilbert, 1961.

———. 1970. "A Theory of the Origin of the State." *Science* 169.

Chambers, J., and Mingay, G. 1966. *The Agrarian Revolution, 1750–1880.* London: Batford.

Chen, L.; Huq, E.; and D'Souza, S. 1981. "Sex Bias in the Family Allocation of Food and Health Care in Rural Bangladesh." *Population and Development Review* 7.

Chenery, H. 1964. "Land: The Effects of Resources on Economic Growth." In Berrill, 1964.

Chesnais, J. 1985. "Progrès economique et transition démographique dans les pays pauvres: trente ans d'expérience (1950–1980)." *Population* 40.

Childe, G. 1952. *New Light on the Most Ancient East.* London: Cassel.

"China's New Marriage Law." 1981. *Population and Development Review* 7.

Chipande, G. 1988. "The Impact of Demographic Changes on Rural Development in Malawi." 1988. In R. D. Lee et al. 1988.

Clark, C. 1967. *The Economics of Irrigation.* Oxford: Pergamon Press.

Clark, C., and Haswell, M. 1964. *The Economics of Subsistence Agriculture.* London: Macmillan.

Coale, A., and Hoover, E. 1958. *Population Growth and Economic Development in Low Income Countries.* Princeton: Princeton University Press.

Cohen, M. 1977. *The Food Crisis in Prehistory.* New Haven: Yale University Press.

Cohen, Y., ed. 1968. *Man in Adaptation.* Chicago: Aldine.

Coleman, D., and Schofield, R., eds. 1986. *The State of Population Theory.* Oxford: Blackwell.

Collins, J. 1983. "Fertility Determinants in a High Andes Community." *Population and Development Review* 9.

Commission of the European Communities. 1984. *Secondary Towns in Africa: Their Role and Functions in National and Regional Development.* Brussels: European Economic Community.

Cowgill, G. 1975. "On Causes and Consequences of Ancient and Modern Population Changes." *American Anthropologist* 77.

Dalrymple, D. 1971. *Survey of Multiple Cropping in Less Developed Nations.* Washington, D.C.: U.S. Agency for International Development.

Dauber, R., and Cain, M., eds. 1981. *Women and Technological Change in Developing Countries.* Boulder: Westview.

David, P. 1984. "The Demographic Transition in the United States." Paper prepared for 1984 meeting of the Population Association of America, quoted in *Population Index* 50.

de Vries, J. 1985. "The Population and Economy of the Preindustrial Netherlands." *Journal of Interdisciplinary History* 15.

Dow, T., and Werner, H. 1983. "Prospects for Fertility Decline in Rural Kenya." *Population and Development Review* 9.

Dumond, D. 1965. "Population Growth and Cultural Change." *Southwestern Journal of Anthropology* 21.

———. 1975. "The Limitations of Human Populations." *Science* 28.

Dumont, R. and Mottin, M. 1983. *Le defi senegalais.* Dakar: Enda.

Dumont, R., and Rosier, B. 1969. *The Hungry Future.* London: Andre Deutsch.

Dyson, T., and Moore, M. 1983. "On Kinship Structure, Female Autonomy, and Demographic Behaviour in India." *Population and Development Review* 9.

Dyson-Hudson, N. 1980. "Strategies of Resource Exploitation among the East African Savannah Pastoralists." In Harris, 1980.

Easterlin, R., ed. 1980. *Population and Economic Change in Developing Countries.* Chicago: University of Chicago Press.

Eighth International Economic History Congress. 1982. *Female Labour before, during, and after the Industrial Revolution.* Budapest: International Economic History Congress.

Ekvall, R. 1972. "Demographical Aspects of Tibetan Nomadic Pastoralism." In Spooner, 1972.

Epstein, T., and Watts, R., eds. 1981. *The Endless Day.* Oxford: Pergamon Press.

Evenson, R. 1983. "Economics of Agricultural Growth: The Case of Northern India." In Nobe and Sampath, 1983.

Faaland, J., ed. 1982. *Population and the World Economy in the Twenty-First Century.* Oxford: Blackwell.

FAO (UN Food and Agriculture Organization). 1966. *Indicative World Plan for Agricultural Development: Near East Subregional Study.* Rome: FAO.

———. 1969. *Provisional Indicative World Plan for Agriculture Development.* Rome: FAO.

———. 1970. *Provisional Indicative Plan for Agriculture Development: Summary and Main Conclusions.* Rome: FAO.

———. 1971a. *Production Yearbook.* Rome: FAO.

———. 1971b. *The State of Food and Agriculture.* Rome: FAO.

———. 1973. "Agricultural Production in Developing Countries in Relation to the Targets for the Second United Nations Development Decade." *Monthly Bulletin of Agricultural Economics and Statistics* 22.

Farooq, G., and Simmons, G., eds. 1985. *Economic Analysis of Fertility Be-*

havior in Developing Countries. New York: Macmillan.

Fauve-Chamoux, A., ed. 1987. *Evolution agraire et croissance demographique.* Liege: Ordina.

Federici, N. 1985. "The Status of Women, Population, and Development." *IUSSP Newsletter* 23.

Finley, M. 1973. *The Ancient Economy.* London: Chatto and Windus.

Flannery, K. 1969. "Origins and Ecological Effects of Early Domestication in Iran and the Near East." In Ucko and Dimbleby, 1969.

Fogel, R., ed. 1986a. "Long-Term Changes in Nutrition and the Standard of Living." Bern: Ninth International Economic History Congress.

————. 1986b. "Nutrition and the Decline of Mortality since 1700." Working Paper 1802. Cambridge: National Bureau of Economic Research.

Fortmann, L. 1981. "The Plight of the Invisible Farmer: The Effect of National Agricultural Policy on Women in Africa." In Dauber and Cain, 1981.

Fourastie, J. 1969. *L'Evolution des Prix a Long Terme.* Paris: Presse Universitaire de France.

Galy, G. 1969. "Pour une geographie de la France prehistorique." *Annales* 24.

Girard, L. 1965. "Transport." *Cambridge Economic History of Europe.* Vol. 4. London: Cambridge University Press.

Gleave, M., and White, H. 1969. "Population Density and Agricultural Systems in West Africa." In Thomas and Whittington, 1969.

Goldstone, J. 1983. "Capitalist Origins of the English Revolution." *Theory and Society* 12.

Griegg, D. 1980. *Population Growth and Agrarian Change: An Historical Perspective.* London: Cambridge University Press.

Hansen, B. 1966. "Marginal Productivity Wage Theory and Subsistence Wage Theory in Egyptian Agriculture." *Journal of Development Studies* 3.

————. 1968. "The Distributive Shares in Egyptian Agriculture." *International Economic Review* 9.

Hansen, S. 1972. *Okonomisk Vaekst i Danmark.* Vol. 1. Copenhagen: G.E.C. Gad.

Harner, M. 1970. "Population Pressure and the Social Evolution of Agriculturalists." *Southwestern Journal of Anthropology* 26.

Harrington, J. 1983. "Nutritional Stress and Economic Responsibility: A Study of Nigerian Women." In Buvinic, Lycette, and McGreevey, 1983.

Harris, D., ed. 1980. *Human Ecology in Savannah Environments.* London: Academic Press.

Harrison, P. and Turner, B., eds. 1978. *Prehistoric Maya Agriculture.* Albuquerque: University of New Mexico Press.

Hayami, Y., and Ruttan, V. 1971. *Agricultural Development: An International Perspective.* Baltimore: Johns Hopkins University Press.

Hole, F. 1968. "Evidence of Social Organization from Western Iran, 8000–4000 B.C." In Binford and Binford, 1968.

IFPRI (International Food Policy Research Institute). 1980. *Agricultural Pro-*

tection in OECD Countries. Washington, D.C.: IFPRI.

ILO (International Labor Office). 1969. *The World Employment Programme: Report of the Director-General to the International Labor Conference.* Geneva: ILO.

International Railway Statistics. 1972. Paris: International Union of Railways.

International Rice Research Institute. 1985. *Report of the Project Design Workshop on Women in Rice Farming Systems.* Los Banos: IRRI.

International Road Federation. 1973. *World Road Statistics.* Washington, D.C.: IRF.

Ishikawa, S. 1967. *Economic Development in Asian Perspective.* Tokyo: Knokuniya Bookshop.

Islam, N. 1974. *Agricultural Policy in Developing Countries.* New York: Macmillan.

———. 1982. "Food." In Faaland, 1982.

ISNAR (International Service for National Agricultural Research). 1985a. *Women and Agricultural Technology.* The Hague: ISNAR.

———. 1985b. *The User's Perspective in International and National Agricultural Research.* The Hague: ISNAR.

Jahan, R., and Papanek, H., eds. 1979. *Women and Development: Perspectives from South and South East Asia.* Dacca: Asiatic Press.

Jain, D. 1975. *Indian Women.* New Delhi. Government of India Publications.

Jejeebhoy, S. 1987. "Reproductive Motivation: The Extent to Which Women Differ from Men." Paper prepared for seminar on Development, Status of Women, and Demographic Change, Italian Institute for Population Research, Rome.

Johnson, G., and Lee, R. D. 1987. *Population Growth and Economic Development.* Madison: University of Wisconsin Press.

Johnson-Stone, M.; Netting, R.; and Stone, G. 1984. "Household Variability and Inequality in Kofyar Subsistence and Cash-Cropping Economies." *Journal of Anthropological Research* 40.

Jones, E. 1981. *The European Miracle: Environments, Economies, and Geopolitics in the History of Europe and Asia.* London: Cambridge University Press.

Jones, G. 1981. "Malay Marriage and Divorce in Peninsular Malaysia: Three Decades of Change." *Population and Development Review* 7.

———. 1982. "Population Trends and Policy in Vietnam." *Population and Development Review* 8.

Jones, R. 1980. "Hunters in the Australian Coastal Savannah." In Harris, 1980.

Kelley, A. 1988. "Economic Consequences of Population Change in the Third World." *Journal of Economic Literature* 26.

Khanam, S., and Nahar, S. 1979. "Class, Patriarchy, and Women's Work in Bangladesh." *Population and Development Review* 5.

Komlos, J. 1985. "Stature and Nutrition in the Habsburg Monarchy." *American Historical Review* 90.

——. 1986. "Patterns of Children's Growth in East-Central Europe in the Eighteenth Century." *Annals of Human Biology* 13.

Kristensen, T. 1969. *The Food Problem of Developing Countries.* Paris: OECD.

Kuznets, S. 1966. *Modern Economic Growth.* New Haven: Yale University Press.

Laslett, P. 1965. *The World We Have Lost.* New York: Scribner's.

Lee, M., ed. 1981. *Toward a New Community Life.* Seoul: National University.

Lee, R. B. 1970. "Work Effort, Group Structure and Land Use in Contemporary Hunter-Gatherers." Paper prepared for research seminar on Archeology and Related Subjects, University of London.

——. 1972. "Population Growth and the Beginning of Sedentary Life." In Spooner, 1972.

Lee, R. B., and de Vore, I., eds. 1968. *Man, the Hunter.* Chicago: University of Chicago Press.

Lee, R. D. 1981. "Short-Term Variation: Vital Rates, Prices, and Weather." In Wrigley and Schofield, 1981.

Lee, R. D., et al., eds. 1988. *Population, Food, and Rural Development.* Oxford: Clarendon.

Leontief, W., et al. 1977. *The Future of the World Economy.* New York: Oxford University Press.

Leontief, W., and Sohn, I. 1982. "Economic Growth." In Faaland, 1982.

Lesthaeghe, R. 1980. "On the Social Control of Human Reproduction." *Population and Development Review* 6.

——. 1984. *Fertility and Its Proximate Determinants in Sub-Saharan Africa.* Liege: International Union for the Scientific Study of Population.

Lewis, W. 1954. "Economic Development with Unlimited Supplies of Labour." *Manchester School of Economic and Social Studies* 22.

Lightbourne, R., and MacDonald, A. 1982. *Family Size Preference.* World Fertility Survey Comparative Studies 14. Vorburg: International Statistical Office.

Loutfi, M. 1980. *Rural Women: Unequal Partners in Development.* Geneva: ILO.

Loza, S. 1981. *Egypt: Studies on Determinants of Fertility Behaviour.* Vol. 2. Liege: International Union for the Scientific Study of Population.

Malthus, T. 1803, 1958. *An Essay on Population.* London: Dent.

Mason, K. 1985. *The Status of Women: A Review of Its Relationship to Fertility and Mortality.* New York: Rockefeller Foundation.

Medina, E. 1980. "Ecology of Tropical American Savannahs." In Harris, 1980.

Mickelwait, D.; Riegelman, M.; and Sweet, C. 1976. *Women in Rural Development.* Boulder: Westview.

Miller, B. 1981. *The Endangered Sex: Neglect of Female Children in Rural North India.* Ithaca: Cornell University Press.

National Academy of Sciences. 1971. *Rapid Population Growth: Conse-*

quences and Policy Implications. Baltimore: Johns Hopkins University Press.

———. 1986. *Population Growth and Economic Development.* Washington, D.C.: National Academy Press.

Netting, R. 1972. "Sacred Power and Centralization: Some Notes on Political Adaptation in Africa." In Spooner, 1972.

Nobe, K., Sampath, R., eds. 1983. *The Third World Development.* Bombay: Western Press, Inc.

North, D. 1966. "Industrialization in the United States." In *Cambridge Economic History Europe.* Vol. 6. London: Cambridge University Press.

———. 1981. *Structure and Change in Economic History.* New York: Norton.

Nurkse, R. 1953. *Problems of Capital Formation in Underdeveloped Countries.* London: Oxford University Press.

OECD (Organization for Economic Cooperation and Development). 1968. *The Food Problems of Developing Countries.* Paris: OECD.

———. 1981. *Development Cooperation, 1981 Review.* Paris: OECD.

Okonjo, C. 1972. "Population Dynamics and Nigerian Development." Paper prepared for the African Population Conference, December 1971.

Oppong, C. 1980. *A Synopsis of Seven Roles and the Status of Women.* Geneva: ILO.

———. 1983. *Paternal Costs, Role Strain, and Fertility Regulation: Some Ghanaian Evidence.* Geneva: ILO.

———. 1985. "Reproduction and Resources: Some Anthropological Evidence from Ghana." In Farooq and Simmons, 1985.

Oppong, C., and Abu, K. 1984. *The Changing Maternal Role of Ghanaian Women: Impacts of Education, Migration and Employment.* Geneva: ILO.

Orans, M. 1966. "Surplus." *Human Organizations* 25.

Pala Okeyo, A. 1984. *Towards Strategies for Strengthening the Position of Women in Food Production: An Overview and Proposals on Africa.* Nairobi: Institute for Development Studies.

Papanek, H., and Minault, G. 1982. *Separate Worlds: Studies of Purdah in South Asia.* Columbia, Mo.: South Asia Books.

Parsons, J. 1980. "Europeanization of the Savannah Lands of Northern South America." In Harris, 1980.

Pawley, W. 1971. "In the Year 2070." *Ceres* 4.

Phelps-Brown, E., and Hopkins, S. 1981. *A Perspective of Wages and Prices.* London: Methuen.

Pingali, P., and Binswanger, H. 1987. "Population Density and Agricultural Intensification." In Johnson and Lee, 1987.

Poffenberger, M. 1983. "Toward a New Understanding of Population Change in Bali." *Population Studies* 37.

Polger, S., ed. 1975. *Population, Ecology, and Social Evolution.* The Hague: Mouton.

Presvelou, C., and Spijkers-Zwart, S., eds. 1980. *The Household, Women, and Agricultural Development.* Wageningen: Veenman and Zonen.

Revelle, R. 1973. "Will the Earth's Land and Water Resources be Sufficient for Future Populations?" Paper prepared for U.N. symposium on Population, Resources, and Environment, Stockholm.

Ricardo, D. 1817, 1951. *The Principles of Political Economy and Taxation.* London: Cambridge University Press.

Rostow, W., ed. 1963. *The Economics of Take-Off into Sustained Growth.* London: Macmillan.

Rotberg, R., and Rabb, T., eds. 1981. *Climate and History.* Princeton: Princeton University Press.

———. 1983. *Hunger and History: The Impact of Changing Food Production and Consumption Patterns on Society.* London: Cambridge University Press.

Saefulla, A. 1979. *The Value of Children among Tea Estate Workers' Families.* Canberra: Development Studies Centre.

Sanders, W. 1972. "Population, Agricultural History, and Societal Evolution in Mesoamerica." In Spooner, 1972.

Sanders, W., and Price, B. 1968. *Mesoamerica: The Evolution of a Civilization.* New York: Random House.

Sarma, J. 1981. *Growth and Equity: Policies and Implementation in Indian Agriculture.* Washington, D.C.: International Food Policy Research Institute.

Schultz, T. P. 1981. *Economics of Population.* Reading: Addison Wesley.

Schultz, T. W. 1964. *Transforming Traditional Agriculture.* New Haven: Yale University Press.

———. 1965. *Economic Crises in World Agriculture.* Ann Arbor: University of Michigan Press.

———. 1968. "What Ails World Agriculture?" *Bulletin of Atomic Scientists* 24.

———. 1973, 1974. "The Economics of the Family." *Journal of Political Economy,* March supplements.

Schutjer, W., and Stokes, C., eds. 1984. *Rural Development and Human Fertility.* New York: Macmillan.

Scudder, T. 1980. "River-basin Development and Local Initiative in African Savannah Environments." In Harris, 1980.

Sen, A. 1985. *Women, Technology and Sexual Divisions.* New York: United Nations.

Sharma, K.; Hussein, S.; and Saharya, A. 1984. *Women in Focus.* New Delhi: Sangam Books.

Simon, J. 1977. *The Economics of Population Growth.* Princeton: Princeton University Press.

Sinha, J. 1975. "Population and Agriculture." In Tabah, 1975.

Slicher van Bath, B. 1963. *The Agrarian History of Western Europe:* A.D. 500– 1500. London: Arnold.

Smith, P., and Young, T. 1972. "The Evolution of Early Agriculture and Culture in Greater Mesopotamia." In Spooner, 1972.

Snell, D. 1981. "Agricultural Seasonal Unemployment, the Standard of Living, and Women's Work in the South and East, 1690–1860." *Economic History Review* 33.

Sopher, D. 1980. "Indian Civilization and the Tropical Savannah Environment." In Harris, 1980.

Som, R. 1968. "Some Demographic Indicators for Africa." In Caldwell and Okonjo, 1968.

Spooner, B., ed. 1972. *Population Growth: Anthropological Implications.* Cambridge: MIT Press.

Stokes, C., and Schutjer, W. 1984. "Access to Land and Fertility in Developing Countries." In Schutjer and Stokes, 1984.

"Symposium on Law and the Status of Women." 1977. *Columbia Human Rights Law Review* 8.

Tabah, L., ed. 1975. *Population Growth and Economic Development in the Third World.* Liege: Ordina.

———. 1982. "Population Growth." In Faaland, 1982.

Tabutin, D. 1984. "La fecondité et la mortalité dans les recensements africains des 25 dernières années." *Population* 39.

Thomas, M., and Whittington, G., eds. 1969. *Environment and Land Use in Africa.* London: Methuen.

Tilly, L. 1972. "La Revolte Frumentaire: Forme de Conflit Politique en France." *Annales* 27.

Tilly, L., and Scott, J. 1978. *Women, Work and Family.* New York: Holt, Rinehart and Winston.

Tinker, I., and Cho, H. 1981. "Women's Participation in Community Development in Korea." In M. Lee, 1981.

Tuchman, B. 1978. *A Distant Mirror: The Calamitous 14th Century.* New York: Ballantine.

Turnham, D., and Jaeger, I. 1971. *The Employment Problem in Less Developed Countries.* Paris: OECD.

Ucko, P., and Dimbleby, G., eds. 1969. *The Domestication and Exploitation of Plants and Animals.* Chicago: Aldine.

UN (United Nations). 1955. "The French Economy." In UN, *Economic Survey of Europe in 1954.* Geneva: UN.

———. 1963. *Report of the ECA Industrial Coordination Mission to East and Central Africa.* Addis Ababa: UN.

———. 1971. *Special Report Prepared by the A.C.C. on the Implications of the Green Revolution.* E/5012, pt. 2. New York: UN.

———. 1973. *Implementation of the International Development Strategy.* Vols. 1, 2. New York: UN.

———. 1974a. *Industrial Development Survey.* Vienna: UNIDO.

———. 1974b. *World Road Statistics.* Vienna: UNIDO.

———. 1975a. *External Finance for Development.* New York: UN.

————. 1975b. *Report of the United Nations World Population Conference.* New York: UN.

————. 1975c. *The Population Debate.* New York: UN.

————. 1976a. *Data Bank of Development Indicators.* Geneva: UNRISD.

————. 1976b. *International Finance, Depressed Regions, and Needed Progress.* New York: UN.

————. 1983. "Recent Trends and Conditions of Fertility." *Population Bulletin of the United Nations* 15.

U.S. Department of Agriculture. 1964. *The World Food Budget.* Washington, D.C.: USDA.

U.S. Department of State. 1970. *World Food-Population Levels.* Washington, D.C.: Government Printing Office.

Utas, B., ed. 1983. *Women in Islamic Societies.* London: Curson.

Valderrama, M., and Moscardi, E. 1977. "Current Policies Affecting Food Production: The Case of Wheat in the Andean Region." In *Proceedings of the World Food Conference 1976.* Ames: Iowa State University Press.

Vlassoff, M., and Vlassoff, C. 1980. "Old Age Security and the Utility of Children in Rural India." *Population Studies* 34.

Wailes, B. 1972. "Plough and Population in Temperate Europe." In Spooner, 1972.

Walker, B. 1980. "Ecology and Management of Savannah Ecosystems in South Central Africa." In Harris, 1980.

Westergaard, K. 1983. *Pauperization and Rural Women in Bangladesh.* Comilla: Samabaya.

Wijemanne, E., and Wijeyesekara, M. 1981. *Sri Lanka: Studies in Determinants of Fertility Behaviour.* Liege: International Union for the Scientific Study of Population.

Wilbert, J., ed. 1961. *The Evolution of Horticultural Systems in Native South America.* Caracas.

Wittvogel, K. 1957. *Oriental Despotism.* New Haven: Yale University Press.

World Bank. 1978. *World Development Report 1978.* Washington, D.C.: World Bank.

————. 1981. *Accelerated Development in Sub-Saharan Africa: An Agenda for Action.* Washington, D.C.: World Bank.

————. 1982. *World Development Report.* Washington, D.C.: World Bank.

————. 1983. *World Development Report.* Washington, D.C.: World Bank.

————. 1984. *World Development Report.* Washington, D.C.: World Bank.

Wrigley, E. 1962. "The Supply of Raw Materials in the Industrial Revolution." *Economic History Review* 15.

————. 1985. "Urban Growth and Agricultural Change: England and the Continent in the Early Modern Period." *Journal of Interdisciplinary History* 15.

Wrigley, E., and Schofield, R., 1981. *The Population History of England 1541–1870.* London: Cambridge University Press.

————. 1983. "English Population History from Family Reconstruction: Summary Results 1600–1799." *Population Studies* 37.

Youssef, N. 1974. "Women's Status and Fertility in Muslim Countries of the Middle East and Asia." Paper prepared for symposium on Women's Status and Fertility, American Psychological Association, New Orleans.
Zelinski, W.; Kosinski, L.; and Prothero, R., eds. 1970. *Geography and a Crowding World.* London: Oxford University Press.

Index

THE JOHNS HOPKINS STUDIES IN DEVELOPMENT

Designed by Martha Farlow
Composed by The Composing Room of Michigan, Inc., in Trump Medieval
Printed by Edwards Brothers, Inc., on 50-lb. Glatfelter B-16